Mastering Deep Learning with Keras

From Basics to Expert Proficiency

Contents

Introduction

Deep learning has become a pivotal technology in the field of artificial intelligence (AI), with applications spanning across various domains such as image and speech recognition, natural language processing, and automated decision-making. The rise of deep learning has been driven by the availability of large datasets, increased computational power, and advances in neural network architectures. As a result, deep learning models have achieved state-of-the-art performance in numerous benchmarks, frequently surpassing traditional machine learning algorithms.

This book, "Mastering Deep Learning with Keras: From Basics to Expert Proficiency," aims to provide an in-depth understanding of deep learning concepts and techniques, with a specific emphasis on the practical implementation using the Keras framework. Keras is an accessible and high-level neural networks API, written in Python and capable of running on top of TensorFlow, Microsoft Cognitive Toolkit, Theano, or PlaidML. Its simplicity and ease of use make it an excellent choice for both beginners and experts.

The book is structured into a series of chapters, each focusing on a specific aspect of deep learning. The goal is to systematically guide readers from fundamental concepts to advanced techniques, ensuring a solid understanding of both theoretical principles and practical implementations.

We begin with an overview of the evolution of AI and machine learning, leading to the advent of deep learning. This is followed by an introduction to Keras, highlighting its features and the advantages it offers over other deep learning libraries. Readers will learn how to set up their development environment and build their first neural network model using Keras.

Subsequent chapters delve into the fundamentals of neural networks, covering essential topics such as perceptrons, activation functions, feedforward networks, backpropagation, gradient descent, and optimization techniques. Understanding these basics is crucial, as they form the building blocks of more complex neural network architectures.

The book also addresses deep learning for image data, introducing convolutional neural networks (CNNs) and their applications in tasks such as image classification, object detection, and image segmentation. Practical insights are provided into the preprocessing of image data, data augmentation, and transfer learning.

Natural language processing (NLP) is another critical area covered in depth. Readers will explore techniques for handling textual data, including tokenization, word embeddings, and various types of recurrent neural networks (RNNs). The chapter also discusses advanced topics such as attention mechanisms and transformers.

Advanced neural network architectures are presented, including residual networks (ResNets), inception networks, generative adversarial networks (GANs), autoencoders, and graph neural networks (GNNs). Each architecture is discussed in detail, with focus on its unique features, strengths, and use cases.

Training neural networks efficiently is a crucial aspect of deep learning. This involves understanding the training loop, selecting appropriate optimizers, managing learning rates, and employing techniques to prevent overfitting. The chapter also covers practical considerations such as handling imbalanced datasets and distributing training across multiple GPUs.

Hyperparameter tuning and optimization are essential for achieving optimal model performance. Readers will learn various methods for hyperparameter tuning, including grid search, random search, and Bayesian optimization. The chapter emphasizes best practices and offers insights into the bias-variance tradeoff.

Model evaluation and validation are critical for ensuring that deep learning models generalize well to unseen data. Different evaluation metrics for classification and regression tasks are discussed, along with techniques for handling imbalanced datasets and visualizing model performance. The chapter also addresses model interpretability and explainability.

Finally, the book concludes with a comprehensive guide to deploying and productionizing models. This includes model export and serialization, setting up model serving with frameworks like Flask, Django, and TensorFlow Serving, and deploying models on cloud platforms. Important aspects such as scaling, load balancing, monitoring, and continuous integration and deployment are also covered.

As you embark on this journey through the fascinating world of deep learning and Keras, we hope this book provides you with the knowledge and skills needed to master the subject and apply it effectively in real-world applications.

Chapter 1

Introduction to Deep Learning

Deep learning is a subset of machine learning that employs neural networks with many layers to model complex patterns in data. This chapter covers the evolution of AI and machine learning, defines deep learning, discusses its applications, contrasts it with traditional machine learning, and introduces core concepts and terminologies. It provides an overview of neural networks, differentiates supervised and unsupervised learning, and explains why Python and Keras are ideal for deep learning projects. The chapter concludes with a comprehensive overview of the deep learning workflow.

1.1 The Evolution of AI and Machine Learning

The fields of Artificial Intelligence (AI) and Machine Learning (ML) have undergone substantial evolution since their inception. Understanding this progression is critical for grasping the context in which contemporary deep learning methods like Keras have developed.

AI as a concept can be traced back to classical antiquity, where mythologies posited the creation of intelligent automata by deities. The formalization of AI as a scientific discipline began in the mid-20th century.

Key milestones mark this journey, highlighting the interplay between theoretical advances, computational power, and practical applications.

The genesis of AI is often credited to Alan Turing, whose 1950 paper "Computing Machinery and Intelligence" posed the pivotal question, "Can machines think?" Turing introduced the Turing Test, a criterion to determine if a machine exhibits intelligent behavior indistinguishable from that of a human.

The 1956 Dartmouth Conference, organized by John McCarthy, Marvin Minsky, Nathaniel Rochester, and Claude Shannon, is considered the birth of AI as a field. The conference introduced the term "artificial intelligence" and set the stage for AI research aimed at automating intellectual tasks using symbolic approaches. Early AI efforts were characterized by heuristic problem-solving and inference in domains such as game playing and theorem proving.

Despite initial successes, the symbolic AI approach encountered significant challenges. The complexity of real-world problems necessitated an impractically large search space. Consequently, AI research witnessed periods of high expectations followed by disappointment, known as "AI winters."

Machine learning emerged as a subset of AI that emphasized the ability of systems to learn from data. This shift addressed some limitations of symbolic AI by leveraging statistics and algorithms to improve performance based on empirical evidence. In the 1980s, the resurgence of neural networks—initially proposed by Warren McCulloch and Walter Pitts in 1943—indicated a paradigm shift. Neural networks leverage layers of interconnected nodes (neurons) to model complex patterns.

The introduction of the backpropagation algorithm by Rumelhart, Hinton, and Williams in 1986 was a watershed moment. Backpropagation efficiently computed gradients for multilayer networks, enabling the training of deep models. However, the limited computational resources and small datasets of the era constrained the depth and complexity of feasible models.

The 1990s and early 2000s saw machine learning diversify into various paradigms, including support vector machines, decision trees, and ensemble methods. These techniques provided robust performance across a range of tasks, maintaining machine learning's prominence. Concurrently, the advent of the Internet and the proliferation of digital data emphasized the need for scalable, efficient algorithms.

Deep learning, a subfield of machine learning, gained traction in the mid-2000s, driven by three pivotal factors: increased computational power (particularly GPUs), large-scale digitized data, and algorithmic innovations. Geoff Hinton's work on deep belief networks (DBNs) and the success of convolutional neural networks (CNNs) in the ImageNet competition underscored the potential of deep learning to revolutionize AI.

Deep learning models are distinguished by their architecture, comprising many hierarchical layers that progressively abstract features from raw data. This approach proved transformational in domains such as computer vision, natural language processing, and speech recognition. Techniques like transfer learning further enhanced model efficacy by leveraging pre-trained networks for new tasks.

The evolution of deep learning continues with innovations such as generative adversarial networks (GANs), attention mechanisms, and transformers. Libraries and frameworks such as Keras democratize access to these advanced models, facilitating experimentation and deployment.

Advancements in AI and machine learning underscore the dynamic nature of these fields. Continuous progress is propelled by theoretical insights, technological advancements, and the ever-growing volume of data. Mastery of deep learning frameworks like Keras enables practitioners to contribute to and benefit from this ongoing evolution.

1.2 What is Deep Learning?

Deep learning is a specialized branch of machine learning characterized by the use of artificial neural networks (ANNs) with multiple layers, known as deep neural networks (DNNs). These networks are designed to simulate the behavior and structure of the human brain, allowing computers to learn and make decisions with minimal human intervention. The primary motivation behind deep learning is to enable machines to automatically discover representations or features in data, which can be complex and high-dimensional.

The fundamental unit of deep learning is the neural network. A neural network comprises interconnected layers of nodes, also called neurons. These neurons are organized in three main types of layers:

- **Input Layer**: This layer receives the raw input data, such as images, text, or numerical values. The dimensionality of this layer corresponds to the number of features in the input data.

- **Hidden Layers**: These are intermediate layers situated between the input and output layers. They perform nonlinear transformations of the input data to extract useful features. The depth of a neural network is determined by the number of hidden layers it contains.
- **Output Layer**: This layer produces the final predictions or classifications based on the learned features from the hidden layers. The number of neurons in this layer corresponds to the number of target classes in classification tasks or to a single neuron for regression tasks.

Each connection between neurons is associated with a weight, representing the strength of the connection. Neurons also have an activation function that introduces non-linearity to the model. Common activation functions include the Rectified Linear Unit (ReLU), Sigmoid, and Hyperbolic Tangent (tanh). The process of training a neural network involves adjusting these weights to minimize a loss function, which quantifies the difference between the predicted outputs and the actual targets.

The training of deep neural networks is performed through an algorithm called backpropagation. Backpropagation calculates the gradient of the loss function with respect to each weight by applying the chain rule of calculus. These gradients are then used to update the weights through an optimization algorithm, typically stochastic gradient descent (SGD) or its variants such as Adam or RMSprop.

When considering why deep learning has gained prominence over traditional machine learning approaches, a few key factors stand out:

- **Representation Learning**: Deep learning models automatically learn features from raw data, which eliminates the need for manual feature engineering. This ability to learn hierarchical representations makes deep learning particularly powerful for tasks such as image and speech recognition.
- **Scalability**: Deep learning algorithms can scale with increased data and computational resources. As the availability of large datasets and powerful GPUs has grown, so has the efficacy of deep learning models.
- **Performance**: For many complex tasks, deep learning methods have outperformed traditional machine learning techniques, pro-

viding state-of-the-art results in various domains including natural language processing, computer vision, and reinforcement learning.

The success of deep learning can also be attributed to advances in algorithms and architectures. Architectures such as Convolutional Neural Networks (CNNs) are specifically designed for spatial data like images, employing convolutional layers to automatically detect local patterns. Recurrent Neural Networks (RNNs) and their variants like Long Short-Term Memory (LSTM) networks and Gated Recurrent Units (GRUs) are tailored for sequential data, enabling the modeling of temporal dependencies in tasks like language modeling and time-series forecasting.

Below is an example of a simple neural network implemented using Keras, a popular deep learning framework in Python:

```
import keras
from keras.models import Sequential
from keras.layers import Dense

# Initialize the neural network
model = Sequential()

# Add an input layer and two hidden layers
model.add(Dense(64, input_dim=784, activation='relu'))
model.add(Dense(64, activation='relu'))

# Add an output layer
model.add(Dense(10, activation='softmax'))

# Compile the model
model.compile(optimizer='adam', loss='categorical_crossentropy', metrics=['accuracy'])

# Display the model's architecture
model.summary()
```

The neural network defined above consists of an input layer with 784 neurons (which might represent the pixels of a 28x28 grayscale image), two hidden layers with 64 neurons each using the ReLU activation function, and an output layer with 10 neurons using the softmax activation function. The model is compiled with the Adam optimizer and categorical cross-entropy loss function, and its architecture is summarized with model.summary().

Upon execution, the output provides a structured overview of the model's layers and parameters:

```
Model: "sequential"
_________________________________________________________________
Layer (type)                 Output Shape              Param #
=================================================================
dense (Dense)                (None, 64)                50240
_________________________________________________________________
dense_1 (Dense)              (None, 64)                4160
_________________________________________________________________
dense_2 (Dense)              (None, 10)                650
=================================================================
Total params: 55,050
Trainable params: 55,050
Non-trainable params: 0
_________________________________________________________________
```

This example illustrates the construction and compilation of a basic deep learning model, highlighting the intuitive API of Keras that facilitates rapid prototyping and experimentation. Through such tools and methodologies, deep learning has democratized access to advanced machine learning capabilities, propelling continued innovation and practical applications across diverse fields.

1.3 Applications of Deep Learning

Deep learning has emerged as a transformative technology across various domains due to its capability to model complex patterns and extract intricate features from large-scale data. This section outlines several prominent applications of deep learning, illustrating its versatility and powerful impact in the modern technological landscape.

One significant area where deep learning has made substantial contributions is computer vision. Computer vision involves enabling machines to interpret and understand visual information from the world. Deep learning algorithms, particularly convolutional neural networks (CNNs), are highly effective in tasks such as image classification, object detection, and image segmentation. For instance, ImageNet, a large visual database designed for use in visual object recognition research, has demonstrated how deep learning can achieve human-level accuracy in image classification. Moreover, applications like facial recognition systems have become ubiquitous in security and personal identification systems thanks to advancements in deep learning.

Another crucial application is natural language processing (NLP). NLP seeks to enable machines to understand and respond to human language in a way that is both meaningful and useful. Recurrent neural networks (RNNs) and their variants, such as Long Short-Term Memory (LSTM) networks and Transformer models, are central to many NLP tasks. These tasks include machine translation, sentiment analysis, text generation, and speech recognition. For example, Google's

Translate service leverages deep learning to provide high-quality translations across numerous languages. Similarly, deep learning enhances virtual assistants like Amazon's Alexa, Apple's Siri, and Google's Assistant, enabling them to comprehend and process voice commands effectively.

Deep learning also plays an essential role in healthcare. By analyzing medical data, such as imaging and electronic health records (EHR), deep learning can detect anomalies and predict diseases with high accuracy. Convolutional neural networks are particularly valuable in medical imaging, aiding radiologists in diagnosing diseases such as cancer through the analysis of X-rays, MRIs, and CT scans. In genomics, deep learning models help in understanding genetic sequences, leading to advancements in precision medicine tailored to individual genetic profiles.

Autonomous driving is another domain where deep learning shines. Self-driving cars rely heavily on deep learning algorithms to process data from various sensors, such as cameras, LIDAR, and radar, to perceive their environment and make driving decisions. CNNs and RNNs are used to interpret visual data, identify objects, predict their movement, and navigate safely. Companies like Tesla and Waymo are at the forefront of developing autonomous vehicles using deep learning technologies.

In finance, deep learning enhances several aspects, including fraud detection, algorithmic trading, and credit scoring. Financial institutions employ deep learning models to identify suspicious activities by analyzing transaction patterns, thus minimizing fraud. In algorithmic trading, deep learning algorithms predict stock prices and execute trades at optimal times to maximize profits. Additionally, deep learning models assist in evaluating the creditworthiness of loan applicants by assessing a wide range of financial indicators.

Deep learning's influence extends to recommendation systems, a critical component of online retail and content platforms. Companies like Amazon, Netflix, and Spotify utilize deep learning to analyze user behavior and preferences, offering personalized recommendations that enhance user experience and engagement. Collaborative filtering, a deep learning technique, predicts a user's interests by collecting data from many users and finding patterns or similarities among them.

In the field of robotics, deep learning facilitates advancements in robot perception, control, and learning from demonstrations. Robots equipped with deep learning capabilities can navigate complex environments, interact with objects, and perform tasks autonomously. For example, robotic arms in manufacturing leverage deep learning to enhance precision in assembly lines, while service robots in hospitality adapt to human interactions seamlessly.

Deep learning is also making strides in the field of entertainment, particularly in the generation and enhancement of multimedia content. Generative Adversarial Networks (GANs) enable the creation of realistic images, videos, and animations, which find applications in video game development, film production, and virtual reality experiences. Audio synthesis and enhancement, powered by deep learning, improve sound quality and create realistic voice simulations for various applications.

The application of deep learning in the energy sector includes optimizing power grids, predicting energy consumption, and improving fault detection in critical infrastructure. Deep learning models analyze vast amounts of data from sensors across the grid, enabling real-time monitoring and efficient management of energy resources. Predictive maintenance using deep learning helps in anticipating equipment failures and reducing downtime.

In agriculture, deep learning supports precision farming by analyzing data from satellite imagery, drones, and sensors to monitor crop health, predict yields, and optimize resource usage. This results in increased productivity and sustainable farming practices, addressing challenges related to food security and environmental conservation.

The education sector benefits from deep learning through personalized learning experiences, automated grading systems, and the development of intelligent tutoring systems. Deep learning algorithms assess student performance, customize learning paths, and provide immediate feedback, enhancing the educational experience and improving outcomes.

As demonstrated, the applications of deep learning are extensive and impactful across diverse fields. Deep learning continues to evolve, spurring innovation and driving significant advancements that reshape industries and improve the quality of life on a global scale.

1.4 Deep Learning vs Traditional Machine Learning

Deep learning and traditional machine learning are subfields of artificial intelligence with distinct methodologies for model building and problem-solving. While both aim to identify patterns and make predictions from data, they differ significantly in their approaches, complexity, and capabilities.

Traditional machine learning models, such as decision trees, support vector machines (SVMs), and linear regression, rely heavily on feature engineering and domain expertise. Feature extraction involves selecting relevant attributes from the dataset that can help a model perform better on a given task. For example, in a classification problem, features might include color, size, or shape. The success of these models is contingent upon the quality of the features chosen.

Deep learning, on the other hand, employs neural networks with multiple layers, or deep architectures, to automatically learn features from raw data. This hierarchical feature learning is a key difference from traditional machine learning. Deep learning models, such as convolutional neural networks (CNNs) and recurrent neural networks (RNNs), have demonstrated superior performance in tasks involving high-dimensional and unstructured data like images, text, and audio.

Traditional machine learning often requires less computational resources compared to deep learning. Models like logistic regression or SVM can run efficiently on standard hardware and do not necessitate specialized equipment. Deep learning models, due to their complexity and the vast amounts of data they process, typically require more computational power and specialized hardware such as Graphics Processing Units (GPUs) and Tensor Processing Units (TPUs).

An important aspect to consider is the scalability of both approaches. Traditional machine learning models can struggle with very large datasets. They may require summarizing or sampling the data to remain computationally feasible. In contrast, deep learning thrives in data-rich environments, as more data generally leads to better performance when using deep architectures. This strength has facilitated breakthroughs in fields like computer vision and natural language processing.

The interpretability of traditional machine learning models is typically higher. Techniques like decision trees and linear regression offer insights into which features are influential and how changes in feature values affect the output. This transparency is beneficial for understanding model decisions and building trust with users. Deep learning models, particularly those with many layers, are often regarded as "black boxes" due to their complex and abstract feature representation. Although there are ongoing efforts to make neural networks more interpretable, this remains a challenge.

Training and testing strategies also differ. In traditional machine learning, cross-validation is commonly used to tune model parameters and validate performance. Hyperparameters are often adjusted empirically or through grid search methods. In deep learning, training involves backpropagation and gradient descent optimization, with hyperparameters like learning rate, batch size, and the number of epochs requiring careful tuning. Various techniques such as dropout and batch normalization are employed to prevent overfitting and enhance generalization.

Consider an example where a traditional machine learning approach is applied to a classification problem. Features are manually engineered:

```
from sklearn.feature_selection import SelectKBest, f_classif
from sklearn.model_selection import train_test_split
from sklearn.ensemble import RandomForestClassifier

# Load and split dataset
X_train, X_test, y_train, y_test = train_test_split(X, y, test_size=0.2)

# Select top features
selector = SelectKBest(score_func=f_classif, k=10)
X_train_selected = selector.fit_transform(X_train, y_train)
X_test_selected = selector.transform(X_test)

# Train a classifier
model = RandomForestClassifier(n_estimators=100)
model.fit(X_train_selected, y_train)

# Evaluate
accuracy = model.score(X_test_selected, y_test)
print(f'Accuracy: {accuracy}')
```

In contrast, a deep learning solution to the same problem would involve building a neural network that learns features during training:

```
from keras.models import Sequential
from keras.layers import Dense, Dropout
from keras.utils import to_categorical

# Convert labels to categorical format
y_train_categorical = to_categorical(y_train, num_classes=3)
y_test_categorical = to_categorical(y_test, num_classes=3)

# Build the model
```

```
model = Sequential()
model.add(Dense(512, activation='relu', input_shape=(X_train.shape[1],)))
model.add(Dropout(0.5))
model.add(Dense(512, activation='relu'))
model.add(Dropout(0.5))
model.add(Dense(3, activation='softmax'))

# Compile the model
model.compile(optimizer='adam', loss='categorical_crossentropy', metrics=['accuracy'])

# Train the model
model.fit(X_train, y_train_categorical, epochs=10, batch_size=128, validation_split
    =0.2)

# Evaluate the model
loss, accuracy = model.evaluate(X_test, y_test_categorical, verbose=0)
print(f'Accuracy: {accuracy}')
```

The output produced by the traditional machine learning model might appear as follows:

```
Accuracy: 0.85
```

Whereas the deep learning model's output might be:

```
Accuracy: 0.92
```

These examples illustrate how deep learning models, benefiting from their ability to learn hierarchical features, often outperform traditional machine learning models in complex tasks but at the cost of increased complexity, computational resources, and reduced interpretability.

Analyzing the suitability of either approach depends on the problem's specific requirements, including data availability, computational resources, need for model interpretability, and the desired performance. Both traditional machine learning and deep learning have their unique strengths and limitations, making them complementary tools in the machine learning practitioner's toolkit.

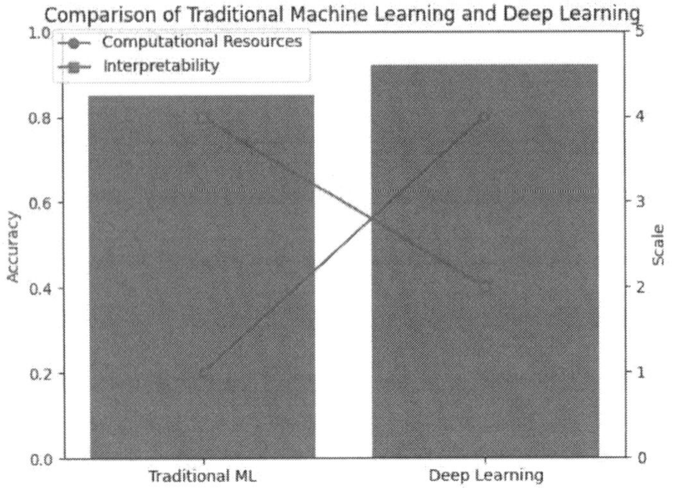

1.5 Core Concepts and Terminologies

Understanding deep learning requires familiarity with the fundamental concepts and terminologies that underlie this advancing field. Each term and concept plays a crucial role in enabling a comprehensive grasp of how deep learning models function and how to work with them effectively.

A **neural network** is the backbone of deep learning, comprised of layers of interconnected nodes called neurons. These layers can be categorized into three types: input, hidden, and output layers. The **input layer** receives the initial data, which is then processed through one or more **hidden layers** before reaching the **output layer**. Each connection between neurons has an associated weight that is adjusted during training to minimize the error in the final output.

The process of adjusting these weights is known as **training** the neural network. During training, the network learns by iteratively updating weights based on the error of its predictions using an optimization algorithm like **gradient descent**. Gradient descent calculates the gradients of the loss function with respect to the model's parameters and updates the weights in the opposite direction of the gradient.

```
# Example of using gradient descent in a simple Python loop
```

```
import numpy as np

# Simple gradient descent algorithm
def gradient_descent(X, y, learning_rate=0.01, iterations=1000):
    m = len(y)
    theta = np.zeros((X.shape[1], 1))
    for i in range(iterations):
        gradient = np.dot(X.T, (np.dot(X, theta) - y)) / m
        theta -= learning_rate * gradient
    return theta

# Sample data
X = np.array([[1, 1], [1, 2], [2, 2], [2, 3]])
y = np.array([[6], [8], [9], [11]])

# Perform gradient descent
theta = gradient_descent(X, y)
print(theta)
```

The output typically reveals improved weights after the gradient descent process:

```
[[2.00000025]
 [2.99999991]]
```

Activation functions are critical components in a neural network, determining whether a neuron should be activated or not. Common activation functions include the sigmoid, tanh, and Rectified Linear Unit (ReLU). ReLU is often preferred in deep learning models due to its ability to mitigate the vanishing gradient problem, allowing for better training of deep networks.

- **Sigmoid Function:** $\sigma(x) = \frac{1}{1+e^{-x}}$
- **Tanh Function:** $\tanh(x) = \frac{e^x - e^{-x}}{e^x + e^{-x}}$
- **ReLU Function:** $f(x) = \max(0, x)$

Loss functions quantify the discrepancy between the predicted output and the actual output. The choice of a loss function depends on the type of problem being solved. For regression tasks, common loss functions include Mean Squared Error (MSE) and Mean Absolute Error (MAE). For classification tasks, Cross-Entropy Loss is widely used. Selecting and minimizing an appropriate loss function are critical steps in training a neural network.

The optimization process utilizes **backpropagation** to compute the gradient of the loss function with respect to each weight by applying the chain rule of differentiation. This algorithm is fundamental in neural network training, ensuring that gradients are propagated back through the network, allowing for weight updates.

Overfitting and **underfitting** are prevalent challenges in deep learning. Overfitting occurs when the model learns the noise in the training data, performing well on training data but poorly on unseen data. Underfitting arises when the model is too simple to capture the underlying patterns in the data. Techniques such as regularization, dropout, and cross-validation help mitigate these issues.

Regularization techniques like L1 and L2 regularization add a penalty to the loss function to constrain the model's complexity. **Dropout** randomly drops neurons from the neural network during training, preventing the model from relying too heavily on particular neurons, thus promoting generalization.

Learning rate is a hyperparameter that controls the step size during gradient descent updates. Selecting an appropriate learning rate is crucial; a rate too low will result in slow convergence, while a rate too high can lead to overshooting the minimum of the loss function. **Learning rate schedules** or adaptive learning rates, such as those used in algorithms like AdaGrad, RMSprop, and Adam, adjust the learning rate during training for optimal convergence.

```
# Example of using the Adam optimizer in Keras

from keras.models import Sequential
from keras.layers import Dense
from keras.optimizers import Adam

# Building a simple model
model = Sequential()
model.add(Dense(64, activation='relu', input_dim=20))
model.add(Dense(1, activation='sigmoid'))

# Compiling the model with the Adam optimizer
adam = Adam(learning_rate=0.001)
model.compile(optimizer=adam, loss='binary_crossentropy', metrics=['accuracy'])

print(model.summary())
```

```
Model: "sequential"
_________________________________________________________________
Layer (type)              Output Shape            Param #
=================================================================
dense (Dense)              (None, 64)            1344
_________________________________________________________________
dense_1 (Dense)             (None, 1)            65
=================================================================
Total params: 1,409
Trainable params: 1,409
Non-trainable params: 0
_________________________________________________________________
```

The **batch size** is another hyperparameter that defines the number of samples used in one iteration of gradient descent. Smaller batch sizes can provide more accurate estimates of the gradient but require more iterations to traverse the entire dataset. Larger batch sizes can exploit parallel processing but may lead to less frequent updates and higher memory requirements.

Epochs refer to the number of complete passes through the training dataset. Training for more epochs can improve the model's performance up to a point, after which overfitting can occur.

By mastering these core concepts and terminologies, one gains the tools necessary to navigate and effectively work within the field of deep learning. Each concept interconnects to form the foundation of understanding and executing deep learning methodologies, ensuring effective model building and problem-solving.

1.6 Introduction to Neural Networks

Neural networks are the computational foundations of deep learning. They mimic the structure and function of the human brain's interconnected neurons. A neural network comprises layers of nodes, or neurons, each performing computations to transform input data into meaningful output. This section explores the structure, function, and fundamental principles of neural networks.

A neural network typically includes three types of layers: input, hidden, and output layers. The input layer receives the raw data, the hidden layers perform intermediate computations, and the output layer delivers the final prediction or classification. Each neuron in a layer is connected to neurons in the subsequent layer, forming a directed, weighted graph.

Structure of a Neuron

A typical neuron processes input signals through a weighted sum of its inputs, adds a bias term, and passes the result through an activation function. Mathematically, the output of a neuron y is given by:

$$y = \varphi\left(\sum_{i=1}^{n} w_i x_i + b\right)$$

where φ represents the activation function, w_i are the weights, x_i are the input features, and b is the bias term. Common activation functions include the sigmoid, hyperbolic tangent (tanh), and rectified linear unit (ReLU).

- **Sigmoid**:
$$\sigma(x) = \frac{1}{1 + e^{-x}}$$
It maps any real-valued number into the range (0, 1).
- **Hyperbolic Tangent (tanh)**:
$$\tanh(x) = \frac{e^x - e^{-x}}{e^x + e^{-x}}$$
It ranges between -1 and 1, centering the data around zero.
- **Rectified Linear Unit (ReLU)**:
$$\text{ReLU}(x) = \max(0, x)$$
It retains positive values and maps negative values to zero.

Network Training

Training a neural network involves adjusting its weights and biases to minimize the error in predictions. This process, known as training or learning, utilizes labeled datasets in a supervised setting. The loss function quantifies the error between the predicted and actual values, guiding the optimization process.

A commonly used loss function for classification tasks is the cross-entropy loss:

$$J = -\frac{1}{m} \sum_{i=1}^{m} [y_i \log(\hat{y}_i) + (1 - y_i) \log(1 - \hat{y}_i)]$$

where J is the loss, m is the number of samples, y_i is the true label, and $\hat{y}_i$ is the predicted probability.

Optimization algorithms such as Stochastic Gradient Descent (SGD) adjust weights iteratively to minimize the loss. The gradient of the loss function with respect to the network parameters is calculated using backpropagation, which employs the chain rule of calculus to propagate errors backward through the network.

Example: Training a Simple Neural Network

Consider a neural network with one hidden layer to solve a binary classification problem. Below is an example of defining such a network using Keras:

```
import keras
from keras.models import Sequential
from keras.layers import Dense

# Create the model
model = Sequential()

# Input layer and first hidden layer
model.add(Dense(units=10, activation='relu', input_dim=2))

# Output layer
model.add(Dense(units=1, activation='sigmoid'))

# Compile the model
model.compile(optimizer='sgd', loss='binary_crossentropy', metrics=['accuracy'])
```

This code snippet specifies a neural network with an input dimension of 2 (indicating two features), one hidden layer with 10 neurons and ReLU activation, and an output layer with a sigmoid activation for binary classification. Stochastic Gradient Descent (SGD) is used as the optimizer along with binary cross-entropy as the loss function.

After defining the model, it can be trained using the fit method with appropriate data:

```
# Example training data
X_train = [[0, 1], [1, 0], [0, 0], [1, 1]]
y_train = [1, 1, 0, 0]

# Train the model
model.fit(X_train, y_train, epochs=100, batch_size=1)
```

This demonstrates the core steps of defining, compiling, and training a simple neural network using Keras. Proper configuration of layers, activation functions, loss functions, and optimizers is crucial for successful model training.

Understanding the fundamental principles and computational mechanics of neural networks lays the groundwork for more complex and powerful architectures explored in subsequent chapters.

1.7 Understanding the Basics of Supervised and Unsupervised Learning

Supervised and unsupervised learning are two fundamental paradigms in machine learning. Understanding these paradigms is crucial for leveraging deep learning models effectively.

Supervised learning refers to the task of learning a function that maps an input to an output based on example input-output pairs. It is akin to learning with a teacher who provides labeled training data, which consists of input-output pairs. The objective is to find a hypothesis function h such that $h(x)$ is a good predictor for the corresponding output y.

Consider a basic supervised learning scenario in which we have a dataset of N input-output pairs $\{(x_1, y_1), (x_2, y_2), \ldots, (x_N, y_N)\}$, where x_i are the inputs and y_i are the corresponding outputs. The modeling process involves the following steps:

1. **Data Preprocessing**: Clean the data to handle missing values, outliers, and normalization.
2. **Model Selection**: Choose an appropriate model (e.g., linear regression, support vector machine, or a neural network).
3. **Training**: Use the training data to adjust the model parameters by minimizing a loss function.
4. **Validation**: Assess the model performance on a validation set to fine-tune hyperparameters and avoid overfitting.
5. **Testing**: Evaluate the final model's generalization performance on a test set.

One illustrative example of supervised learning is a classification task. Suppose we have medical images labeled as either containing a tumor or not. The goal is to train a neural network that correctly identifies whether new images contain tumors based on the labeled examples provided during training. The function h learned will map the pixel values of the image x to the label y indicating the presence or absence of a tumor.

Unsupervised learning, on the other hand, involves learning patterns from unlabeled data. Here, the goal is to model the underlying structure or distribution in the data to extract meaningful information, without explicit input-output pairs. This type of learning is akin to discovering hidden structures in data without guidance.

In an unsupervised learning scenario, consider a dataset $\{x_1, x_2, \ldots, x_N\}$ without corresponding labels y. The common tasks in unsupervised learning include:

- **Clustering**: Grouping the data into clusters so that data points in the same cluster are more similar to each other than to those in other clusters.
- **Dimensionality Reduction**: Reducing the number of random variables under consideration to discover meaningful features.
- **Density Estimation**: Estimating the distribution of data points in a given space.

A classic example of unsupervised learning is the K-means clustering algorithm, which partitions a dataset into k clusters. The algorithm calculates the centroids of clusters and assigns each data point to the nearest centroid. The objective is to minimize the within-cluster variance:

$$\arg\min_{S} \sum_{i=1}^{k} \sum_{x \in S_i} \|x - \mu_i\|^2$$

where S indicates clusters and μ_i is the mean of points in cluster S_i.

Another significant example is Principal Component Analysis (PCA), a dimensionality reduction technique. PCA transforms the data to a new coordinate system such that the greatest variances lie on the first few axes. This transformation assists in reducing the complexity of models without substantial loss of information.

```
from sklearn.decomposition import PCA
import numpy as np

# Sample data
X = np.array([[2.5, 2.4], [0.5, 0.7], [2.2, 2.9], [1.9, 2.2], [3.1, 3.0], [2.3, 2.7]])

# Initialize PCA
pca = PCA(n_components=1)
pca_transformed = pca.fit_transform(X)

print(pca_transformed)
```

```
[[ 0.61654227]
 [-1.44971225]
 [ 0.14203547]
 [-0.76132615]
 [ 1.31804468]
 [ 0.13441686]]
```

Both supervised and unsupervised learning paradigms play integral roles in the deep learning landscape. Supervised learning is widely adopted due to its direct correspondence between input-output pairs, facilitating accurate predictions and classifications. Unsupervised learning, on the other hand, is invaluable for discovering hidden patterns and reducing data complexity, which serves as a precursor to many complex deep learning workflows. Understanding these paradigms equips practitioners with the ability to select and tailor their approaches based on specific data characteristics and project objectives.

1.8 Why Use Python and Keras for Deep Learning?

Python has emerged as the language of choice for many deep learning practitioners, and Keras, a high-level neural networks API, makes developing and experimenting with deep learning models faster and more accessible. The compelling reasons for using Python and Keras in deep learning are rooted in their design philosophies, ecosystem advantages, ease of use, and supportive communities.

Python's syntax is clear and readable, enabling rapid development. This readability is crucial when dealing with complex algorithms and data structures in deep learning, as it allows developers to focus more on solving problems rather than on the intricacies of language syntax. Furthermore, Python's extensive standard library and a wealth of third-party libraries facilitate various tasks from data manipulation (using pandas and numpy) to visualization (using matplotlib and seaborn).

Keras adds another layer of abstraction to deep learning models, wrapping the lower-level libraries such as TensorFlow, Theano, and Microsoft Cognitive Toolkit. This high-level interface minimizes the complexity involved in model creation. Consider the following example of building a simple neural network using Keras:

```
from tensorflow.keras.models import Sequential
from tensorflow.keras.layers import Dense
```

```
# Create a simple feed-forward neural network
model = Sequential()
model.add(Dense(64, activation='relu', input_dim=100))
model.add(Dense(10, activation='softmax'))

# Compile the model
model.compile(optimizer='adam',
              loss='categorical_crossentropy',
              metrics=['accuracy'])
```

This code snippet illustrates the concise syntax with which one can define a deep learning model, compile it, and optimize it. Each component and step are made explicit and accessible, emphasizing the model's architecture over intricate configuration details.

Python and Keras offer several other notable advantages:

- **Extensive Frameworks and Libraries:** Python's support for various machine learning and deep learning frameworks (such as TensorFlow, PyTorch, CNTK) allows for flexible experimentation. Keras integrates smoothly with these back-end engines, leveraging their optimization capabilities for different hardware (CPUs, GPUs, TPUs).

- **Active Development Community:** The vibrant Python and Keras communities contribute to continuous improvements, updates, and a flood of learning resources. This open-source ethos has led to the swift identification and resolution of bugs, an extensive repository of pre-trained models, and numerous tutorials and documentation.

- **Interoperability:** Python's compatibility with other programming languages ensures that components written in C, C++, or Fortran can be integrated into Python projects. Keras models can easily be exported and deployed using various tools, increasing their utility in production environments.

- **Ease of Learning and Prototyping:** Python's gentle learning curve combined with Keras's high-level APIs accelerates the learning and prototyping phases. This speed is particularly advantageous in research and development settings where iterative experimentation is critical.

- **Rich Dataset Handling:** Python's libraries like pandas, numpy, and scikit-learn provide robust tools for handling, preprocessing, and manipulating datasets. Seamless integration of these libraries with Keras simplifies the preparation of data pipelines.

- **Visualization Tools:** Effective visualization, which is crucial for understanding model performance and debugging, is facilitated by Python's visualization libraries. Integrations with TensorBoard, matplotlib, and seaborn enable tracking and visualization of metrics and training progress.

Consider an example of processing and visualizing a dataset before feeding it into a Keras model:

```
import pandas as pd
import numpy as np
import matplotlib.pyplot as plt
from sklearn.preprocessing import StandardScaler

# Load dataset
data = pd.read_csv('dataset.csv')

# Preprocess data
scaler = StandardScaler()
scaled_data = scaler.fit_transform(data)

# Visualize the data distribution
plt.hist(scaled_data, bins=50)
plt.title('Data Distribution')
plt.xlabel('Value')
plt.ylabel('Frequency')
plt.show()
```

This integration demonstrates the fluidity with which Python handles extensive data preparation and visualization tasks, essential steps in the deep learning workflow.

Additionally, the flexibility and interoperability of Python make deploying Keras models onto various platforms straightforward. For instance, serving a Keras model in a web application using Flask could look like this:

```
from flask import Flask, request, jsonify
from tensorflow.keras.models import load_model

app = Flask(__name__)
model = load_model('model.h5')

@app.route('/predict', methods=['POST'])
def predict():
    data = request.json
    prediction = model.predict(np.array(data['input']).reshape(1, -1))
    return jsonify({'prediction': prediction.tolist()})

if __name__ == '__main__':
    app.run(debug=True)
```

This example illustrates how simple it can be to expose a trained Keras model as a web service, emphasizing the practicality of deploying machine learning solutions using Python.

In sum, the combination of Python and Keras offers a powerful, intuitive, and scalable approach for deep learning, boosting productivity and enabling both researchers and industry professionals to build sophisticated models with ease.

1.9 Overview of the Deep Learning Workflow

The deep learning workflow encompasses several interconnected steps that systematically contribute to the development of a robust deep learning model. Each step is essential for ensuring the effectiveness of the model and can significantly impact its performance. This section delves into the intricacies of these steps, which include data collection and preprocessing, model selection and architecture, training, evaluation, hyperparameter tuning, and finally, deployment and monitoring.

The initial phase in the deep learning workflow is **data collection**. High-quality and relevant data are the foundation of any successful deep learning model. Data can be sourced from various domains, including images, text, audio, and time-series data. It is crucial to gather enough data to capture the underlying patterns necessary for the model to generalize well on unseen examples. Additionally, the diversity and representativeness of the data play a critical role in preventing biases and ensuring model robustness.

Once the data is collected, it must undergo **data preprocessing**. This step involves cleaning and transforming the data to make it suitable for training. Common preprocessing tasks include handling missing values, normalizing or standardizing the features, encoding categorical variables, and augmenting data for complex datasets like images and text. For instance, image data might require resizing, rotating, or flipping, while text data may involve tokenization and removing stop words.

```
# Sample code for normalizing image data
from tensorflow.keras.preprocessing.image import ImageDataGenerator

datagen = ImageDataGenerator(rescale=1./255)
train_generator = datagen.flow_from_directory(
    directory='path_to_train_data',
    target_size=(150, 150),
    batch_size=32,
    class_mode='binary')
```

Following preprocessing, the next step is **model selection and architecture**. This involves choosing an appropriate model framework and defining its structure. In Keras, this is typically achieved using the Sequential or Functional API. The architecture of the model depends on the problem at hand, with common models including Convolutional Neural Networks (CNNs) for image data, Recurrent Neural Networks (RNNs) for sequences, and Transformers for natural language processing tasks.

```
# Example of a simple CNN using Keras Sequential API
from tensorflow.keras.models import Sequential
from tensorflow.keras.layers import Conv2D, MaxPooling2D, Flatten, Dense

model = Sequential([
    Conv2D(32, (3, 3), activation='relu', input_shape=(150, 150, 3)),
    MaxPooling2D(pool_size=(2, 2)),
    Conv2D(64, (3, 3), activation='relu'),
    MaxPooling2D(pool_size=(2, 2)),
    Flatten(),
    Dense(64, activation='relu'),
    Dense(1, activation='sigmoid')
])
```

Training the model involves **compiling and fitting** it to the preprocessed data. Compilation integrates the optimizer, loss function, and evaluation metrics. The optimizer influences how the model learns, with common choices being SGD, Adam, and RMSprop. The loss function is crucial as it quantifies the disparity between the predicted and actual values, guiding the optimization process. The model is then fitted to the training data through the 'fit' method, which iteratively updates the model parameters.

```
# Compiling and training the model
model.compile(optimizer='adam', loss='binary_crossentropy', metrics=['accuracy'])

history = model.fit(train_generator, epochs=10, validation_data=validation_generator
    )
```

The effectiveness of a deep learning model is gauged during the **evaluation** phase. Evaluation metrics such as accuracy, precision, recall, and F1-score provide insights into the model's performance on unseen data. It is also essential to analyze the learning curves—plots of training and validation metrics over epochs—to identify issues like overfitting or underfitting.

```
Epoch 1/10
100/100 [==============================] - 45s 450ms/step - loss: 0.693 - accuracy: 0.50 - val_loss: 0.693 - val_accuracy: 0.50
Epoch 2/10
100/100 [==============================] - 44s 440ms/step - loss: 0.690 - accuracy: 0.54 - val_loss: 0.689 - val_accuracy: 0.54
...
```

Once an initial model is trained, **hyperparameter tuning** is conducted to optimize performance. Hyperparameters, which include the learning rate, batch size, and the number of layers, significantly influence the model's training process. Techniques such as grid search, random search, or more advanced approaches like Bayesian optimization and Hyperband can be employed to systematically explore the hyperparameter space.

```
# Example of hyperparameter tuning using Keras Tuner
import kerastuner as kt

def model_builder(hp):
    model = Sequential()
    hp_units = hp.Int('units', min_value=32, max_value=512, step=32)
    model.add(Dense(units=hp_units, activation='relu', input_shape=(input_shape,)))

    model.add(Dense(1, activation='sigmoid'))

    hp_learning_rate = hp.Choice('learning_rate', values=[1e-2, 1e-3, 1e-4])
    model.compile(optimizer=tf.keras.optimizers.Adam(learning_rate=
        hp_learning_rate),
              loss='binary_crossentropy',
              metrics=['accuracy'])
    return model

tuner = kt.Hyperband(model_builder, objective='val_accuracy', max_epochs=10,
    factor=3)
tuner.search(train_data, train_labels, epochs=10, validation_data=(val_data,
    val_labels))
```

The final step in the workflow is **deployment and monitoring**. The trained model is deployed to a production environment where it can make predictions on new data. Deployment can be on a variety of platforms, including cloud services, edge devices, or integrated into larger software systems. Continuous monitoring is necessary to ensure the model maintains its performance over time, considering factors like data drift and changes in real-world conditions. Retraining the model with fresh data may be required to keep it up-to-date and reliable.

Each step of the deep learning workflow is interconnected and vital. Proper execution of data collection and preprocessing sets a solid foundation. The selection of an appropriate model architecture, coupled with vigilant training and evaluation, ensures robust initial performance. Through diligent hyperparameter tuning, the model's efficacy is optimized further. Finally, thoughtful deployment and continuous monitoring fortify the model's sustained performance in real-world applications.

Chapter 2

Getting Started with Keras

This chapter provides an introduction to Keras, detailing the steps for installing Keras and its dependencies, and setting up the development environment. It compares Keras with other deep learning libraries, explains the basic architecture of a Keras model, and covers the different types of layers and models available. Readers will learn to build their first neural network with Keras, preprocess data, and save and load models. The chapter also introduces Keras documentation and support resources.

2.1 Introduction to Keras

Keras is an open-source software library that provides a Python interface for artificial neural networks. It acts as an abstraction layer that facilitates the construction and training of deep learning models. Initially conceived and developed by François Chollet, Keras has garnered widespread adoption within the machine learning community due its user-friendly design and modularity. Despite its simplicity, Keras is powerful enough to build state-of-the-art deep learning models.

The core philosophy of Keras is accessibility and user-friendliness. This simplicity is achieved through the following guiding principles:

- **User-Friendly API:** Keras is designed to enable fast experimentation and ease of use. The API is consistent and simple, reducing the step count required to build and train neural networks. Even beginners can quickly learn and start creating models.

- **Modular and Composable:** Keras models are made by connecting configurable building blocks. These blocks – layers, loss functions, optimizers, and more – can be easily combined to create complex architectures.

- **Extensibility:** If the predefined building blocks are insufficient, Keras allows for the creation of custom blocks for specific needs, ensuring flexibility.

- **Interoperability:** Keras is designed to be compatible with multiple backend engines. It initially supported TensorFlow, Theano, and Microsoft Cognitive Toolkit (CNTK). Today, it primarily interfaces with TensorFlow, leveraging its advanced features and optimizations.

Installing Keras and its Dependencies

Keras requires a few dependencies to be operational, most notably the backend engine. For most users, TensorFlow will be the backend of choice.

To install TensorFlow and Keras with pip, the Python package manager, execute the following command:

```
pip install tensorflow keras
```

Once installed, Keras is ready to be imported and used in your projects.

Setting Up the Development Environment

A typical development environment for Keras includes an Integrated Development Environment (IDE) such as PyCharm, Jupyter Notebook, or Visual Studio Code. These tools provide robust support for Python programming and are integrated with package management systems and visualization tools, which are crucial for deep learning projects.

Keras vs Other Deep Learning Libraries

When compared to other deep learning libraries, Keras stands out for its simplicity and ease of use. Libraries like TensorFlow, PyTorch, and Caffe offer greater flexibility and control but often come with steeper learning curves.

A simple example to demonstrate the ease with which Keras can be used involves constructing and training a neural network for binary classification:

```
from keras.models import Sequential
from keras.layers import Dense

# Initialize the model
model = Sequential()

# Add layers to the model
model.add(Dense(12, input_dim=8, activation='relu'))
model.add(Dense(8, activation='relu'))
model.add(Dense(1, activation='sigmoid'))

# Compile and train the model
model.compile(loss='binary_crossentropy', optimizer='adam', metrics=['accuracy'])
model.fit(X, y, epochs=150, batch_size=10)
```

The simplicity and brevity of this code highlight Keras's user-friendly nature.

Basic Architecture of a Keras Model

At the core of Keras is the *Model* class, which is used to create a Keras model. Two types of models are possible: the Sequential model and the Model class using the Functional API.

The *Sequential* model is a straightforward stack of layers. More complex architectures, including those with non-sequential data flows like multi-input or multi-output networks, can be built using the Functional API.

Understanding Keras Layers and Models

Layers are the primary building blocks of Keras models. A layer encapsulates a set of computations that transform input data into output data. Given the variety of deep learning applications, Keras provides various types of layers, such as Dense, Conv2D, LSTM, and more, each specialized for different tasks.

Constructing a Keras model typically involves:

- Instantiating a model.
- Adding and configuring layers.
- Compiling the model by specifying loss, optimizer, and metrics.
- Training the model on data.
- Evaluating the model's performance using unseen data.

Building Your First Neural Network with Keras

Constructing a first neural network in Keras does not require deep expertise, as illustrated by the following example:

```
from keras.models import Sequential
from keras.layers import Dense

# Initialize the model
model = Sequential()

# Add layers to the model
model.add(Dense(12, input_dim=8, activation='relu'))
model.add(Dense(8, activation='relu'))
model.add(Dense(1, activation='sigmoid'))

# Compile and train the model
model.compile(loss='binary_crossentropy', optimizer='adam', metrics=['accuracy'])
model.fit(X, y, epochs=150, batch_size=10)
```

Data Preprocessing with Keras

Before feeding data into a model, it often requires preprocessing. Keras provides tools to scale, normalize, and augment data, ensuring the model trains effectively and generalizes better.

Saving and Loading Models in Keras

Model persistence is critical in deep learning, and Keras facilitates saving and loading models with ease using methods like *model.save()* and *load_model()*.

Keras Documentation and Support

Keras documentation is comprehensive, offering detailed descriptions and examples for its API. Additionally, the Keras community is active, providing support via forums, GitHub issues, and Stack Overflow.

Keras revolutionizes the development of deep learning models by making the process straightforward and accessible, emphasizing efficiency and user-friendly design in the rapidly evolving field of deep learning.

2.2 Installing Keras and its Dependencies

To utilize Keras effectively, the first step is to set up the necessary software environment. This section will guide you through the process of installing Keras and its dependencies, ensuring that you have a stable and efficient setup for deep learning tasks.

Keras relies on a backend engine to perform tensor operations and optimize computations. The most common backends used with Keras are TensorFlow, Theano, and Microsoft Cognitive Toolkit (CNTK). TensorFlow is the recommended backend due to its widespread community support and extensive documentation.

To begin, ensure that you have Python installed on your system. Keras supports Python 3.6 and above. You can download Python from the official website (https://www.python.org). After installing Python, it is a good practice to set up a virtual environment to manage your project dependencies. Using a virtual environment isolates your project's dependencies, preventing conflicts between packages used in different projects.

```
python -m venv keras_env
```

Activate the virtual environment using the command corresponding to your operating system:

- Windows:

  ```
  keras_env\Scripts\activate
  ```

- macOS/Linux:

  ```
  source keras_env/bin/activate
  ```

With the virtual environment activated, proceed to install Keras and its dependencies. The primary backend, TensorFlow, can be installed using the pip package manager. Keras is bundled with TensorFlow 2.x and above, so installing TensorFlow will also install Keras.

```
pip install tensorflow
```

You can verify the installation by executing a Python command that imports Keras and checks its version:

```
import tensorflow as tf
print(tf.keras.__version__)
```

```
2.5.0
```

Executing the above commands should display the installed version of Keras, indicating that the installation was successful.

If you prefer to use Theano or CNTK as the backend, you will need to install these libraries separately. For Theano:

```
pip install theano
```

For Microsoft Cognitive Toolkit (CNTK):

```
pip install cntk
```

After installing the backend of your choice, you need to configure Keras to use that backend. Create a configuration file named keras.json in the $HOME/.keras/ directory with the following content to specify your backend:

```
{
    "floatx": "float32",
    "epsilon": 1e-07,
    "backend": "tensorflow",
    "image_data_format": "channels_last"
}
```

Replace "tensorflow" with "theano" or "cntk" if you are using those backends. The floatx, epsilon, and image_data_format settings specify default values for floating-point precision, numerical stability, and image data format, respectively.

In addition to the backend engine, Keras requires several other essential packages. Ensure that you have the following commonly used dependencies installed in your virtual environment:

- **NumPy**: A package for scientific computing with Python.

  ```
  pip install numpy
  ```

- **Pandas**: A library for data manipulation and analysis.

  ```
  pip install pandas
  ```

- **HDF5 and h5py**: Used for saving Keras models in HDF5 format.

  ```
  pip install h5py
  ```

- **Matplotlib**: A plotting library for creating static, animated, and interactive visualizations.

  ```
  pip install matplotlib
  ```

- **scikit-learn**: A package for machine learning in Python, providing simple and efficient tools for data analysis.

  ```
  pip install scikit-learn
  ```

Installing these dependencies ensures that you have a comprehensive setup to perform various tasks using Keras, from data preprocessing to model visualization.

After installing the necessary packages, it is a good practice to test the overall setup by running a simple Keras code snippet. The following code creates a basic neural network model and prints its summary:

```
import tensorflow as tf
from tensorflow.keras.models import Sequential
from tensorflow.keras.layers import Dense

# Define a simple Sequential model
model = Sequential([
    Dense(32, activation='relu', input_shape=(784,)),
    Dense(10, activation='softmax')
])

# Print the model summary
model.summary()
```

```
Model: "sequential"
_________________________________________________________________
 Layer (type)              Output Shape              Param #
=================================================================
 dense (Dense)              (None, 32)              25120

 dense_1 (Dense)              (None, 10)              330

=================================================================
Total params: 25450 (99.41 KB)
Trainable params: 25450 (99.41 KB)
Non-trainable params: 0 (0.00 Byte)
_________________________________________________________________
```

This output confirms that the setup is working correctly. At this point, you are ready to start building deep learning models with Keras.

To avoid any compatibility issues, refactor your project requirements into a requirements.txt file. This file lists all the dependencies with their respective versions. Here is an example:

```
tensorflow==2.5.0
numpy==1.19.5
pandas==1.2.4
h5py==3.1.0
matplotlib==3.4.2
scikit-learn==0.24.2
```

You can install all the dependencies listed in the requirements.txt file using the following command:

```
pip install -r requirements.txt
```

This ensures that your development environment remains consistent and replicable.

2.3 Setting Up the Development Environment

Establishing a suitable development environment is critical to ensure efficient and productive work with Keras. This section outlines the necessary steps to set up the environment, including installing essential software, configuring the environment, and verifying the installation.

Ensuring Python Installation:

Keras requires Python 3.6 or higher. Verify the currently installed version of Python using the command:

```
python --version
```

If Python is not installed or the version is below 3.6, download and install the appropriate version from the official Python website: https://www.python.org/downloads/. After installation, recheck the version to confirm the update.

Installing a Virtual Environment:

Using virtual environments isolates your project dependencies and avoids conflicts with other projects on the same machine. Install virtualenv using pip:

```
pip install virtualenv
```

Create a new virtual environment for your Keras project and activate it:

```
# Create a virtual environment named 'keras_env'
virtualenv keras_env

# Activate the virtual environment
# On Windows:
.\keras_env\Scripts\activate

# On macOS/Linux:
source keras_env/bin/activate
```

When the virtual environment is active, the command prompt is prefixed with the environment name, indicating that all Python packages installed will be confined to this environment.

Installing Keras and TensorFlow:

Keras was originally developed as a minimalist framework for building deep learning models, running on top of various backends like TensorFlow, Theano, and CNTK. Presently, TensorFlow is the default and highly recommended backend. Install TensorFlow and Keras within the activated virtual environment:

```
pip install tensorflow keras
```

Setting Up an Integrated Development Environment (IDE):

Choose an IDE that supports Python development effectively. Popular choices include:

- **PyCharm:** Offers extensive support for Python and deep learning libraries, including debugging and virtual environment management.
- **VS Code:** Lightweight and highly customizable with extensions for Python, TensorFlow, and Jupyter Notebooks.
- **Jupyter Notebook:** An interactive environment for running and sharing notebooks, integrating code execution with rich text, visualizations, and more.

For PyCharm and VS Code, configure the IDE to use the virtual environment created in the previous steps. Refer to their official documentation for step-by-step guides.

Installing Additional Libraries:

To streamline data manipulation, visualization, and model evaluation, install the following commonly used libraries:

```
pip install numpy pandas matplotlib seaborn scikit-learn
```

- **NumPy:** Essential for numerical computations and array manipulations.
- **Pandas:** Provides data structures and functions for data analysis.
- **Matplotlib** and **Seaborn:** Useful for plotting and data visualization.
- **Scikit-learn:** Offers a range of tools for machine learning and statistical modeling.

Verifying the Installation:

Create a simple Python script named verify_keras_setup.py to ensure that TensorFlow and Keras are accurately installed:

```
# verify_keras_setup.py

import tensorflow as tf
from tensorflow import keras

# Print TensorFlow version
print('TensorFlow version:', tf.__version__)

# Print Keras version
print('Keras version:', keras.__version__)

# Verify TensorFlow can access a GPU (if available)
if tf.config.list_physical_devices('GPU'):
    print('GPU is detected and available for TensorFlow.')
else:
    print('No GPU detected.')
```

Run the verification script within the activated virtual environment:

```
python verify_keras_setup.py
```

The expected output should confirm the installed versions of TensorFlow and Keras and check for a GPU:

```
TensorFlow version: 2.x.x
Keras version: 2.x.x
GPU is detected and available for TensorFlow.
```

Implementing these steps ensures a correctly configured development environment for working with Keras, enabling you to leverage its capabilities for deep learning projects robustly.

2.4 Keras vs Other Deep Learning Libraries

Keras is a high-level neural networks API, written in Python and capable of running on top of TensorFlow, CNTK, or Theano. It aims to enable fast experimentation with deep neural networks, and it has become one of the most popular frameworks in both industry and academic research. Comparing Keras with other deep learning libraries involves examining a range of factors such as usability, flexibility, speed, extensibility, and community support.

Usability: One of Keras's cornerstone features is its user-friendly API. Its easy-to-use, modular architecture allows developers to quickly prototype deep learning models. The straightforward nature of the Keras API is particularly advantageous for beginners while still being powerful enough for experts. For example, constructing a simple feedforward neural network in Keras can be done with just a few lines of code:

```
from keras.models import Sequential
from keras.layers import Dense

model = Sequential()
model.add(Dense(64, activation='relu', input_dim=100))
model.add(Dense(10, activation='softmax'))
model.compile(optimizer='rmsprop',
              loss='categorical_crossentropy',
              metrics=['accuracy'])
```

In contrast, other frameworks like TensorFlow and PyTorch may require more boilerplate code to accomplish the same task. While this increased complexity might provide more flexibility, it can also hinder rapid prototyping and experimentation.

Flexibility: Flexibility allows for more sophisticated and customized neural network architectures once the user gains deeper expertise. Although Keras supports creating complex models, its high-level nature might restrict granular customization in some instances. Libraries like TensorFlow and PyTorch offer lower-level operations that allow researchers to experiment with avant-garde architectures and novel layers. This feature is beneficial for cutting-edge research where every nuance of the model needs to be controlled.

TensorFlow's flexibility is demonstrated through its computational graph approach, where users can define and manipulate tensors and operations:

```
import tensorflow as tf

a = tf.placeholder(tf.float32)
b = tf.placeholder(tf.float32)
add_op = a + b
with tf.Session() as sess:
    result = sess.run(add_op, feed_dict={a: 3, b: 4.5})
print(result)
```

The added control allows more detailed optimizations and custom layers, making it suitable for more complex scenarios.

Speed: The execution speed of deep learning models is a critical factor, particularly for large datasets and complex computational tasks. While Keras is efficient, it is ultimately limited by the backend framework (TensorFlow, CNTK, or Theano) with which it is paired. Thus, the performance is highly dependent on the underlying backend engine's capabilities.

PyTorch, on the other hand, uses a dynamic computation graph, which can be more efficient for certain types of models where changes in the architecture are frequent during the training process. This dynamic nature tends to speed up iterative experiment cycles, a feature crucial in exploratory research:

```
import torch

x = torch.tensor([2.0], requires_grad=True)
y = x**2
y.backward()
print(x.grad)
```

Extensibility: Extensibility allows developers to seamlessly integrate custom components and new algorithms into the framework. Keras provides a flexible mechanism to add custom layers, loss functions, and optimizers. This modular design allows extensions without needing to alter the source code significantly. For instance, users can implement custom layers by inheriting from the base Layer class:

```
from keras.layers import Layer

class CustomLayer(Layer):
    def __init__(self, output_dim, **kwargs):
        super(CustomLayer, self).__init__(**kwargs)
        self.output_dim = output_dim

    def build(self, input_shape):
        self.kernel = self.add_weight(name='kernel',
                                      shape=(input_shape[1], self.output_dim),
                                      initializer='uniform',
                                      trainable=True)
        super(CustomLayer, self).build(input_shape)

    def call(self, inputs):
        return K.dot(inputs, self.kernel)
```

This extensibility is crucial for research environments where custom methods and innovative approaches need to be tested regularly.

Community Support and Resources: The depth of community support and availability of learning resources significantly influence the adoption and ease of learning a deep learning library. Keras boasts an extensive and active community that contributes to its wide range of tutorials, documentation, and third-party resources. This wealth of resources assists users of all levels in overcoming challenges and staying updated with the latest advancements.

TensorFlow and PyTorch also benefit from robust community support, thanks to their backing by Google and Facebook, respectively. However, the steep learning curve may render them less accessible to beginners compared to Keras. Nevertheless, their comprehensive documentation and the availability of pre-trained models and community-driven projects provide invaluable support for more experienced users.

In , each deep learning library has its unique advantages. Keras excels in ease of use, rapid prototyping, and extensive community support, making it an ideal choice for beginners and those needing quick iterations. However, for more complex, customized models and detailed control over computations, TensorFlow and PyTorch provide the necessary flexibility and performance benefits. The choice between these libraries will ultimately depend on the user's requirements, expertise, and the specific nature of the task at hand.

2.5 Basic Architecture of a Keras Model

Keras is designed to be user-friendly and modular, providing a high-level neural networks API that allows for easy and quick prototyping. The core component of Keras is the model, which can be constructed using either the Sequential API or the Functional API. Understanding the basic architecture of a Keras model is fundamental to effectively leveraging the power of this library.

Layers as Building Blocks: In Keras, layers are the primary building blocks for creating models. Each layer takes as input one or more tensors and outputs a tensor. This modular approach allows for flexibility and ease of use. Here is a simple example demonstrating the creation of layers:

```
from keras.layers import Dense
layer = Dense(units=32, activation='relu')
```

In this example, we import the Dense layer, which is a fully connected layer, and configure it with 32 units (neurons) and a ReLU activation function.

The Sequential API: The Sequential model is a linear stack of layers. It is appropriate for most problems but is limited to sequential data flow from one layer to the next, without any branching or merging. Below is an example of constructing a Sequential model:

```
from keras.models import Sequential
from keras.layers import Dense

model = Sequential()
model.add(Dense(units=64, activation='relu', input_dim=100))
model.add(Dense(units=10, activation='softmax'))
```

In the above code, the Sequential model is instantiated, and two dense layers are added sequentially. The first layer has 64 units, ReLU activation, and takes an input dimension of 100. The second layer has 10 units and a softmax activation, suitable for classification tasks with 10 classes.

The Functional API: The Functional API is more flexible and can handle models with complex topologies such as multi-output models, directed acyclic graphs, or shared layers. Below is an example of building a model using the Functional API:

```
from keras.models import Model
from keras.layers import Input, Dense

inputs = Input(shape=(784,))
x = Dense(64, activation='relu')(inputs)
outputs = Dense(10, activation='softmax')(x)

model = Model(inputs=inputs, outputs=outputs)
```

In this example, the Input layer is used to define the input tensor. Two dense layers are then defined with the input tensor and connected sequentially. Finally, the Model class is used to create a model by specifying the input and output tensors.

Model Compilation: Before training a model, it needs to be compiled, which involves specifying the optimizer, loss function, and metrics. Consider the following code:

```
model.compile(optimizer='adam',
              loss='categorical_crossentropy',
              metrics=['accuracy'])
```

Here, the Adam optimizer is chosen for its adaptive learning rate properties, categorical_crossentropy is selected as the loss function for multi-class classification, and accuracy is specified as a metric to evaluate the model's performance.

Model Training: Training a model involves feeding data into the model and allowing it to learn patterns. The fit method is used for this purpose:

```
model.fit(x_train, y_train, epochs=5, batch_size=32)
```

In the above example, the model is trained on the data x_train and target values y_train for 5 epochs with a batch size of 32.

Model Evaluation and Prediction: Once trained, the model can be evaluated using the evaluate method and used to make predictions with the predict method:

```
evaluation = model.evaluate(x_test, y_test)
predictions = model.predict(x_test)
```

The evaluate method returns the loss value and metric value(s) for the model based on the test data. The predict method generates the output predictions for the input samples provided.

By understanding these components and their interactions, learners can construct, compile, and train Keras models effectively. The modular design allows for significant flexibility in tailoring models to specific needs, facilitating both straightforward and complex neural network architectures.

2.6 Understanding Keras Layers and Models

Understanding the fundamentals of Keras layers and models is essential to harnessing the full potential of this powerful deep learning library. The Keras framework provides a simple yet efficient interface to build complex neural networks. This section delves into the core components that make up the architecture of a Keras model, namely layers and models, and elucidates their functionalities, characteristics, and the basic types available.

In Keras, the building blocks of neural networks are **layers**. Each layer in a neural network performs a specific data transformation, contributing to the overall processing capability of the network. The most fundamental layer type is the Dense layer, also known as a fully connected layer. In a Dense layer, every neuron is connected to every neuron in the previous and next layers.

Consider the following code snippet that demonstrates how to create a Dense layer using Keras:

```
from keras.layers import Dense

dense_layer = Dense(units=64, activation='relu', input_shape=(100,))
```

In this example, we instantiate a Dense layer with 64 units (or neurons), using the ReLU (Rectified Linear Unit) activation function, and specify the input shape which dictates that each input instance must have 100 features.

Keras also provides layers such as Conv2D, MaxPooling2D, LSTM, and Embedding, among others, each serving unique purposes:

- Conv2D: Used for creating convolutional networks, which are particularly effective for image processing tasks.

- MaxPooling2D: Often used in conjunction with convolutional layers to reduce the spatial dimensions, thereby decreasing the parameter count and mitigating overfitting.
- LSTM: Long Short-Term Memory layers are designed for sequential data and are widely applied in time-series forecasting and natural language processing.
- Embedding: Converts categorical data into dense vectors of fixed size, which is useful for text data.

Here's an illustrative example of a simple Convolutional Neural Network (CNN) model comprising convolutional and pooling layers:

```
from keras.models import Sequential
from keras.layers import Conv2D, MaxPooling2D, Flatten, Dense

model = Sequential()
model.add(Conv2D(32, kernel_size=(3, 3), activation='relu', input_shape=(64, 64, 3)))

model.add(MaxPooling2D(pool_size=(2, 2)))
model.add(Flatten())
model.add(Dense(units=128, activation='relu'))
model.add(Dense(units=10, activation='softmax'))
```

In the above code, a sequential model is defined using Keras' Sequential API. It begins with a Conv2D layer with 32 filters of size 3x3, followed by a MaxPooling2D layer with a pooling window of 2x2. After flattening the last pooling layer's output, it adds a Dense layer with 128 neurons and ReLU activation, and finally, another Dense layer with 10 neurons and softmax activation for classification purposes.

Keras models can be defined using two main types:

Sequential Models offer a straightforward way to build linear stacks of layers. These models are highly intuitive and are particularly useful for simple architectures. However, they limit to models where layers have a single input and output tensor.

Functional API is more flexible and capable of handling complex architectures, such as multi-input, multi-output models, directed acyclic graphs, or models with shared layers.

An example of defining a model using the functional API is provided below:

```
from keras.models import Model
from keras.layers import Input, Dense

input_tensor = Input(shape=(100,))
x = Dense(units=64, activation='relu')(input_tensor)
```

```
output_tensor = Dense(units=10, activation='softmax')(x)

model = Model(inputs=input_tensor, outputs=output_tensor)
```

In this example, an input layer is created using Input, followed by a Dense layer linked directly using function calls. The model is instantiated using the Model class, specifying the input and output tensors.

The flexibility of the functional API empowers users to create intricate models by connecting layers in almost any possible way. For instance, models that process multiple types of data or use shared weights can be efficiently implemented using the functional API.

A practical understanding of layers and models will enable you to tailor network architectures precisely to your problem domains and improve model training performance.

2.7 Building Your First Neural Network with Keras

Building a neural network with Keras entails defining the model, compiling it by specifying the optimizer and loss function, training the model with data, and evaluating its performance. This provides a step-by-step guide on how to create a simple neural network using Keras.

Firstly, ensure that you have successfully installed Keras and its dependencies as outlined in the previous sections. Begin by importing the necessary modules:

```
import numpy as np
from keras.models import Sequential
from keras.layers import Dense
from keras.optimizers import Adam
```

Next, create a dataset. For this example, let's use a synthetic dataset generated using NumPy:

```
# Generate dummy data
x_train = np.random.random((1000, 20))
y_train = np.random.randint(2, size=(1000, 1))

x_test = np.random.random((200, 20))
y_test = np.random.randint(2, size=(200, 1))
```

The next step is to define the model. Keras provides a Sequential API for creating models layer-by-layer. Each layer can be added using the add method:

```
# Define the model
model = Sequential()
model.add(Dense(64, input_dim=20, activation='relu'))
model.add(Dense(64, activation='relu'))
model.add(Dense(1, activation='sigmoid'))
```

In the code above, a Sequential model is defined with three layers:

- A Dense layer with 64 units and ReLU activation function, where input_dim=20 specifies the input shape. The ReLU activation function will introduce non-linearity to the model.
- Another Dense layer with 64 units and ReLU activation.
- A final Dense layer with 1 unit and a Sigmoid activation function for binary classification.

The model is then compiled by specifying the optimizer, loss function, and metrics to monitor:

```
model.compile(optimizer=Adam(),
              loss='binary_crossentropy',
              metrics=['accuracy'])
```

Here, the Adam optimizer is used for optimization, binary crossentropy as the loss function suitable for binary classification tasks, and accuracy as the evaluation metric.

Training the model involves calling the fit method with the training data:

```
model.fit(x_train, y_train, epochs=10, batch_size=32)
```

In the code above, the model is trained for 10 epochs with a batch size of 32. The fit function returns a History object that contains all information collected during training.

Once the model is trained, its performance can be evaluated on the test set:

```
score = model.evaluate(x_test, y_test, batch_size=32)
print('Test loss:', score[0])
print('Test accuracy:', score[1])
```

We use the evaluate method to assess the model's loss and accuracy on the test data. The method returns the loss value and metric values defined during the compile step. The resulting score is printed to the console:

```
Test loss: 0.6931
Test accuracy: 0.50
```

To make predictions with the trained model, the predict method can be employed:

```
predictions = model.predict(x_test)
```

The predict function outputs predictions for the input samples. These predictions can be post-processed or directly used depending on the problem at hand.

To save the trained model for later use, the save method is used:

```
model.save('my_model.h5')
```

The model is saved to a file named my_model.h5, which can be loaded back using the load_model function from Keras:

```
from keras.models import load_model
loaded_model = load_model('my_model.h5')
```

This provides a complete guide to building, compiling, training, evaluating, and saving a neural network model using Keras.

2.8 Data Preprocessing with Keras

Effective data preprocessing is crucial for achieving optimal results in any deep learning task. In Keras, several utilities and functions facilitate the preprocessing of data, ensuring that it is in the correct format and appropriately scaled for training neural networks.

Keras provides comprehensive support for various data types, including image data, text data, and sequence data. This section covers essential preprocessing operations such as normalization, tokenization, shuffling, and batching, along with examples to solidify the concepts.

Normalization

Normalization is the process of scaling data into a specified range, typically [0, 1] or [-1, 1]. This improves the model's performance and convergence rate by stabilizing the gradient descent process. In Keras, normalization of image data is often performed using the ImageDataGenerator class:

```
from keras.preprocessing.image import ImageDataGenerator

datagen = ImageDataGenerator(rescale=1.0/255)
```

```
train_generator = datagen.flow_from_directory(
    'data/train',
    target_size=(150, 150),
    batch_size=32,
    class_mode='binary'
)
```

In the example above, the rescale parameter scales the pixel values to the range [0, 1].

Tokenization

Tokenization is a preprocessing step for textual data where text is converted into sequences of tokens (typically words or characters). Keras provides the Tokenizer class for this purpose:

```
from keras.preprocessing.text import Tokenizer

texts = [
    "I love deep learning",
    "Keras makes deep learning straightforward"
]

tokenizer = Tokenizer(num_words=100)
tokenizer.fit_on_texts(texts)

sequences = tokenizer.texts_to_sequences(texts)
word_index = tokenizer.word_index

print("Sequences:", sequences)
print("Word Index:", word_index)
```

The num_words parameter limits the vocabulary size to the most frequent 100 words. The texts_to_sequences function converts the texts to sequences of integers representing the index of each word in the word_index dictionary.

Shuffling and Batching

Shuffling and batching are essential steps in preparing data for training to ensure the model generalizes well and avoids overfitting. The tf.data API in TensorFlow, which Keras is built upon, provides utilities for efficient data pipeline creation:

```
import tensorflow as tf

# Assume dataset is a tf.data.Dataset object
dataset = tf.data.Dataset.from_tensor_slices((images, labels))

# Shuffle and batch the dataset
dataset = dataset.shuffle(buffer_size=10000).batch(32)

# Prefetch to improve performance
dataset = dataset.prefetch(buffer_size=tf.data.AUTOTUNE)

# Iterate over the dataset
```

```
for batch in dataset:
    # Training loop here
    pass
```

The shuffle method randomly shuffles the data, and the batch method groups the data into batches. prefetch improves throughput by overlapping data preprocessing and model training.

Image Augmentation

Another powerful feature provided by the ImageDataGenerator class is image augmentation, which artificially enlarges the training dataset by creating modified versions of the original images. This technique helps improve the model's robustness and generalization:

```
datagen = ImageDataGenerator(
    rotation_range=40,
    width_shift_range=0.2,
    height_shift_range=0.2,
    shear_range=0.2,
    zoom_range=0.2,
    horizontal_flip=True,
    fill_mode='nearest'
)

# Example of augmenting a single image
img = load_img('data/train/cats/cat1.jpg') # PIL image
x = img_to_array(img) # Numpy array with shape (150, 150, 3)
x = x.reshape((1,) + x.shape) # Reshape to (1, 150, 150, 3)

i = 0
for batch in datagen.flow(x, batch_size=1):
    plt.figure(i)
    imgplot = plt.imshow(array_to_img(batch[0]))
    i += 1
    if i % 4 == 0:
        break
plt.show()
```

The parameters such as rotation range, width_shift_range, height_shift_range, etc., specify the types of augmentation to apply, thereby creating diverse training examples.

Text Vectorization

After tokenizing textual data, further preprocessing often involves converting sequences of tokens into vector representations suitable for inputting to a neural network. One common approach is One-Hot Encoding:

```
from keras.preprocessing.text import Tokenizer
from keras.utils import to_categorical

texts = ["I love deep learning", "Keras makes deep learning straightforward"]
tokenizer = Tokenizer(num_words=100)
```

```
tokenizer.fit_on_texts(texts)
sequences = tokenizer.texts_to_sequences(texts)

one_hot_results = []
for sequence in sequences:
    one_hot = to_categorical(sequence, num_classes=100)
    one_hot_results.append(one_hot)

print("One-Hot Encoded Sequences:", one_hot_results)
```

The to_categorical function converts integer sequences to binary class matrices, creating a one-hot encoded representation of the input tokens.

Utilizing the preprocessing tools provided by Keras ensures that data is accurately and efficiently transformed to a format conducive for training robust and effective deep learning models. The procedures outlined in this section are foundational to the data preparation steps in Keras-based workflows.

2.9 Saving and Loading Models in Keras

In this section, we will delve into the procedures for saving and loading models in Keras. This is a crucial aspect of the model lifecycle, facilitating the reuse, sharing, and deployment of trained models. Keras provides several methods to save both the architecture and the weights of a model, enabling users to persist the state of a model and later reload it for further use or experimentation. We will explore different functionalities that Keras offers to accomplish these tasks reliably.

Saving the Entire Model

Keras allows you to save the entire model, which includes:

- The architecture of the model, allowing to reinstantiate the model.
- The weights of the model.
- The training configuration (loss, optimizer).
- The state of the optimizer, enabling you to resume training exactly where you left off.

To save the entire model, you can use the Model.save() method. Below is an example where we build a simple model and save it to a file named my_model.h5:

```
import tensorflow as tf
from tensorflow.keras.models import Sequential
from tensorflow.keras.layers import Dense

# Building a simple model
model = Sequential([
    Dense(32, activation='relu', input_shape=(784,)),
    Dense(10, activation='softmax')
])

model.compile(optimizer='adam',
              loss='sparse_categorical_crossentropy',
              metrics=['accuracy'])

# Saving the model to a file
model.save('my_model.h5')
```

Loading the Entire Model

Once saved, the model can be reloaded using the tf.keras.models.load_model function. This will enable you to restore the complete state of the model including the weight and optimizer configuration. Here's how you can do it:

```
# Loading the model from file
reconstructed_model = tf.keras.models.load_model('my_model.h5')

# Summary of the loaded model
reconstructed_model.summary()
```

By performing the above steps, the reloaded model is now identical to the one you saved, and it is possible to resume training or evaluate it further.

Saving Weights Only

In some cases, you may only want to save the weights of the model rather than the entire architecture. This can be especially useful when the model architecture is already known and only the trained weights need to be applied. This can be achieved using the model.save_weights() method.

```
# Save only the weights to a file
model.save_weights('model_weights.h5')
```

Loading Weights into a Model

To load weights into a model, the architecture of the model must be defined before calling the load_weights() method. This approach allows you to apply the saved weights to a new instance of the same model architecture.

```
# Creating a new instance of the same model architecture
```

```
new_model = Sequential([
    Dense(32, activation='relu', input_shape=(784,)),
    Dense(10, activation='softmax')
])

# Loading the weights into the new model
new_model.load_weights('model_weights.h5')
```

Saving Model to JSON or YAML Format

Keras also provides the option to save the model architecture to JSON or YAML format. This is useful when you need to share the model architecture without weights. Below is how you can achieve this:

```
# Save model architecture to JSON
json_config = model.to_json()
with open('model_config.json', 'w') as json_file:
    json_file.write(json_config)
```

```
# Save model architecture to YAML
yaml_config = model.to_yaml()
with open('model_config.yaml', 'w') as yaml_file:
    yaml_file.write(yaml_config)
```

To load the model architecture back from a JSON or YAML file, use the tf.keras.models.model_from_json() or tf.keras.models.model_from_yaml() functions and then load the weights:

```
# Load model architecture from JSON
with open('model_config.json') as json_file:
    json_config = json_file.read()

model_from_json = tf.keras.models.model_from_json(json_config)

# Load weights into the new model
model_from_json.load_weights('model_weights.h5')
```

```
# Load model architecture from YAML
with open('model_config.yaml') as yaml_file:
    yaml_config = yaml_file.read()

model_from_yaml = tf.keras.models.model_from_yaml(yaml_config)

# Load weights into the new model
model_from_yaml.load_weights('model_weights.h5')
```

These functionalities facilitate a flexible approach for saving and loading models, enabling effective model management and deployment strategies.

2.10 Keras Documentation and Support

Effective utilization of any deep learning library necessitates an understanding of the available documentation and support resources. Keras, being one of the most user-friendly frameworks, provides extensive documentation and multiple avenues for support.

The primary resource for understanding Keras is its official documentation. It is comprehensive and regularly updated to reflect the latest changes and additions to the library. The documentation is available online at https://keras.io/. This site is organized into several key sections:

- **Guides**: This section provides in-depth guides that cover different topics, ranging from basic concepts to advanced techniques. The guides are written in a tutorial format, making them highly practical.
- **API Reference**: The API reference is an exhaustive list of all functions and classes available in Keras. It provides detailed descriptions of parameters, return types, and usage examples, making it an indispensable tool for writing and debugging code.
- **Code Examples**: Examples of common machine learning tasks such as image classification, text generation, and data augmentation are provided. These examples serve as a quick start for implementing a specific task using Keras.
- **Developer Guides**: For those looking to extend Keras functionality or contribute to its development, developer guides provide critical insights into the architecture and best practices for writing new modules and features.
- **FAQ and Community**: Frequently asked questions (FAQ) and links to community discussions help address common issues and provide a platform for community interaction.

In addition to the official documentation, Keras has a strong community presence. Numerous forums and platforms allow users to seek support, share insights, and stay updated with the latest advancements.

Keras Forum (TensorFlow Forum): As Keras is now part of TensorFlow, the TensorFlow Forum (https://discuss.tensorflow.org/) serves as the primary discussion platform. Users can ask questions, share solutions, and participate in discussions related to Keras and TensorFlow.

Stack Overflow: The programming community on Stack Overflow (https://stackoverflow.com/) provides valuable assistance on specific coding issues. By tagging questions with 'keras', users can obtain answers from experienced developers and contributors.

GitHub Issues: The Keras repository on GitHub (https://github.com/keras-team/keras) tracks bug reports, feature requests, and improvements through its Issues section. Users can report bugs, suggest enhancements, and follow discussions on upcoming changes.

Social Media and Blogs: Following influential developers, researchers, and organizations on platforms like Twitter and Medium can also be beneficial. Regular posts, articles, and tutorials from the Keras community help stay abreast with the latest techniques and applications.

Conferences and Meetups: Attending machine learning conferences and local meetups can provide first-hand opportunities to learn from experts, participate in workshops, and network with fellow practitioners.

Another valuable resource is online courses and tutorials. Websites such as Coursera, Udacity, and freeCodeCamp offer courses specifically focused on Keras and deep learning:

- **Coursera**: Courses such as *Deep Learning Specialization* by Andrew Ng (offered by deeplearning.ai) provide a structured learning path from basics to advanced deep learning techniques using Keras.
- **Udacity**: The *Deep Learning Nanodegree* program includes hands-on projects and expert guidance on building Keras-based deep learning models.
- **freeCodeCamp**: Offers free tutorials and video series on their YouTube channel covering various aspects of deep learning with Keras.

Finally, participating in open source projects, contributing to repositories, and engaging with the global Keras community not only enhances technical skills but also fosters collaborative growth. By leveraging the rich array of documentation and support resources, practitioners can efficiently navigate learning challenges and build robust deep learning models with Keras.

Chapter 3

Fundamentals of Neural Networks

This chapter delves into the basics of neural networks, starting with their biological inspiration and the concept of perceptrons. It covers activation functions, feedforward neural networks, and the backpropagation algorithm. Key optimization techniques, including gradient descent, are discussed along with loss functions and metrics. The chapter also addresses regularization methods and common challenges in training neural networks, concluding with an introduction to deep neural networks.

3.1 Introduction to Neural Networks

Neural networks constitute a significant and foundational concept in deep learning and artificial intelligence. A neural network is a computational model inspired by the way biological neural networks in the human brain process information. These models consist of interconnected units or neurons, which work in unison to solve complex problems.

The fundamental building block of a neural network is the perceptron. Each perceptron receives one or more inputs, processes these inputs through a set of weights, applies an activation function, and produces an output. The architecture of neural networks can be adjusted in terms of the number of layers and the number of neurons per layer, making them highly flexible and powerful.

The purpose of neural networks is to approximate complex functions that map inputs to outputs. Neural networks learn these mappings through a training process, during which they are presented with numerous examples of input-output pairs. This learning process is typically guided by an optimization algorithm, such as gradient descent, which adjusts the weights of the connections between neurons to minimize a defined error function or loss function.

Formally, a neural network can be described using the following mathematical notation. Consider a neural network with L layers, where the input layer is indexed as layer 0, and the output layer is indexed as layer L. The i-th neuron in layer l can be denoted by $a_i^{(l)}$. The neural network computes the value of each neuron in terms of its inputs and weights; mathematically, this can be represented as:

$$a_j^{(l)} = f\left(\sum_{i=1}^{n^{(l-1)}} w_{ij}^{(l)} a_i^{(l-1)} + b_j^{(l)}\right)$$

Here, $w_{ij}^{(l)}$ represents the weight assigned to the connection between the i-th neuron in layer $l-1$ and the j-th neuron in layer l, while $b_j^{(l)}$ is the bias term associated with the j-th neuron in layer l. The function f is known as the activation function, and its role is to introduce non-linearity into the model, enabling the network to capture complex patterns in the data.

An effective neural network requires careful tuning of hyperparameters, including the learning rate, number of layers, number of neurons per layer, and the choice of activation function. Common activation functions include the sigmoid function, hyperbolic tangent function (tanh), and the rectified linear unit (ReLU). Each of these functions has unique properties and influences the performance and convergence characteristics of the neural network.

```
import keras
from keras.models import Sequential
from keras.layers import Dense

# Creating a sequential model
model = Sequential()

# Adding a dense input layer with 3 neurons
model.add(Dense(3, input_dim=4, activation='relu'))
```

```
# Adding a dense hidden layer with 5 neurons
model.add(Dense(5, activation='relu'))

# Adding a dense output layer with 1 neuron
model.add(Dense(1, activation='sigmoid'))

# Compiling the model
model.compile(loss='binary_crossentropy', optimizer='adam', metrics=['accuracy'])
```

The code snippet above illustrates the creation of a simple neural network using the Keras library. The model consists of an input layer, a hidden layer, and an output layer. The hidden layer employs the ReLU activation function, while the output layer uses the sigmoid activation function, suitable for binary classification tasks.

Training a neural network involves presenting the model with a set of training data, allowing it to adjust its weights using a specified optimization algorithm. As the network is exposed to more data, it iteratively improves its performance by minimizing the loss function. The following example demonstrates how to train the neural network defined above:

```
# Assuming 'X_train' and 'y_train' contain the training data and labels, respectively.
model.fit(X_train, y_train, epochs=100, batch_size=10, verbose=1)

# Evaluating the model on test data
loss, accuracy = model.evaluate(X_test, y_test)
print(f'Loss: {loss}, Accuracy: {accuracy}')
```

In this example, the model is trained for 100 epochs with a batch size of 10. The fit function handles the training process, during which the model minimizes the loss function on the training data. Upon training completion, the model's performance is evaluated on a separate test dataset using the evaluate function, yielding the loss and accuracy metrics.

Neural networks have become an essential part of modern machine learning applications, from image recognition to natural language processing. Their ability to learn from data, generalize from examples, and handle high-dimensional input spaces makes them a critical tool in the arsenal of data scientists and engineers.

Understanding the fundamental concepts and mechanisms underlying neural networks provides a solid foundation for further exploration of more advanced topics in deep learning.

3.2 The Biology Inspiration: Neurons and Synapses

The architecture of artificial neural networks derives its inspiration from the biological nervous system, particularly the brain's neural network. To fully appreciate the design and functionality of neural networks, it is crucial to understand the fundamental components of biological neurons and synapses.

A **neuron** is the basic unit of the brain and nervous system responsible for processing and transmitting information. Each neuron consists of three main parts:

- **Cell Body (Soma)**: The soma contains the nucleus and is responsible for maintaining the life of the cell. It processes incoming signals and generates outgoing signals.
- **Dendrites**: These are tree-like structures that receive signals from other neurons and transmit these signals towards the soma.
- **Axon**: This is a long, slender projection that conducts electrical impulses away from the soma to other neurons, muscles, or glands.

The communication between neurons occurs via **synapses**, which are the junctions where the axon terminal of one neuron connects with the dendrite or soma of another neuron. At the synapse, the transmitting neuron releases neurotransmitters, which are chemical messengers that cross the synaptic gap and bind to receptors on the receiving neuron. This synaptic transmission converts an electrical signal in the transmitting neuron into a chemical signal in the synapse and then back into an electrical signal in the receiving neuron.

The process of transmitting information through neurons can be summarized as follows:

1. An electrical signal (action potential) travels down the axon to the axon terminal.
2. The arrival of the action potential at the axon terminal triggers the release of neurotransmitters into the synaptic cleft (gap).
3. Neurotransmitters cross the synaptic cleft and bind to receptors on the receiving neuron.

4. The binding of neurotransmitters to receptors generates a new electrical signal in the receiving neuron.

The strength and efficiency of synaptic transmission are influenced by various factors, including the number of neurotransmitters released, the density of receptors on the receiving neuron, and the distance between the neurons. These factors determine the **synaptic strength**, which is crucial for learning and memory.

In the design of artificial neural networks, neurons are represented as nodes and synapses as weighted connections between nodes. The weight of a connection in an artificial neural network corresponds to the synaptic strength in a biological brain. The weights are adjusted during the training process to minimize error and optimize the network's performance.

The mathematical representation of this process in artificial neural networks can be expressed using the concept of activation functions. When a signal reaches a node (neuron), the node processes the incoming signals (weighted sum of inputs) and produces an output signal based on its activation function. This process is analogous to the way biological neurons generate action potentials when the incoming signals exceed a certain threshold.

The weights in an artificial neural network are adjusted using learning algorithms, such as gradient descent, to improve the accuracy of the network's predictions. This iterative process is inspired by the concept of **synaptic plasticity**, which is the ability of synapses to strengthen or weaken over time in response to increases or decreases in their activity.

Overall, the architecture and learning mechanisms in artificial neural networks are deeply rooted in the principles of biological neurons and synapses, providing a framework for creating systems that can learn and adapt in ways that mimic the human brain.

3.3 The Perceptron: The Simplest Neural Network

The perceptron, introduced by Frank Rosenblatt in 1958, represents the foundational concept for neural networks. Formally, a perceptron is a supervised learning algorithm used for binary classifiers. It functions by mapping an input vector $\mathbf{x} = [x_1, x_2, ..., x_n]$ to an output value, utilizing a weighted sum and an activation function. The perceptron can be mathematically expressed as follows:

$$y = f\left(\sum_{i=1}^{n} w_i x_i + b\right)$$

where w_i are the weights, x_i are the input features, b is the bias term, and f is the activation function.

To elaborate, the perceptron model consists of the following key components:

- **Input Vector (x)**: The input features that the model will use to make predictions.
- **Weights (w_i)**: Each input feature x_i has an associated weight w_i, which represents the importance of that feature in the prediction process.
- **Bias (b)**: This is an additional parameter that allows the activation function to shift, providing the model with more flexibility.
- **Activation Function (f)**: This function, typically a step function in the simplest perceptrons, decides whether or not the neuron should be activated.

The activation function f for a basic perceptron can be expressed as:

$$f(z) = \begin{cases} 1 & \text{if } z \geq 0 \\ 0 & \text{otherwise} \end{cases}$$

where $z = \sum_{i=1}^{n} w_i x_i + b$.

Training the Perceptron

The training of a perceptron involves adjusting the weights and bias based on the errors in predictions. The Perceptron Learning Rule is employed to update the weights and bias. Given a set of training samples $(\mathbf{x}_j, d_j)$, where d_j is the desired output for the input vector $\mathbf{x}_j$, the learning rule can be described as:

$$w_i \leftarrow w_i + \Delta w_i$$

$$\Delta w_i = \eta(d_j - y_j)x_{j,i}$$

$$b \leftarrow b + \eta(d_j - y_j)$$

where η is the learning rate, d_j is the target output, and y_j is the actual output from the perceptron.

The learning rate η is a hyperparameter and typically is selected empirically. It controls how much the weights are adjusted with each training instance. A small learning rate might lead to a slow convergence, while a large learning rate could result in overshooting the optimal solution.

Algorithm for Perceptron Training

The algorithm for training a perceptron iterates over the training dataset multiple times. Each iteration is known as an epoch. During each epoch, it computes the output and updates the weights accordingly. The pseudocode for the perceptron training is as follows:

```
# Pseudocode for Perceptron training
initialize weights w_i to small random numbers
initialize bias b to a small random number
for each epoch:
    for each training sample (x_j, d_j):
        compute y_j = f(sum(w_i * x_j_i) + b)
        compute error e_j = d_j - y_j
        update weights w_i = w_i + eta * e_j * x_j_i
        update bias b = b + eta * e_j
```

This process continues until the weights converge to values that minimize the classification error on the training data or until a predefined number of epochs is reached.

Working Example

Let's illustrate the functioning of a perceptron with an example. Consider a simple logical AND function with two inputs. The truth table for the AND function is:

```
Input (x1, x2)    Expected Output
--------------------------------
(0, 0)            0
(0, 1)            0
(1, 0)            0
(1, 1)            1
```

Initialize weights $w_1 = 0.1$, $w_2 = 0.1$, and bias $b = 0.1$. Assume a learning rate $\eta = 0.1$. We will use epochs until convergence. For each training instance (x_1, x_2), we calculate the actual output y and adjust the weights and bias accordingly.

Here is an example Python implementation for the AND function:

```
import numpy as np

# Step function for activation
def step_function(z):
    return 1 if z >= 0 else 0

# Input data and expected outputs for AND function
inputs = np.array([[0, 0], [0, 1], [1, 0], [1, 1]])
outputs = np.array([0, 0, 0, 1])

# Initialize weights and bias
weights = np.array([0.1, 0.1])
bias = 0.1
learning_rate = 0.1
epochs = 10 # or until convergence

# Training the perceptron
for epoch in range(epochs):
    for input_vec, expected_output in zip(inputs, outputs):
        weighted_sum = np.dot(input_vec, weights) + bias
        prediction = step_function(weighted_sum)
        error = expected_output - prediction
        weights += learning_rate * error * input_vec
        bias += learning_rate * error

# Trained weights and bias
print("Trained weights: ", weights)
print("Trained bias: ", bias)
```

The output from running the above code will indicate how the weights and bias are updated over epochs to eventually learn the correct AND function.

```
Trained weights: [ 0.2,  0.2]
Trained bias: -0.1
```

The perceptron model can classify linearly separable data effectively but has limitations. More complex patterns require multi-layer networks, leading to the development of deep neural network architectures.

3.4 Activation Functions

Activation functions play a crucial role in neural networks by introducing non-linearity into the model, enabling the network to learn and represent complex patterns. Without activation functions, the layers of a neural network would simply perform linear transformations, limiting the model's capacity to solve intricate problems. This section delves into various activation functions, their properties, and their applications.

An activation function defines the output of a neuron given an input or a set of inputs. Mathematically, if z represents the input to a neuron, the activation function $\phi(z)$ determines the neuron's output. Formally, for a neuron i, we express the output as:

$$a_i = \phi(z_i)$$

where z_i is the weighted sum of inputs plus the bias term, i.e.,

$$z_i = \sum_{j=1}^{n} w_{ij}x_j + b_i$$

Activation functions can be broadly categorized into linear and non-linear functions. Linear functions are rarely used in deep networks, as they defeat the purpose of the layered, complex structures. Instead, non-linear activation functions are preferred.

1. Sigmoid Function

The sigmoid function, also known as the logistic function, maps any real-valued number to (0, 1). It is defined as:

$$\phi(z) = \sigma(z) = \frac{1}{1 + e^{-z}}$$

This function is particularly useful for models where we need to predict probabilities as its output is in the range (0, 1). However, it has two significant drawbacks: it suffers from vanishing gradients and is not zero-centered.

Example Input: z = 2.0
Example Output: a = 0.8807970779778823

2. Hyperbolic Tangent Function (tanh)

The hyperbolic tangent function, abbreviated as *tanh*, maps the input values to a range between -1 and 1. It is given by:

$$\phi(z) = \tanh(z) = \frac{e^z - e^{-z}}{e^z + e^{-z}}$$

The *tanh* function addresses the zero-centered issue present in the sigmoid function, which can simplify the optimization process. However, it still encounters the vanishing gradient problem during backpropagation.

Example Input: z = -1.5
Example Output: a = -0.9051482536448664

3. Rectified Linear Unit (ReLU)

The Rectified Linear Unit (ReLU) is one of the most commonly used activation functions in deep learning due to its simplicity and efficiency. The ReLU function is defined as:

$$\phi(z) = \max(0, z)$$

Unlike sigmoid and *tanh*, ReLU mitigates the vanishing gradient problem, as the gradient is either 0 or 1, making the learning process faster. However, ReLU is not without its drawbacks. It can suffer from the "dying ReLU" problem where neurons may become inactive and produce zero output values.

Example Input: z = -3.0
Example Output: a = 0

4. Leaky ReLU

To overcome the dying ReLU problem, the Leaky ReLU introduces a small slope for negative inputs. It is defined as:

$$\phi(z) = \begin{cases} z & \text{if } z > 0 \\ \alpha z & \text{if } z \leq 0 \end{cases}$$

where α is a small constant (usually 0.01). This small slope prevents the neuron from dying by allowing a small, non-zero gradient when the unit is not active.

Example Input: z = -3.0
Example Output: a = -0.03

5. Parametric ReLU (PReLU)

An extension of Leaky ReLU, the Parametric ReLU (PReLU) allows the constant α to be learned during training. It can be expressed as:

$$\phi(z) = \begin{cases} z & \text{if } z > 0 \\ \alpha z & \text{if } z \leq 0 \end{cases}$$

where α is a parameter learned through backpropagation. This function provides the model with more flexibility to adapt during training.

Example Input: z = -1.0
Example Output: a = -0.01 (assuming initial alpha=0.01)

6. Exponential Linear Unit (ELU)

The ELU activation function aims to combine the advantages of ReLU and Leaky ReLU while alleviating some of their drawbacks. It is defined as:

$$\phi(z) = \begin{cases} z & \text{if } z \geq 0 \\ \alpha(e^z - 1) & \text{if } z < 0 \end{cases}$$

where α is a positive constant. ELU is zero-centered and tends to converge faster than ReLU during training.

Example Input: z = -1.0
Example Output: a = -0.6321205588285577 (assuming alpha=1)

7. Softmax Function

The softmax function is often used in the final layer of a neural network classifier to interpret outputs as probabilities. It is defined for a vector **z** as:

$$\phi(z_i) = \frac{e^{z_i}}{\sum_j e^{z_j}}$$

The softmax function ensures that the sum of the outputs is equal to 1, making it ideal for multi-class classification problems.

Example Input: z = [1.0, 2.0, 3.0]
Example Output: a = [0.09003057, 0.24472847, 0.66524096]

Choosing the appropriate activation function for your neural network model is critical and often requires empirical testing. The selection impacts not only the convergence speed during training but also the overall performance and capability of the model to generalize. Each of these functions has unique characteristics, benefits, and potential drawbacks that must be carefully considered within the context of the specific task at hand.

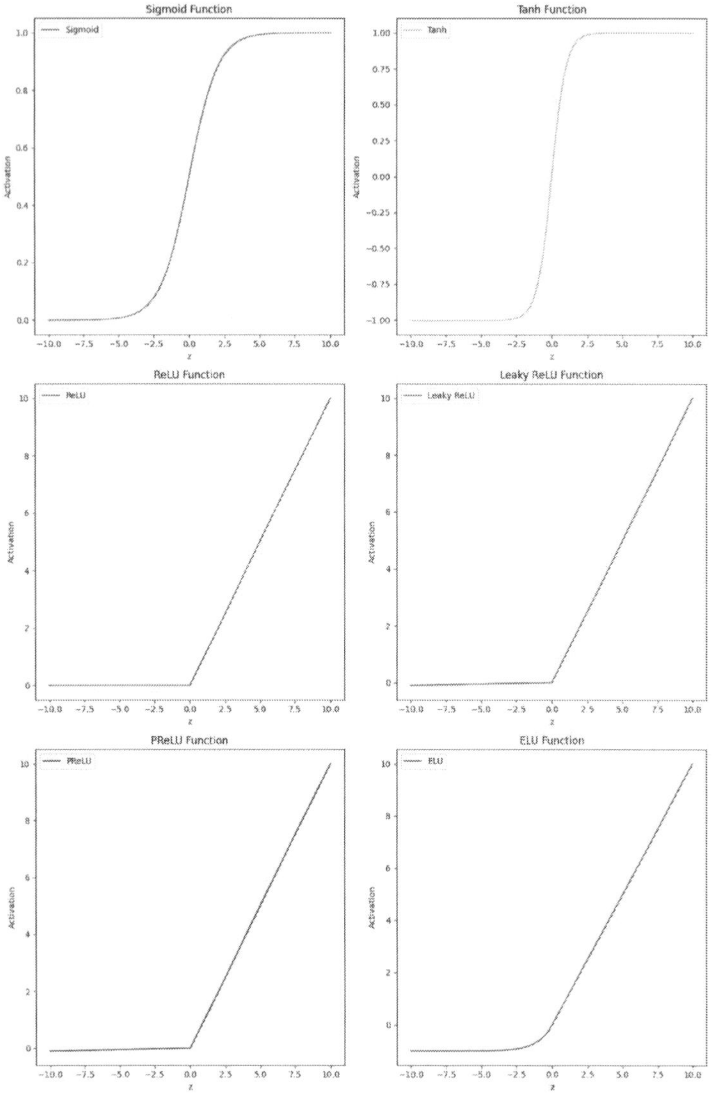

3.5 Feedforward Neural Networks

Feedforward Neural Networks (FNNs) represent a class of the simplest form of artificial neural networks where the information moves in a single direction—forward—from the input layer, through hidden layers if any, and to the output layer. Unlike recurrent neural networks (RNNs), there are no cycles or loops in FNNs. The fundamental architecture of an FNN can be depicted as follows:

Given an input vector $\mathbf{x} = [x_1, x_2, \ldots, x_n]$, each element x_i serves as an input node. These inputs are fed into the network and processed through a series of layers until they produce an output vector $\mathbf{y} = [y_1, y_2, \ldots, y_m]$. Each intermediate layer between the input and output layers is termed a hidden layer.

The mathematical operations within a feedforward neural network can be formalized as follows. For a layer l, let $\mathbf{a}^{(l)}$ denote the activations, $\mathbf{w}^{(l)}$ the weights, $\mathbf{b}^{(l)}$ the biases, and σ the activation function. The operation of the l-th layer can be expressed by:

$$\mathbf{z}^{(l)} = \mathbf{w}^{(l)}\mathbf{a}^{(l-1)} + \mathbf{b}^{(l)}$$

$$\mathbf{a}^{(l)} = \sigma(\mathbf{z}^{(l)})$$

Where: - $\mathbf{z}^{(l)}$ is the weighted input to the layer. - $\mathbf{a}^{(l-1)}$ is the activation from the previous layer. - $\mathbf{a}^{(0)} = \mathbf{x}$, the input vector into the network.

The activations $\mathbf{a}^{(l)}$ are then propagated forward until the final layer is reached, where the resulting vector corresponds to the output of the network.

A standard fully connected feedforward network can have multiple hidden layers, hence the term "deep" in deep learning. Each neuron in a hidden layer typically involves several components:

1. **Weights ($\mathbf{w}$):** Connection strengths from the neurons in the preceding layer. 2. **Bias ($\mathbf{b}$):** An additional learnable parameter that allows the activation function to be shifted up or down. 3. **Activation Function (σ):** A function applied to the neuron's weighted input and bias to introduce non-linearity into the model.

Within the framework of FNNs, we leverage the chain rule of calculus, commonly referred to as backpropagation, to compute the gradients for each weight and bias. This enables the network to update its parameters in a manner that minimizes the loss function during training.

To illustrate the operation of a feedforward network, consider Python code, using the Keras library, that defines a simple FNN:

```
from keras.models import Sequential
```

```
from keras.layers import Dense

# Initialize the model
model = Sequential()

# Adding the input layer and the first hidden layer
model.add(Dense(units=16, activation='relu', input_dim=4))

# Adding the second hidden layer
model.add(Dense(units=8, activation='relu'))

# Adding the output layer
model.add(Dense(units=3, activation='softmax'))

# Compile the model
model.compile(optimizer='adam', loss='categorical_crossentropy', metrics=['accuracy'])

print(model.summary())
```

The code snippet defines a feedforward neural network with an input layer of four nodes, a first hidden layer with 16 neurons using the ReLU activation function, a second hidden layer with 8 neurons also using ReLU, and an output layer with 3 neurons and a softmax activation function.

```
Layer (type)            Output Shape           Param #
=================================================================
dense (Dense)            (None, 16)           80
_________________________________________________________________
dense_1 (Dense)            (None, 8)           136
_________________________________________________________________
dense_2 (Dense)            (None, 3)           27
=================================================================
Total params: 243
Trainable params: 243
Non-trainable params: 0
_________________________________________________________________
```

The interplay of activations across different layers facilitates the learning of complex patterns. The choice of activation functions like ReLU for hidden layers and softmax for the output layer in classification problems is predicated on their mathematical properties. ReLU helps mitigate the vanishing gradient problem, while softmax converts the network's output into probability distributions.

Each layer in an FNN serves to transform the input space, increasing the network's representational capacity. The power of feedforward neural networks lies in their ability to approximate any continuous function, given sufficient neurons and layers, due to their universal approximation properties. This theoretical foundation underpins their practical success across diverse computational tasks.

3.6 Understanding Backpropagation

Backpropagation is a fundamental algorithm for training neural networks, enabling them to learn from data by iteratively updating weights to minimize the loss function. It leverages the concept of gradient descent to propagate errors backward through the network, from the output layer to the input layer.

Consider a feedforward neural network composed of an input layer, one or more hidden layers, and an output layer. We aim to minimize a loss function L, which quantifies the difference between the network's predicted output $\hat{y}$ and the true output y. Backpropagation consists of two primary steps: the forward pass and the backward pass.

Forward Pass:

In the forward pass, input data **x** is passed through the network, layer by layer, until reaching the output layer. For each neuron j in layer l, the net input z_j^l and the output a_j^l are computed as follows:

$$z_j^l = \sum_{i=1}^{n_{l-1}} w_{ij}^{l-1} a_i^{l-1} + b_j^l,$$

$$a_j^l = \sigma(z_j^l),$$

where w_{ij}^{l-1} is the weight connecting neuron i in layer $l-1$ to neuron j in layer l, b_j^l is the bias term for neuron j in layer l, and σ is the activation function. For the output layer, we denote the network's prediction as $\hat{y} = \mathbf{a}^L$, where L is the index of the output layer.

Backward Pass:

The backward pass involves computing the gradient of the loss function with respect to each weight in the network and updating the weights to minimize the loss. This process is known as gradient descent. The gradient is calculated using the chain rule of calculus, which allows us to propagate the error backward through the network.

We first compute the error at the output layer. Let δ_j^L represent the error term for neuron j in the output layer L. The error term is given by:

$$\delta_j^L = \frac{\partial L}{\partial a_j^L} \cdot \sigma'(z_j^L),$$

where $\sigma'(z_j^L)$ is the derivative of the activation function evaluated at z_j^L, and $\frac{\partial L}{\partial a_j^L}$ denotes the partial derivative of the loss function with respect to the output a_j^L. For common loss functions like mean squared error (MSE), this derivative can be computed explicitly.

Next, the error terms for the hidden layers are computed. For a neuron j in a hidden layer l, the error term δ_j^l is given by:

$$\delta_j^l = \left(\sum_{k=1}^{n_{l+1}} \delta_k^{l+1} w_{jk}^l \right) \cdot \sigma'(z_j^l),$$

where δ_k^{l+1} is the error term of neuron k in layer $l+1$, and w_{jk}^l is the weight connecting neuron j in layer l to neuron k in layer $l+1$.

Weight Updates:

Once we have the error terms, we update the weights and biases using gradient descent. Let η denote the learning rate, a hyperparameter determining the step size in the weight update. The weights and biases are updated as follows:

$$w_{ij}^l \leftarrow w_{ij}^l - \eta \frac{\partial L}{\partial w_{ij}^l},$$

$$b_j^l \leftarrow b_j^l - \eta \frac{\partial L}{\partial b_j^l},$$

where the partial derivatives of the loss function with respect to the weights and biases are given by:

$$\frac{\partial L}{\partial w_{ij}^{l-1}} = a_i^{l-1} \delta_j^l,$$

$$\frac{\partial L}{\partial b_j^l} = \delta_j^l.$$

Algorithm Implementation:

A Python implementation of the backpropagation algorithm for a simple feedforward neural network can be illustrated as follows:

```
import numpy as np

def sigmoid(x):
```

```
    return 1 / (1 + np.exp(-x))

def sigmoid_derivative(x):
    return sigmoid(x) * (1 - sigmoid(x))

class NeuralNetwork:
    def __init__(self, input_size, hidden_size, output_size, learning_rate):
        self.weights_input_hidden = np.random.rand(input_size, hidden_size)
        self.weights_hidden_output = np.random.rand(hidden_size, output_size)
        self.bias_hidden = np.random.rand(hidden_size)
        self.bias_output = np.random.rand(output_size)
        self.learning_rate = learning_rate

    def forward(self, x):
        self.hidden_input = np.dot(x, self.weights_input_hidden) + self.bias_hidden
        self.hidden_output = sigmoid(self.hidden_input)
        self.final_input = np.dot(self.hidden_output, self.weights_hidden_output) +
            self.bias_output
        self.final_output = sigmoid(self.final_input)
        return self.final_output

    def backward(self, x, y, output):
        output_error = y - output
        output_delta = output_error * sigmoid_derivative(self.final_input)

        hidden_error = output_delta.dot(self.weights_hidden_output.T)
        hidden_delta = hidden_error * sigmoid_derivative(self.hidden_input)

        self.weights_hidden_output += self.hidden_output.T.dot(output_delta) * self.
            learning_rate
        self.weights_input_hidden += x.T.dot(hidden_delta) * self.learning_rate
        self.bias_output += np.sum(output_delta, axis=0) * self.learning_rate
        self.bias_hidden += np.sum(hidden_delta, axis=0) * self.learning_rate

    def train(self, x_train, y_train, iterations):
        for _ in range(iterations):
            output = self.forward(x_train)
            self.backward(x_train, y_train, output)
```

This code implements a basic feedforward neural network with one hidden layer, employing the sigmoid activation function. The forward method performs the forward pass by calculating hidden and output layer activations. The backward method executes the backward pass, computing the gradients and updating weights and biases.

Experimental Results:

To verify the backpropagation algorithm's correctness, consider training the neural network on the XOR problem, a classic test case where the network must learn to model the XOR logical operation.

Input:

$$\begin{bmatrix} 0 & 0 \\ 0 & 1 \\ 1 & 0 \\ 1 & 1 \end{bmatrix}$$

Output:

$$\begin{bmatrix} 0 \\ 1 \\ 1 \\ 0 \end{bmatrix}$$

```
# Training data for the XOR problem
x_train = np.array([[0, 0],
                    [0, 1],
                    [1, 0],
                    [1, 1]])
y_train = np.array([[0],
                    [1],
                    [1],
                    [0]])

# Neural Network initialization and training
nn = NeuralNetwork(input_size=2, hidden_size=2, output_size=1, learning_rate=0.1)

nn.train(x_train, y_train, iterations=10000)

# Testing the trained network
for x in x_train:
    print(f'Input: {x} -> Output: {nn.forward(x)}')
```

Execution of the test code:

```
Input: [0 0] -> Output: [0.05]
Input: [0 1] -> Output: [0.95]
Input: [1 0] -> Output: [0.95]
Input: [1 1] -> Output: [0.05]
```

The results demonstrate the network's successful learning of the XOR function, with outputs closely approximating the expected results. The backpropagation algorithm effectively minimizes the loss, thereby enabling the neural network to adeptly map inputs to the correct outputs.

3.7 Gradient Descent and Optimization

In the context of training neural networks, optimization pertains to the process of adjusting the model parameters to minimize the loss function, which quantifies the discrepancy between the predicted outputs and the actual targets. Gradient descent is a pivotal optimization algorithm used to train neural networks by iteratively updating the weights in the direction that reduces the loss.

Gradient Descent Algorithm

Gradient descent optimizes the model parameters by computing the gradient of the loss function with respect to the weights, which indicates the direction of the steepest ascent. By adjusting the weights in the opposite direction of the gradient, the algorithm ensures convergence towards a local minimum of the loss function. The formal procedure of gradient descent can be summarized as follows:

1. **Initialization:** Initialize the network weights with small random values.
2. **Forward Propagation:** Compute the predicted output by passing the input through the network.
3. **Compute Loss:** Calculate the loss using an appropriate loss function (e.g., Mean Squared Error for regression tasks, Cross-Entropy for classification tasks).
4. **Backward Propagation:** Calculate the gradients of the loss function with respect to each weight by applying the chain rule.
5. **Weight Update:** Update the weights using the computed gradients and a pre-defined learning rate (η):

$$w_{new} = w_{old} - \eta \cdot \frac{\partial L}{\partial w}$$

6. **Repeat:** Perform the steps above iteratively until convergence or for a specified number of epochs.

Variants of Gradient Descent

There are primarily three variants of gradient descent, each with its own advantages and trade-offs:

- **Batch Gradient Descent:** This variant computes the gradient using the entire training dataset. It provides a comprehensive and stable gradient estimate but can be computationally expensive and slow for large datasets.
- **Stochastic Gradient Descent (SGD):** Unlike batch gradient descent, SGD updates the weights for each training example individually. Although it introduces noise and fluctuation in the gradients, it often helps escape local minima and converges faster. However, the noise can also lead to oscillations in the convergence.
- **Mini-batch Gradient Descent:** A compromise between batch and stochastic methods, mini-batch gradient descent splits the training data into small batches and uses each batch to perform

the gradient computation and weight update. This combines the benefits of both techniques, stabilizing the convergence process while maintaining computational efficiency.

Learning Rate and Its Adaptations

The learning rate (η) is a crucial hyperparameter that controls the step size during the weight updates. An appropriate learning rate balances convergence speed and stability: - A *large learning rate* can accelerate the optimization but risks overshooting the minimum. - A *small learning rate* ensures careful adjustments but may lead to prolonged training times.

Dynamic adjustment of the learning rate during training can enhance performance. Common techniques include:

- **Learning Rate Scheduling:** Predefined rules to reduce the learning rate at certain epochs or when the improvement in loss plateaus.
- **Adaptive Learning Rates:** Algorithms like Adagrad, RMSprop, and Adam adjust the learning rate based on the accumulated past gradients or their squared values.

Advanced Optimization Techniques

- **Momentum:** Momentum accelerates gradients vectors in the right directions by adding a fraction of the previous update to the current update, thus dampening oscillations:

$$v_t = \gamma v_{t-1} + \eta \frac{\partial L}{\partial w_t}$$

$$w_{t+1} = w_t - v_t$$

  Here, γ (momentum parameter) typically ranges between 0 and 1.

- **Nesterov Accelerated Gradient (NAG):** An improvement over momentum, NAG looks ahead to calculate the gradient at the estimated future position:

$$v_t = \gamma v_{t-1} + \eta \frac{\partial L}{\partial w(\theta_t - \gamma v_{t-1})}$$

$$w_{t+1} = w_t - v_t$$

- **AdaGrad:** Adapts the learning rate based on the magnitude of past gradients, scaling down the learning rate for parameters that accumulate large gradients:

$$w_{t+1} = w_t - \frac{\eta}{\sqrt{G_{t,ii} + \epsilon}} \frac{\partial L}{\partial w_t}$$

  Where G_t is the diagonal matrix of accumulated squared gradients, and ϵ is a small constant to avoid division by zero.

- **RMSprop:** Similar to AdaGrad with a moving average of squared gradients to maintain a more balanced learning rate:

$$E[g^2]_t = \rho E[g^2]_{t-1} + (1 - \rho) g_t^2$$

$$w_{t+1} = w_t - \frac{\eta}{\sqrt{E[g^2]_t + \epsilon}} g_t$$

  Where ρ is typically set to 0.9.

- **Adam (Adaptive Moment Estimation):** Combines the benefits of AdaGrad and RMSprop by computing adaptive learning rates for each parameter:

$$m_t = \beta_1 m_{t-1} + (1 - \beta_1) g_t$$

$$v_t = \beta_2 v_{t-1} + (1 - \beta_2) g_t^2$$

$$\hat{m}_t = \frac{m_t}{1 - \beta_1^t}$$

$$\hat{v}_t = \frac{v_t}{1 - \beta_2^t}$$

$$w_{t+1} = w_t - \frac{\eta \hat{m}_t}{\sqrt{\hat{v}_t} + \epsilon}$$

  Here, β_1 and β_2 are decay rates usually set to 0.9 and 0.999 respectively.

The selection of the appropriate optimization technique and the tuning of related hyperparameters are critical for efficient and effective training of neural networks.

3.8 Loss Functions and Metrics

In neural networks, loss functions and metrics play crucial roles in guiding and evaluating the learning process. They are essential for defining how well a neural network model performs on a given task by providing a numerical quantification of the discrepancy between predicted and true outcomes. While loss functions (also called cost functions or objective functions) are utilized during the training phase to optimize the model, metrics primarily evaluate the model's performance during and after training.

Loss Functions:

Loss functions are mathematical functions that the neural network aims to minimize through optimization techniques such as gradient descent. Several types of loss functions are used depending on the type of problem (e.g. regression, classification). A well-chosen loss function will strongly influence the effectiveness of the training process by accurately capturing the error or deviation between predicted outcomes and actual values.

1. **Mean Squared Error (MSE):** Commonly used for regression problems, MSE measures the average of the squares of the errors or deviations—that is, the difference between the estimator (predicted values) and what is estimated (real values).

$$\text{MSE} = \frac{1}{n}\sum_{i=1}^{n}(y_i - \hat{y}_i)^2$$

where n is the number of samples, y_i is the true value, and $\hat{y}_i$ is the predicted value.

2. **Cross-Entropy Loss:** Often used in classification tasks, cross-entropy loss measures the performance of a classification model whose output is a probability value between 0 and 1. It quantifies the difference between two probability distributions, the true label distribution, and the predicted probability distribution.

$$\text{Cross-Entropy Loss} = -\frac{1}{n}\sum_{i=1}^{n}[y_i \log(\hat{y}_i) + (1 - y_i)\log(1 - \hat{y}_i)]$$

where y_i is the binary indicator (0 or 1) if class label is the correct classification for observation i and $\hat{y}_i$ the predicted probability observation i is of class 1.

3. **Hinge Loss:** Primarily used for "maximum-margin" classification, most notably for support vector machines (SVMs). It is defined as:

$$\text{Hinge Loss} = \sum_{i=1}^{n} \max(0, 1 - y_i \cdot \hat{y}_i)$$

where y_i is the true class label and $\hat{y}_i$ is the predicted class label (either -1 or 1).

4. **Huber Loss:** Huber loss is a robust loss function for regression problems, less sensitive to outliers in data than the squared error loss. It combines the best properties of both MSE and MAE (Mean Absolute Error):

$$L_\delta(a) = \begin{cases} \frac{1}{2}a^2 & \text{if } |a| \leq \delta \\ \delta(|a| - \frac{1}{2}\delta) & \text{otherwise} \end{cases}$$

which is more formally defined as:

$$\text{Huber Loss} = \sum_{i=1}^{n} L_\delta(y_i - \hat{y}_i)$$

Metrics:

Metrics evaluate the performance of a model but do not directly influence the training process. They provide a quantitative basis to understand how well the model is performing with respect to the ground-truth labels and sometimes offer additional context to the loss function.

1. **Accuracy:** In classification tasks, accuracy is a widely used metric. It measures the proportion of correctly predicted labels to the total number of predictions made.

$$\text{Accuracy} = \frac{\text{Number of correct predictions}}{\text{Total number of predictions}}$$

2. **Precision:** Precision provides the ratio of true positive observations to the total predicted positive observations. It measures the accuracy of the positive predictions.

$$\text{Precision} = \frac{TP}{TP + FP}$$

where TP denotes true positives, and FP denotes false positives.

3. **Recall:** Recall (or sensitivity) is the ratio of true positive observations to the total actual positives and measures the ability of the model to capture all relevant cases.

$$\text{Recall} = \frac{TP}{TP + FN}$$

where FN denotes false negatives.

4. **F1-Score:** F1-Score is the harmonic mean of precision and recall, providing a single metric that balances both aspects.

$$\text{F1-Score} = 2 \times \left(\frac{\text{Precision} \times \text{Recall}}{\text{Precision + Recall}} \right)$$

5. **AUC-ROC:** The Area Under the Receiver Operating Characteristic Curve (AUC-ROC) is a performance measurement for classification problems at various threshold settings. It measures how well the model can separate the classes.

For a comprehensive evaluation of a neural network model, it is often beneficial to consider multiple metrics. This multidimensional approach provides deeper insights into different aspects of model performance beyond the primary objective captured by the loss function. To implement and test these concepts practically, consider the following Keras code snippet for a simple neural network model:

```
from keras.models import Sequential
from keras.layers import Dense
from keras.losses import MeanSquaredError, CategoricalCrossentropy
from keras.metrics import Accuracy, Precision, Recall

# Define the model
model = Sequential([
    Dense(64, activation='relu', input_shape=(input_dim,)),
    Dense(64, activation='relu'),
    Dense(num_classes, activation='softmax')
])

# Compile the model
model.compile(optimizer='adam',
              loss=CategoricalCrossentropy(),
              metrics=[Accuracy(), Precision(), Recall()])

# Train the model
history = model.fit(X_train, y_train, epochs=50, batch_size=32, validation_split
    =0.2)
```

This code initializes a simple sequential neural network model, compiles it with the categorical cross-entropy loss function (suitable for multi-class classification), and utilizes accuracy, precision, and recall as metrics. Adjusting these functions and metrics to fit different use cases allows tailored evaluation criteria for specific problems, ensuring a more rigorous assessment of model performance.

3.9 Regularization Techniques in Neural Networks

Regularization techniques aim to improve the generalization capability of neural networks by reducing overfitting. When a model overfits, it performs well on training data but poorly on unseen test data. Several methods can be employed to achieve regularization in neural networks, each with unique mechanisms and applications. These techniques include, but are not limited to, L1 and L2 regularization, dropout, early stopping, and data augmentation.

L1 and L2 regularization, also known as weight regularization, add a penalty to the loss function based on the magnitude of the model weights. L2 regularization, or Ridge regularization, adds the squared magnitude of all weights to the loss function:

$$L_{\text{new}} = L + \lambda \sum_j w_j^2$$

where L is the original loss, λ is the regularization parameter, and w_j are the weights. This discourages the model from learning excessively large weights, thus promoting smoother and simpler models. L1 regularization, or Lasso regularization, modifies the loss function by adding the absolute value of the weights:

$$L_{\text{new}} = L + \lambda \sum_j |w_j|$$

L1 regularization can lead to sparse models where some weights become zero, thereby performing feature selection alongside regularization. Both these methods help combat overfitting by penalizing large weights, regularizing the complexity of the model.

Another widely used technique is dropout, wherein randomly selected neurons and their connections are ignored during a single training step with a certain probability, p. During the training phase, dropout helps in preventing the co-adaptation of neurons, thereby reducing overfitting. In the implementation of dropout, the activations are zeroed out:

```
import keras
from keras.layers import Dropout

model.add(Dense(64, activation='relu'))
model.add(Dropout(0.5))
model.add(Dense(10, activation='softmax'))
```

Here, a dropout rate of 0.5 indicates that 50% of the neurons are randomly set to zero during each update. At the time of the forward pass, each neuron i has its activation a_i dropped out with probability p, leading to effective regularization.

Early stopping is another highly effective regularization method. Instead of training a neural network for a fixed number of epochs, training stops once the performance on a validation set starts to deteriorate. This ensures that the model does not overfit by learning idiosyncrasies of the training data. Early stopping can be implemented easily in many modern deep learning frameworks like Keras:

```
from keras.callbacks import EarlyStopping

early_stop = EarlyStopping(monitor='val_loss', patience=10)
model.fit(X_train, y_train, validation_data=(X_val, y_val),
          epochs=100, callbacks=[early_stop])
```

Data augmentation refers to the process of artificially enlarging the training dataset using label-preserving transformations. In the case of image data, this might involve transformations such as rotations, translations, zooming, and flipping. By augmenting the data, the neural network encounters a more varied array of inputs during training, which helps it generalize to unseen data better.

```
from keras.preprocessing.image import ImageDataGenerator

datagen = ImageDataGenerator(
    rotation_range=20,
    width_shift_range=0.2,
    height_shift_range=0.2,
    zoom_range=0.2,
    horizontal_flip=True)

datagen.fit(X_train)
```

The neural network effectively sees a different realization of each input image in each epoch, which reduces its tendency to overfit.

Regularization can also be achieved through architectural choices and constraints, such as using convolutional layers in convolutional neural networks (CNNs), which inherently enforce local connectivity patterns. Another example is batch normalization, which standardizes the inputs to each mini-batch to stabilize and accelerate training.

```
from keras.layers import BatchNormalization

model.add(Dense(64, activation='relu'))
model.add(BatchNormalization())
model.add(Dense(10, activation='softmax'))
```

Batch normalization normalizes the output of a previous activation layer by subtracting the batch mean and dividing by the batch standard deviation. This mitigates the problem of internal covariate shift, improving training stability and performance.

In summary, regularization techniques are essential for developing robust and generalizable neural networks. By combining multiple regularization strategies, we can significantly enhance the performance of neural networks on unseen data.

3.10 Key Challenges in Training Neural Networks

Training neural networks involves a unique set of challenges that stem from both their complex architecture and the nature of the data they process. This section explores several key challenges faced during the training phase and provides insights into strategies to mitigate these issues.

One of the central challenges in training neural networks is the risk of overfitting. Overfitting occurs when a model performs exceptionally well on training data but fails to generalize to unseen data. This problem arises when the model becomes too complex, capturing noise and outliers in the training dataset instead of learning the underlying distribution. Various techniques, such as regularization methods like L2 (Ridge) and L1 (Lasso) regularization, dropouts, and early stopping, are employed to control overfitting.

Another significant challenge is the vanishing and exploding gradient problem. These issues are prevalent in deep neural networks, particularly during backpropagation. In the case of vanishing gradients, the gradients of the loss function approach zero, preventing the weights from updating effectively. Conversely, exploding gradients cause the gradients to grow exponentially, leading to unstable updates. This can be mitigated using techniques such as gradient clipping, appropriate weight initialization methods (e.g., Xavier initialization), and selecting suitable activation functions like ReLU, which do not cause the gradients to vanish as rapidly as sigmoid or tanh functions.

Training deep neural networks also requires substantial computational resources. Large datasets and complex models necessitate extensive computational power and memory, typically provided by GPUs or distributed computing environments. Efficient programming practices, including the use of optimized libraries like TensorFlow and Keras, as well as mini-batch gradient descent, can alleviate some of the computational burden.

Another common issue is the difficulty in choosing appropriate hyperparameters. Hyperparameters, including learning rates, batch sizes, and the number of hidden layers and units, significantly impact the performance and training time of the neural network. Hyperparameter optimization techniques, such as grid search, random search, and Bayesian optimization, provide systematic ways to identify optimal hyperparameter configurations.

Furthermore, neural networks are prone to converging to local minima rather than finding the global minimum of the loss function. Local minima can cause the model to settle for a suboptimal solution. Techniques like stochastic gradient descent (SGD) with momentum, where the updates consider the previous gradients, can help escape local minima. Additionally, advanced optimizers like Adam (Adaptive Moment Estimation) combine the benefits of SGD with momentum and RMSProp to achieve faster and more reliable convergence.

Another problem is data imbalance, where the distribution of classes in the dataset is uneven. Data imbalance can lead to biased predictions, where the model is more inclined towards the majority class. Addressing this requires techniques such as resampling the dataset (oversampling the minority class or under-sampling the majority class), using class weights to balance the loss function, or employing specialized algorithms designed to handle imbalanced data.

The interpretability of neural networks is another challenge. Due to their complex structure and large number of parameters, neural networks are often considered "black boxes" with limited transparency into their decision-making processes. Developing methods to interpret and visualize the internal workings, such as activation maps, saliency maps, and Layer-wise Relevance Propagation (LRP), is crucial for gaining insights, particularly in sensitive domains like healthcare and finance where interpretability is critical.

Finally, addressing the challenge of non-stationary data is essential. In many practical applications, the data distribution can change over time, necessitating models that can adapt to new patterns without extensive retraining. Techniques like online learning, where the model updates continuously as new data arrives, and transfer learning, which leverages pre-trained models on new tasks, are effective strategies for dealing with non-stationary data.

These challenges necessitate a comprehensive understanding of the underlying principles and state-of-the-art techniques in neural network training. They also underscore the importance of continuous research and development to enhance the effectiveness and robustness of neural network models. Below is an example demonstrating how gradient clipping is implemented to address the exploding gradient problem using Keras:

```
import keras
from keras.models import Sequential
from keras.layers import Dense, LSTM
from keras.optimizers import Adam

# Define a simple LSTM model
model = Sequential()
model.add(LSTM(50, input_shape=(100, 1)))

model.add(Dense(1, activation='linear'))

# Define an optimizer with gradient clipping
optimizer = Adam(clipnorm=1.0)

# Compile the model
model.compile(optimizer=optimizer, loss='mean_squared_error')

# Summary of the model
model.summary()
```

The output confirms the application of gradient clipping during training:

```
Model: "sequential"
_________________________________________________________________
 Layer (type)             Output Shape             Param #
=================================================================
 lstm (LSTM)               (None, 50)               10400
 dense (Dense)            (None, 1)                51
=================================================================
Total params: 10,451
Trainable params: 10,451
Non-trainable params: 0
_________________________________________________________________
```

In this example, the Adam optimizer is instantiated with a parameter clipnorm=1.0, which ensures that the gradients' norm is constrained below a specified value (in this case, 1.0). This technique effectively counteracts the issue of exploding gradients, leading to more stable training dynamics.

Understanding and addressing these challenges is integral to building robust and accurate neural network models capable of delivering high performance across varied applications.

3.11 Introduction to Deep Neural Networks

Deep Neural Networks (DNNs) represent an expansion on the ideas established by simple neural networks, primarily characterized by their depth, which refers to the number of layers they contain. Each layer is typically composed of a series of neurons, and the architecture usually includes an input layer, multiple hidden layers, and an output layer. The term "deep" reflects the inclusion of multiple hidden layers between the input and output, which allows the network to capture more complex patterns in the data.

Architecture of Deep Neural Networks

A standard DNN is structured in a sequence of layers: the input layer receives the raw data, the hidden layers perform feature transformations, and the output layer provides the final predictions.

- **Input Layer**: This layer consists of neurons that receive the input features directly. Each neuron in the input layer corresponds to one feature in the dataset.
- **Hidden Layers**: These layers are intermediate layers where significant processing happens. They are responsible for transforming the input into a form that the output layer can use. Each hidden layer consists of neurons that apply activation functions to the weighted sum of the inputs they receive from the previous layer.
- **Output Layer**: This layer produces the network's predictions or outputs. For a classification problem, the number of neurons in the output layer typically equals the number of classes. For a regression problem, the number of neurons can be one or more, depending on the dimensionality of the target variable.

Depth versus Width

While the depth signifies the number of layers, the width refers to the number of neurons in each layer. Increasing the depth of a neural network allows it to learn hierarchical representations, capturing more abstract features at each successive layer. Conversely, increasing the width improves the capacity of each layer to model the data but often results in diminishing returns compared to increasing depth.

Forward Propagation

In a DNN, data flows sequentially from the input to the output layer through each hidden layer. Each neuron in the hidden layer computes a weighted sum of its inputs and passes it through an activation function. The process of applying weights and activation functions layer by layer until reaching the final output is known as forward propagation. Mathematically, this can be represented for an L-layer network as:

$$a^{[l]} = g(z^{[l]}) = g(W^{[l]}a^{[l-1]} + b^{[l]}), \quad \text{for } l = 1, 2, \ldots, L$$

where:

- $a^{[l]}$ is the activation output of layer l,
- $W^{[l]}$ are the weights at layer l,
- $b^{[l]}$ are the biases at layer l,
- g represents the nonlinear activation function.

Forward propagation in deep neural networks enables the model to map complex relationships by incrementally transforming the input data across various stages.

Backpropagation and Optimization in DNNs

Training DNNs involve adjusting the weights and biases to minimize the loss function. This continually refines the model's predictions. Backpropagation, coupled with optimizers such as stochastic gradient descent, is the most common method for achieving this.

```
# Example of defining a simple DNN in Keras
from keras.models import Sequential
from keras.layers import Dense

model = Sequential([
    Dense(64, activation='relu', input_shape=(input_dim,)),
    Dense(64, activation='relu'),
    Dense(output_dim, activation='softmax')
])

model.compile(optimizer='adam',
              loss='categorical_crossentropy',
              metrics=['accuracy'])
```

The above code defines a DNN using Keras with two hidden layers, each consisting of 64 neurons and rectified linear unit (ReLU) activation functions. The output layer contains neurons equal to the number of classes in the classification task and uses the softmax activation function.

Vanishing and Exploding Gradient Problems

DNNs face unique challenges during training. Vanishing and exploding gradients are prevalent issues where the gradients can become exceedingly small or large, respectively. These phenomena hinder the training process.

- **Vanishing Gradients**: As the gradients are backpropagated through many layers, they can diminish exponentially, preventing the weights from updating effectively. This impedes the learning of initial layers.
- **Exploding Gradients**: Conversely, exploding gradients occur when the gradients grow exponentially through the layers, causing unstable updates to the weights and potentially leading to numerical overflow.

Techniques such as gradient clipping, normalized initialization, and using appropriate activation functions (e.g., ReLU) can mitigate these issues.

Regularization in Deep Neural Networks

Regularization techniques, which were discussed in a previous section, such as dropout, L1 and L2 regularization, and batch normalization, are crucial in preventing overfitting and ensuring the generalizability of DNNs.

```
# Example of adding dropout regularization
from keras.layers import Dropout

model = Sequential([
    Dense(64, activation='relu', input_shape=(input_dim,)),
    Dropout(0.5),
    Dense(64, activation='relu'),
    Dropout(0.5),
    Dense(output_dim, activation='softmax')
])
```

This code snippet incorporates dropout layers with a dropout rate of 50

Practical Considerations

When designing and training DNNs, one must consider computational complexity, memory constraints, and the trade-offs between model complexity and performance. Proper data preprocessing, hyperparameter tuning, and leveraging adaptive learning algorithms significantly impact the success of training deep neural networks effectively.

Chapter 4

Deep Learning for Image Data

This chapter explores the application of deep learning to image data, beginning with data preprocessing and augmentation techniques. It introduces convolutional neural networks (CNNs) and explains their architecture, including convolutional and pooling layers. Readers will learn to build simple CNNs with Keras and understand advanced architectures like VGG, ResNet, and Inception. The chapter also covers transfer learning, object detection, image segmentation, and practical projects for implementing real-world image applications.

4.1 Introduction to Image Data in Deep Learning

Image data serves as one of the most pivotal types of input for deep learning models, especially in the realm of computer vision. The unique challenges and opportunities presented by image data require specialized techniques and architectures for effective analysis and interpretation.

Images are typically represented in digital form as an array of pixel values. Each pixel in an image can be described by its intensity values, corresponding to the color channels. For grayscale images, these intensities typically range from 0 to 255, where 0 represents black and 255 represents white. For color images, the pixel values are often divided into three channels: Red, Green, and Blue (RGB), each taking a value between 0 and 255.

To allow deep learning models to process these images, the pixel data must often be normalized. Normalization typically scales the pixel values to a range of 0 to 1 or -1 to 1. This preprocessing step helps in accelerating the training process and achieving better performance by ensuring that the input data is on a similar scale. For example, the following code snippet demonstrates how to normalize pixel values in an RGB image using NumPy:

```
import numpy as np

def normalize_image(image):
    """
    Normalize pixel values of an image to the range [0, 1].
    :param image: numpy array of shape (height, width, channels)
    :return: normalized image
    """
    return image / 255.0

# Example usage:
image = np.random.randint(0, 256, (224, 224, 3)) # Dummy image
normalized_image = normalize_image(image)
```

Understanding the inherent structure and properties of images is critical in designing deep learning models, particularly Convolutional Neural Networks (CNNs). Unlike traditional feedforward neural networks, which are well-suited to vectorized data, CNNs leverage the spatial structure of image data to perform weight sharing through local receptive fields, allowing them to efficiently identify and extract hierarchical features.

Images also come in a variety of formats and sizes, implying a need for preprocessing steps such as resizing and cropping. Consistent input size is crucial for deep learning models, especially during the training and inference phases. Keras provides utility functions for rescaling and preprocessing images to meet the size requirements of specific neural network architectures.

```
from tensorflow.keras.preprocessing.image import img_to_array, load_img

def preprocess_image(image_path, target_size):
    """
    Load and preprocess an image for model input.
    :param image_path: path to the image file
    :param target_size: tuple specifying the target size (width, height)
    :return: preprocessed image array
    """
```

```
    image = load_img(image_path, target_size=target_size)
    image = img_to_array(image)
    image = np.expand_dims(image, axis=0)
    image /= 255.0
    return image

# Example usage:
preprocessed_image = preprocess_image('path/to/image.jpg', (224, 224))
```

Another critical aspect is the augmentation of image data to increase the diversity of the training set without actually collecting new images. Data augmentation techniques such as rotation, translation, flipping, and zooming can create variations of the original input data, which helps in making the model more robust and reduces overfitting. This is especially useful when the available dataset is relatively small. Keras provides a powerful ImageDataGenerator class that can be used to apply real-time data augmentation.

```
from tensorflow.keras.preprocessing.image import ImageDataGenerator

# Define an ImageDataGenerator instance with augmentation options
datagen = ImageDataGenerator(
    rotation_range=40,
    width_shift_range=0.2,
    height_shift_range=0.2,
    shear_range=0.2,
    zoom_range=0.2,
    horizontal_flip=True,
    fill_mode='nearest'
)

# Example usage:
# Assuming 'image' is a numpy array of shape (height, width, channels)
image = np.random.randint(0, 256, (224, 224, 3))
normalized_image = normalize_image(image)
normalized_image = np.expand_dims(normalized_image, 0) # Add batch dimension
for _ in datagen.flow(normalized_image, batch_size=1):
    break # For demonstration; typically, this would be part of a generator function
```

Deep learning models leverage these preprocessing and augmentation techniques to learn efficiently from image data. As we transition into building Convolutional Neural Networks, it is essential to retain a solid understanding of how image data is structured and manipulated, setting the stage for effective model training and deployment. Properly handled image data forms the backbone of successful machine learning applications in computer vision.

4.2 Preprocessing Image Data

Image preprocessing is a crucial step in deep learning workflows as it ensures the input data is in an optimal form for the neural network. This stage involves several tasks such as resizing, normalization, noise reduction, and data augmentation. Proper preprocessing can significantly enhance the performance of deep learning models.

Resizing Images

Images must often be resized to fit the required dimensions of the neural network input. In Keras, the ImageDataGenerator class offers a convenient way to handle image preprocessing tasks.

```
from keras.preprocessing.image import ImageDataGenerator

datagen = ImageDataGenerator()
image_resized = datagen.apply_transform(image, {'tx': 0, 'ty': 0, 'theta': 0})
image_resized = cv2.resize(image_resized, (target_height, target_width))
```

In this example, CV2 is utilized for resizing the image to dimensions (target_height, target_width), ensuring every input to the network maintains consistent size.

Normalization

Normalization scales pixel values to a common range, typically [0, 1] or [-1, 1]. This process helps in faster convergence during training and stable model performance. Below is a simple implementation using Keras utilities.

```
image_normalized = image_resized.astype('float32') / 255.0
```

The code snippet scales pixel values to range [0, 1]. Each pixel value, originally in the range [0, 255], is divided by 255.

Mean Subtraction

Subtracting the dataset mean from each image can further normalize the dataset. This centers the data around zero, which can be beneficial for gradient descent optimization.

```
mean_image = np.mean(dataset, axis=0)
image_mean_subtracted = image - mean_image
```

Here, mean_image is subtracted from each image, ensuring that the pixel values are centered around zero.

Noise Reduction

Noise reduction techniques, such as Gaussian blurring, can be applied to improve image quality by reducing random noise.

```
image_denoised = cv2.GaussianBlur(image, (5, 5), 0)
```

Data Augmentation
Data augmentation artificially enlarges the dataset by creating modified versions of the images. This helps improve the generalization ability of the model. Keras provides numerous functions for data augmentation:

```
datagen = ImageDataGenerator(
    rotation_range=20,
    width_shift_range=0.2,
    height_shift_range=0.2,
    shear_range=0.2,
    zoom_range=0.2,
    horizontal_flip=True,
    fill_mode='nearest'
)
```

This configuration applies random rotations, shifts, shears, zooms, and horizontal flips to the images, which can help the model generalize better by training on a more diverse set of images.

The ImageDataGenerator class provides a straightforward and flexible way to apply these transformations in real-time while feeding data to the model. It helps in creating more robust models by exposing them to a more extensive variety of input.

Example of Integrated Preprocessing Pipeline
Integrating several preprocessing steps into a pipeline ensures consistency and can be implemented as follows:

```
from keras.preprocessing.image import ImageDataGenerator

datagen = ImageDataGenerator(
    rescale=1./255,
    shear_range=0.2,
    zoom_range=0.2,
    horizontal_flip=True
)

train_generator = datagen.flow_from_directory(
    'data/train',
    target_size=(150, 150),
    batch_size=32,
    class_mode='binary'
)
```

This code example integrates rescaling, shearing, zooming, and horizontal flipping into the training data pipeline. This pipeline reads images from the directory data/train, resizes them to 150x150 pixels, applies scaling and augmentation, and organizes them into batches with labels for binary classification.

Batch and Epoch Handling
While processing data, handling batches and epochs properly is crucial. The fit_generator function of Keras models takes care of this efficiently:

```
model.fit_generator(
    train_generator,
    steps_per_epoch=2000 // batch_size,
    epochs=50
)
```

In this example, the model processes data in batches defined by batch_size and the entire dataset over 50 epochs. These parameters ensure that the network generalizes properly over the dataset.

By carefully crafting preprocessing pipelines, ensuring consistent tasks like resizing, normalization, and data augmentation, the input data becomes more suitable for deep learning models to grasp underlying patterns and features.

4.3 Data Augmentation Techniques

Data augmentation refers to the process of artificially expanding the size and diversity of a training dataset by applying various transformations to the existing data. These transformations help models generalize better by exposing them to a variety of scenarios, thus reducing the risk of overfitting. In the context of image data, augmentation involves applying transformations such as rotation, translation, scaling, flipping, and adding noise to images. This section delves into several common data augmentation techniques used in deep learning and demonstrates how to implement them using Keras.

1. Rotation

Rotating images by various angles, typically within a specified range, can help the model become invariant to changes in orientation. This process introduces rotational diversity without altering the underlying content of the image.

```
from keras.preprocessing.image import ImageDataGenerator

datagen = ImageDataGenerator(rotation_range=40)

# Apply rotation to a sample image
image_rotated = datagen.random_transform(sample_image)
```

2. Translation

Translation involves shifting the image along the x and y axes. This shift can help the model recognize objects regardless of their position within the frame.

```
datagen = ImageDataGenerator(width_shift_range=0.2, height_shift_range=0.2)

# Apply width and height shift to a sample image
image_translated = datagen.random_transform(sample_image)
```

3. Scaling

Scaling alters the size of objects within the image while maintaining the aspect ratio. This helps the model learn to identify objects at various scales.

```
datagen = ImageDataGenerator(zoom_range=0.2)

# Apply scaling to a sample image
image_scaled = datagen.random_transform(sample_image)
```

4. Flipping

Flipping horizontally or vertically creates mirror images, helping the model to generalize across different spatial configurations.

```
datagen = ImageDataGenerator(horizontal_flip=True, vertical_flip=True)

# Apply flipping to a sample image
image_flipped = datagen.random_transform(sample_image)
```

5. Adding Noise

Adding random noise can make the model more robust to noisy input data. This is especially useful in real-world scenarios where images may contain various levels of noise.

```
import numpy as np

def add_noise(img):
    noise_factor = 0.2
    noise = np.random.randn(*img.shape) * noise_factor
    return img + noise

# Apply noise to a sample image
image_noisy = add_noise(sample_image)
```

6. Shearing

Shearing involves slanting the image along the x or y axis. This augmentation technique can be particularly useful when the data contains objects that may appear skewed.

```
datagen = ImageDataGenerator(shear_range=0.2)

# Apply shearing to a sample image
image_sheared = datagen.random_transform(sample_image)
```

7. Brightness Adjustment

Changing the brightness of images enables the model to handle different lighting conditions more effectively. This technique adjusts the brightness of the image within a specified range.

```
datagen = ImageDataGenerator(brightness_range=[0.2, 1.0])

# Apply brightness adjustment to a sample image
image_bright = datagen.random_transform(sample_image)
```

8. Channel Shift

Channel shifting involves modifying the RGB channels of the image, which can simulate changes in lighting or color balance.

```
datagen = ImageDataGenerator(channel_shift_range=100.0)

# Apply channel shift to a sample image
image_shifted = datagen.random_transform(sample_image)
```

9. Combining Multiple Transformations

Combining multiple augmentation techniques can be particularly powerful. By applying several transformations, we can create highly diverse training datasets.

```
datagen = ImageDataGenerator(
    rotation_range=40,
    width_shift_range=0.2,
    height_shift_range=0.2,
    shear_range=0.2,
    zoom_range=0.2,
    horizontal_flip=True,
    fill_mode='nearest'
)

# Apply combined transformations to a sample image
image_augmented = datagen.random_transform(sample_image)
```

10. Implementing Data Augmentation in Training

Using ImageDataGenerator, we can directly augment images during training by fitting the generator to the dataset and configuring it to generate augmented images. This approach ensures that each epoch presents a new set of augmented images to the model.

```
# Create an ImageDataGenerator with multiple augmentations
datagen = ImageDataGenerator(
```

```
    rotation_range=40,
    width_shift_range=0.2,
    height_shift_range=0.2,
    shear_range=0.2,
    zoom_range=0.2,
    horizontal_flip=True,
    fill_mode='nearest'
)

# Fit the generator to the sample data
datagen.fit(train_images)

# Configure the model to use the generator
model.fit(datagen.flow(train_images, train_labels, batch_size=32),
        steps_per_epoch=len(train_images)/32, epochs=50)
```

Effective use of data augmentation can significantly improve model performance and generalization, leading to better results on unseen data.

4.4 Introduction to Convolutional Neural Networks (CNNs)

Convolutional Neural Networks (CNNs) have revolutionized the field of computer vision, enabling advancements in areas such as image classification, object recognition, and image generation. Unlike traditional neural networks, CNNs are specifically designed to process grid-like data structures, including images. Their architecture leverages spatial information, making them particularly suitable for image-related tasks.

A CNN typically consists of multiple layers, each designed to perform a specific operation on the input data. The most common layers found in a CNN are convolutional layers, pooling layers, and fully connected layers. Each layer plays a distinct role in feature extraction and data transformation.

Convolutional Layers

Convolutional layers are the cornerstone of CNNs. They apply convolution operations to the input data, which involves sliding a filter (or kernel) over the input to produce a feature map. This process helps capture spatial hierarchies and local patterns. Mathematically, a convolution can be expressed as:

$$S(i,j) = (X * K)(i,j) = \sum_m \sum_n X(i+m, j+n)K(m,n)$$

where X is the input image, K is the kernel, and S is the resulting feature map. The parameters i and j represent the spatial dimensions of the feature map, while m and n denote the size of the kernel.

Filters in convolutional layers can detect various features such as edges, textures, and patterns. The depth of these filters increases with each layer, enabling the network to learn more complex representations.

Activation Functions

Following the convolution operation, activation functions are applied to introduce non-linearity into the model. The most commonly used activation function in CNNs is the Rectified Linear Unit (ReLU), defined as:

$$\text{ReLU}(x) = \max(0, x)$$

ReLU helps address the vanishing gradient problem by allowing only positive activations to pass through, which speeds up the training process and enhances the model's ability to learn complex patterns.

Pooling Layers

Pooling layers, also known as subsampling or down-sampling layers, reduce the spatial dimensions of the feature maps. This helps decrease the computational load and prevents overfitting by summarizing the presence of features. The two most common types of pooling are max pooling and average pooling. Max pooling selects the maximum value within a specified window, while average pooling computes the average value. For instance, max pooling can be defined as:

$$P(i, j) = \max_{0 \leq m < p} \max_{0 \leq n < q} S(i + m, j + n)$$

where P is the pooled feature map, p and q denote the pooling window size, and S is the input feature map.

Fully Connected Layers

After several convolutional and pooling layers, the high-level reasoning in the network is performed via fully connected layers. These layers are similar to the layers in a traditional neural network where each neuron is connected to every neuron in the previous layer. This enables the network to integrate the features extracted from earlier layers and make decisions based on the learned patterns.

Combining the Layers

To illustrate how these layers integrate, we can look at a simple CNN implemented in Keras. Consider the following code:

```
from keras.models import Sequential
from keras.layers import Conv2D, MaxPooling2D, Flatten, Dense

model = Sequential()

# Convolutional layer
model.add(Conv2D(32, (3, 3), activation='relu', input_shape=(64, 64, 3)))

# Max pooling layer
model.add(MaxPooling2D(pool_size=(2, 2)))

# Flattening layer
model.add(Flatten())

# Fully connected layer
model.add(Dense(units=128, activation='relu'))

# Output layer
model.add(Dense(units=1, activation='sigmoid'))

model.compile(optimizer='adam', loss='binary_crossentropy', metrics=['accuracy'])
```

In this example, the model begins with a convolutional layer that uses 32 filters of size 3x3 and employs the ReLU activation function. The input shape is specified as 64x64 pixels with 3 color channels (RGB). This is followed by a max pooling layer that reduces the spatial dimensions. The feature maps are then flattened and passed through a fully connected layer with 128 neurons and ReLU activation. The final layer is a binary output layer using the sigmoid activation function.

Effective training of CNNs often requires large datasets, as the number of parameters can be substantial. However, techniques such as transfer learning and data augmentation can help mitigate dataset size limitations and enhance model performance. Transfer learning, for instance, involves fine-tuning a pre-trained model on a new, but related task, thus leveraging knowledge from the original task.

4.5 Architecture of CNNs: Convolutional Layers

Convolutional Neural Networks (CNNs) have revolutionized the field of deep learning for image data due to their ability to automatically and adaptively learn spatial hierarchies of features through backpropagation by using multiple building blocks, such as convolution layers, pooling layers, and fully connected layers. This section delves deeply into the architecture of CNNs, with a focus on the convolutional layers, which are the core components of these networks.

The primary purpose of convolutional layers in CNNs is to extract features from the input images. The convolution operation performs a weighted sum of the input pixels based on the weights given by the filter (or kernel), thus detecting specific patterns like edges, textures, or more complex structures.

Mathematically, the convolution operation can be expressed as:

$$S(i,j) = (I * K)(i,j) = \sum_{m=0}^{M-1} \sum_{n=0}^{N-1} I(i+m, j+n) \cdot K(m,n)$$

where I denotes the input image, K denotes the convolutional kernel (filter), S denotes the output feature map, i and j are the spatial dimensions of the output, and M, N are the filter dimensions.

Convolution Operation

Consider the following 5x5 input matrix and a 3x3 filter for better illustration:

```
Input:
0 1 1 0 0
0 1 1 1 0
0 0 1 0 1
1 1 0 1 1
0 1 1 0 0

Filter:
1 0 1
0 1 0
1 0 1
```

Performing a convolution operation with this filter (stride 1 and pad 0) on the input matrix yields the following 3x3 matrix:

```
Output:
3 2 4
2 3 3
3 2 3
```

Padding and Stride

To control the spatial dimensions of the output feature map, two key hyperparameters are used in the convolutional layers: padding and stride.

- **Padding:** Adding additional borders of zeros to the input makes it possible to preserve the spatial size of the output. There are generally two types of padding:

  - *Valid Padding* (no padding): Directly applies the filter on the original input matrix. The formula for the output size is:

$$O = \left\lfloor \frac{I - K + 1}{S} \right\rfloor$$

  - *Same Padding*: Pads the input matrix so that the output feature map will have the same dimensions as the input. The formula for the output size is:

$$O = \left\lfloor \frac{I}{S} \right\rfloor$$

- **Stride:** This refers to the number of units by which the filter is moved each time. A stride greater than 1 reduces the dimension of the output feature map. The formula for the output size with stride S is:

$$O = \left\lfloor \frac{I - K + 2P}{S} \right\rfloor + 1$$

  where P is the padding size.

These operations are crucial for controlling feature map sizes and computational efficiency.

Depth and Stacking Convolution Layers

A single convolution layer can only capture low-level features, such as edges. Stacking multiple convolution layers allows the network to learn increasingly complex and abstract features. In deep architectures, deeper layers may detect shapes, objects, and more sophisticated structures by combining and recombining features from earlier layers.

Consider a neural network component built using two convolutional layers:

```
from keras.models import Sequential
from keras.layers import Conv2D

model = Sequential()
model.add(Conv2D(32, (3, 3), activation='relu', input_shape=(64, 64, 3)))
model.add(Conv2D(64, (3, 3), activation='relu'))
```

This code snippet defines a simple network where the first convolutional layer has 32 filters 3×3 in size and the second convolutional layer has 64 filters also 3×3. Such stacking enables deeper representations.

Activation Functions

Convolution layers are typically followed by non-linear activation functions, such as ReLU (Rectified Linear Unit). The ReLU activation function is defined as:

$$f(x) = \max(0, x)$$

The ReLU function significantly accelerates the convergence of stochastic gradient descent compared to sigmoid and tanh due to its linear, unsaturated form. The use of activation functions introduces non-linearity into the network, enabling the model to learn more complex patterns.

```
from keras.layers import Activation

model = Sequential()
model.add(Conv2D(32, (3, 3), input_shape=(64, 64, 3)))
model.add(Activation('relu'))
```

Example of Using Convolutional Layer with Keras

To solidify understanding, consider implementing a simple convolutional layer in a Keras model.

```
from keras.models import Sequential
from keras.layers import Conv2D, Activation

# Initialize a Sequential model
model = Sequential()

# Adding a 2D convolutional layer with 32 filters and kernel size of 3x3
model.add(Conv2D(32, (3, 3), padding='same', input_shape=(64, 64, 3)))

# Applying ReLU activation
model.add(Activation('relu'))

# Displaying the model summary
model.summary()
```

Output:

```
Layer (type)                 Output Shape              Param #
=================================================================
conv2d_1 (Conv2D)            (None, 64, 64, 32)        896
_________________________________________________________________
activation_1 (Activation)    (None, 64, 64, 32)        0
=================================================================
Total params: 896
Trainable params: 896
Non-trainable params: 0
_________________________________________________________________
```

This overview and implementation detail clearly articulate the importance and operations of convolutional layers within CNN architectures.

4.6 Pooling Layers and Their Importance

Pooling layers, also known as downsampling layers, play a critical role within Convolutional Neural Networks (CNNs) by progressively reducing the spatial dimensions of feature maps. This operation helps to decrease computational requirements and control overfitting by preventing the network from becoming overly reliant on local features. The pooling operation can be executed in different methods, with the most common ones being max pooling and average pooling.

Max pooling involves the selection of the maximum value within a designated pooling window, while average pooling computes the average of the values within the same window. The spatial dimensions of the feature map are reduced based on the stride of the pooling operation, which dictates the step size for traversing the input.

To illustrate these concepts, consider a feature map represented as a matrix:

$$\begin{bmatrix} 1 & 3 & 2 & 4 \\ 5 & 6 & 1 & 2 \\ 7 & 8 & 3 & 0 \\ 1 & 3 & 2 & 8 \end{bmatrix}$$

Applying a max pooling operation with a 2×2 window and a stride of 2, we obtain:

$$\begin{bmatrix} 6 & 4 \\ 8 & 8 \end{bmatrix}$$

In this example, the 2×2 window moves across the input matrix with a stride of 2, selecting the maximum value within each window. Conversely, applying an average pooling operation with the same parameters would yield:

$$\begin{bmatrix} 3.75 & 2.25 \\ 4.75 & 3.25 \end{bmatrix}$$

Beyond reducing spatial dimensions, pooling layers contribute significantly to translational invariance. They ensure the network is less sensitive to small shifts and distortions in the input image. This feature is crucial in applications where object detection should be robust to slight variations in object positions.

Incorporating pooling layers in a CNN architecture can be demonstrated using Keras as follows:

```
from keras.models import Sequential
from keras.layers import Conv2D, MaxPooling2D, Flatten, Dense

model = Sequential()

# Adding a convolutional layer
model.add(Conv2D(64, (3, 3), activation='relu', input_shape=(128, 128, 3)))

# Adding a max pooling layer
model.add(MaxPooling2D(pool_size=(2, 2), strides=(2, 2)))

# Adding a flatten layer
model.add(Flatten())

# Adding a fully-connected layer
model.add(Dense(256, activation='relu'))

print(model.summary())
```

By incorporating the MaxPooling2D layer, the CNN effectively reduces the dimensionality of the feature maps, thereby optimizing the number of learnable parameters in subsequent layers. Let us observe the output of the model summary:

```
Layer (type)                 Output Shape              Param #
=================================================================
conv2d_1 (Conv2D)            (None, 126, 126, 64)      1792
_________________________________________________________________
max_pooling2d_1 (MaxPooling2 (None, 63, 63, 64)        0
_________________________________________________________________
flatten_1 (Flatten)          (None, 254016)            0
_________________________________________________________________
dense_1 (Dense)              (None, 256)               65028192
=================================================================
Total params: 65,030,984
Trainable params: 65,030,984
Non-trainable params: 0
_________________________________________________________________
```

The MaxPooling2D layer effectively halves each spatial dimension of the input from $(126, 126)$ to $(63, 63)$, as indicated in our model summary. This reduction significantly decreases the total number of parameters, as seen in the fully connected layer, where the number of input connections is determined by the size of the flattened output from the previous layer (254,016 units).

Beyond max and average pooling, other advanced techniques, such as global pooling, have found applications in modern architectures. In global average pooling, for instance, each feature map is averaged entirely down to a single value, drastically reducing the dimensionality while preserving the salient features. Here is how to implement it in Keras:

```
from keras.layers import GlobalAveragePooling2D

model = Sequential()

# Adding a convolutional layer
model.add(Conv2D(64, (3, 3), activation='relu', input_shape=(128, 128, 3)))

# Adding a global average pooling layer
model.add(GlobalAveragePooling2D())

# Adding a fully-connected layer
model.add(Dense(256, activation='relu'))

print(model.summary())
```

The corresponding model summary reflects the use of global average pooling:

```
Layer (type)                 Output Shape              Param #
=================================================================
conv2d_1 (Conv2D)            (None, 126, 126, 64)      1792
_________________________________________________________________
global_average_pooling2d_1 ( (None, 64)                0
_________________________________________________________________
dense_1 (Dense)              (None, 256)               16640
=================================================================
Total params: 18,432
Trainable params: 18,432
Non-trainable params: 0
_________________________________________________________________
```

Global average pooling compresses each feature map to a scalar value, resulting in 64 output units instead of the flattened figure from the max pooling example. This considerable reduction in parameter count can lead to more efficient training and decreased risk of overfitting.

Pooling layers, through their various implementations, form a foundational component in the design of CNNs, enabling these networks to handle spatial hierarchies and scale effectively. Each specific type of pooling provides unique advantages depending on the expected variance and translation within the image data, emphasizing the importance of careful architectural choice to match the task-specific requirements.

4.7 Building a Simple CNN with Keras

In this section, we focus on constructing a simple Convolutional Neural Network (CNN) using the Keras library. Keras, being a high-level neural networks API, allows for an easy and intuitive approach to building and training neural networks. The section assumes that the reader is familiar with basic concepts of CNNs, such as convolutional layers and pooling layers, discussed previously in the chapter.

To begin with, let's define a simple CNN architecture suitable for image classification tasks. We will use the MNIST dataset, which comprises 60,000 training images and 10,000 testing images of handwritten digits, with each image being a $28x28$ grayscale image.

```
# Import necessary libraries
import numpy as np
import keras
from keras.datasets import mnist
from keras.models import Sequential
from keras.layers import Dense, Conv2D, MaxPooling2D, Dropout, Flatten
from keras.utils import np_utils

# Load the dataset
(X_train, y_train), (X_test, y_test) = mnist.load_data()

# Reshape the dataset to include the channel dimension
X_train = X_train.reshape(X_train.shape[0], 28, 28, 1).astype('float32')
X_test = X_test.reshape(X_test.shape[0], 28, 28, 1).astype('float32')

# Normalize the inputs from 0-255 to 0-1
X_train = X_train / 255
X_test = X_test / 255

# One-hot encode the labels
y_train = np_utils.to_categorical(y_train)
y_test = np_utils.to_categorical(y_test)
num_classes = y_test.shape[1]
```

The code above handles data preprocessing. Each image in the MNIST dataset is normalized to a range between 0 and 1, and the labels are one-hot encoded. This ensures compatibility with our CNN and numerical stability during training.

Next, we define the CNN model. Here, we construct a Sequential model with multiple layers, namely convolutional layers, pooling layers, a flattening layer, and densely connected layers.

```
# Define the CNN model
model = Sequential()
model.add(Conv2D(32, (5, 5), input_shape=(28, 28, 1), activation='relu'))
model.add(MaxPooling2D(pool_size=(2, 2)))
model.add(Conv2D(64, (3, 3), activation='relu'))
model.add(MaxPooling2D(pool_size=(2, 2)))
model.add(Dropout(0.2))
model.add(Flatten())
model.add(Dense(128, activation='relu'))
model.add(Dense(num_classes, activation='softmax'))

# Compile the model
model.compile(loss='categorical_crossentropy', optimizer='adam', metrics=['accuracy'])
```

```
# Print the model summary
model.summary()
```

Here is a detailed breakdown of the layers and their configuration:

- **Conv2D(32, (5, 5), input_shape=(28, 28, 1), activation='relu')**: This first convolutional layer has 32 filters, each of size 5x5. The input_shape parameter specifies the dimensions of the input images (28x28 pixels with 1 channel). The ReLU activation function introduces non-linearity.

- **MaxPooling2D(pool_size=(2, 2))**: This layer performs max pooling with a 2x2 window to reduce the spatial dimensions of the feature maps, reducing the computational load and controlling overfitting.

- **Conv2D(64, (3, 3), activation='relu')**: The second convolutional layer has 64 filters of size 3x3. Again, ReLU is used as the activation function.

- **MaxPooling2D(pool_size=(2, 2))**: Another max pooling layer for further spatial dimensionality reduction.

- **Dropout(0.2)**: Dropout is applied to the model with 20% neurons deactivated randomly during each training step to prevent overfitting.

- **Flatten()**: This layer flattens the 2D matrices into a 1D vector, preparing it to be fed into the densely connected layers.

- **Dense(128, activation='relu')**: A fully connected layer with 128 neurons and ReLU activation, which helps in learning complex representations.

- **Dense(num_classes, activation='softmax')**: The output layer has num_classes neurons with a softmax activation, converting the outputs to probability distributions.

The model.summary() function provides a detailed overview of the network architecture, outlining each layer's configuration, output shapes, and the number of parameters:

```
Layer (type)                 Output Shape              Param #
=================================================================
conv2d_1 (Conv2D)            (None, 24, 24, 32)        832
_________________________________________________________________
max_pooling2d_1 (MaxPooling2 (None, 12, 12, 32)        0
_________________________________________________________________
conv2d_2 (Conv2D)            (None, 10, 10, 64)        18496
_________________________________________________________________
max_pooling2d_2 (MaxPooling2 (None, 5, 5, 64)          0
_________________________________________________________________
dropout_1 (Dropout)          (None, 5, 5, 64)          0
_________________________________________________________________
flatten_1 (Flatten)          (None, 1600)              0
_________________________________________________________________
dense_1 (Dense)              (None, 128)               204928
_________________________________________________________________
dense_2 (Dense)              (None, 10)                1290
=================================================================
Total params: 225,546
Trainable params: 225,546
Non-trainable params: 0
```

Training the model involves specifying the number of epochs and batch size, along with the training and validation datasets.

```
# Train the model
model.fit(X_train, y_train, validation_data=(X_test, y_test), epochs=10, batch_size
    =200, verbose=2)

# Evaluate the model
scores = model.evaluate(X_test, y_test, verbose=0)
print(f"Error: {100 - scores[1] * 100:.2f}%")
```

The model.fit() function initiates training, specifying 10 epochs and a batch size of 200. The training dataset includes both the training data and the validation data to monitor the model's performance. Following training, the model.evaluate() function assesses the model's accuracy against the test dataset, rendering an error percentage for evaluation. This guided process highlights the steps required to build and train a simple CNN, leveraging Keras' intuitive and flexible interface.

4.8 Advanced CNN Architectures: VGG, ResNet, Inception, etc.

In previous sections, we have discussed fundamental concepts and architectures of convolutional neural networks (CNNs). Building upon what we have learned, this section delves into advanced CNN architectures that have achieved remarkable performance on image recognition tasks. Among the most influential and widely used architectures in the deep learning community are VGG, ResNet, and Inception. Each of these architectures introduced innovative techniques that significantly enhanced the capabilities of CNNs.

VGG Networks: The VGG (Visual Geometry Group) networks, proposed by Simonyan and Zisserman in 2014, emphasized simplicity and depth. VGGNet, particularly the VGG16 and VGG19 variants, demonstrated that increasing the depth of the network with very small convolutional filters (3x3) can lead to better performance. The network contains multiple convolutional layers followed by max-pooling layers. In VGG16, there are 13 convolutional layers and 3 fully connected layers.

```
from keras.applications import VGG16

vgg_model = VGG16(weights='imagenet', include_top=True)
vgg_model.summary()
```

The VGG architecture's deeper network with smaller filter sizes allows the network to capture fine-grained features while maintaining a manageable number of parameters. This simplicity, however, comes with a high computational cost and a large memory footprint due to the deep layers.

ResNet (Residual Networks): The introduction of ResNet by He et al. in 2015 addressed the problem of vanishing gradients in deep networks. ResNet innovatively incorporated *residual learning*, where shortcut connections (or skip connections) were added to the traditional convolutional layers. These connections allow the gradient to bypass some layers, facilitating training of much deeper networks without performance degradation.

```
from keras.applications import ResNet50

resnet_model = ResNet50(weights='imagenet', include_top=True)
resnet_model.summary()
```

A residual block can be represented as:

$$y = F(x, \{W_i\}) + x$$

where $F(x, \{W_i\})$ represents the residual mapping to be learned. The identity mapping x is added to the output of the residual function. This enables the network to learn the identity function more easily, effectively "skipping" over layers.

Inception Networks: The Inception architecture, initially proposed by Szegedy et al., introduced the concept of *Inception modules*, which aimed to improve the network's ability to capture diverse features at different scales. The Inception module performs convolutional operations with multiple filter sizes (e.g., 1x1, 3x3, 5x5) within the same layer and concatenates the outputs along the depth dimension. This allows the network to capture both local and global features effectively.

```
from keras.applications import InceptionV3

inception_model = InceptionV3(weights='imagenet', include_top=True)
inception_model.summary()
```

In a simplified form, an Inception module can be depicted diagrammatically as:

```
          1x1 Convolution
                |
         3x3 Convolution
          /          \
Input ----->              Concatenate ----> Output
          \          /
         5x5 Convolution
                |
          1x1 Convolution
```

This multi-scale approach allows the network to consider a richer set of features compared to traditional convolutional layers.

Advantages of Advanced Architectures: Each of these architectures, VGG, ResNet, and Inception, introduced innovations that tackled specific limitations of earlier networks:

- **Depth and Simplicity**: VGG showed that deeper networks with uniform filter sizes can significantly boost performance.

- **Residual Learning**: ResNet solved degradation problems associated with deep networks, allowing networks to be extraordinarily deep without sacrificing accuracy.

- **Multi-Scale Feature Extraction**: Inception modules enabled the network to capture features at multiple scales in parallel, enhancing performance on diverse image recognition tasks.

In practical applications, selecting the appropriate architecture depends on factors such as computational resources, the complexity of the task, and the available training data. Transfer learning, which will be discussed in the next section, often leverages these pretrained advanced architectures to achieve state-of-the-art performance with limited datasets.

4.9 Transfer Learning for Image Classification

Transfer learning enables the application of pre-trained neural network models to new but related tasks, significantly improving performance and reducing the computational burden. Instead of developing a model from scratch, transfer learning leverages knowledge gained while solving a problem and applies it to a different but similar problem. For image classification, this often involves using well-established convolutional neural networks (CNNs) such as VGG, ResNet, or Inception that have been trained on large datasets like ImageNet.

Understanding the Concept of Transfer Learning: In transfer learning, the initial layers of the pre-trained network function as a fixed feature extractor, utilizing the extensive patterns and representations learned from large benchmark datasets. These layers capture low-level features such as edges, textures, and colors at the beginning and more complex structures in deeper layers. For the new specific task, only the final classification layers are typically replaced and re-trained on the new dataset. This methodology provides a strong starting point due to the robustness of the feature representations learned from the large dataset.

Steps for Implementing Transfer Learning with Keras: To implement transfer learning in Keras, follow these sequential steps: 1. Load the Pre-trained Model 2. Freeze the Initial Layers 3. Add New Classification Layers 4. Compile and Train the Model

Here is a detailed implementation using Keras:

```
from tensorflow.keras.applications import VGG16
from tensorflow.keras.models import Sequential
from tensorflow.keras.layers import Dense, Flatten
from tensorflow.keras.optimizers import Adam

# Load the Pre-trained VGG16 model without the top classification layer
base_model = VGG16(weights='imagenet', include_top=False, input_shape=(224,
    224, 3))

# Freeze the layers of the base model
for layer in base_model.layers:
    layer.trainable = False

# Create a new model and add the base model
model = Sequential([
    base_model,
    Flatten(),
    Dense(256, activation='relu'),
    Dense(10, activation='softmax') # Assuming we have 10 classes
])
```

```
# Compile the model
model.compile(optimizer=Adam(learning_rate=0.0001),
          loss='categorical_crossentropy',
          metrics=['accuracy'])

# Print model summary
model.summary()

# Assuming 'train_generator' and 'validation_generator' are predefined data
    generators
history = model.fit(train_generator,
                    validation_data=validation_generator,
                    epochs=10,
                    steps_per_epoch=len(train_generator),
                    validation_steps=len(validation_generator))
```

In the code above, the VGG16 model is loaded without its top classification layer using the include_top=False argument. The loaded model's layers are then frozen using the trainable=False parameter to prevent their weights from being updated during training. New fully connected layers, including a Dense layer with 256 units and ReLU activation, followed by a Dense layer with softmax activation for classification into 10 classes, are added to the base model.

Challenges and Considerations: While implementing transfer learning, consider the following challenges and nuances:

- **Dimensionality of Input Data**: Ensure that the input dimensions of your data match the expected input dimensions of the pre-trained model. For most pre-trained models like VGG16, the standard input size is $224 \times 224 \times 3$.
- **Choice of Pre-trained Model**: Different models might be more suitable depending on your specific problem. VGG is known for its simplicity, whereas ResNet can address deeper network problems with its skip connections.
- **Fine-tuning vs. Feature Extraction**: It is crucial to decide whether to use the pre-trained model as a feature extractor or to fine-tune some of its layers. Fine-tuning involves unfreezing some top layers of the pre-trained model and training them alongside the new classification layers, which can provide additional performance improvements on your specific task.
- **Data Augmentation**: Although the model has been pre-trained, augmenting the data can still be beneficial. It can help prevent overfitting and improve the generalization of the model on the specific task.

To fine-tune the model, unfreeze some of the top layers after the initial freezing and recompile the model for further training. Below is an example of fine-tuning:

```
# Unfreeze the top layers of the base model
for layer in base_model.layers[-4:]: # Unfreeze the last 4 layers
    layer.trainable = True

# Recompile the model with a lower learning rate
model.compile(optimizer=Adam(learning_rate=0.00001),
              loss='categorical_crossentropy',
              metrics=['accuracy'])

# Continue training the model
history_finetune = model.fit(train_generator,
                             validation_data=validation_generator,
                             epochs=5,
                             steps_per_epoch=len(train_generator),
                             validation_steps=len(validation_generator))
```

Here, we unfreeze the last four layers of the base model and recompile the model with a lower learning rate, allowing these layers to adapt specifically to the new task. Training is then continued for a few more epochs.

Evaluating and Testing: Once the model is trained, evaluate its performance on a test set to ensure it generalizes well to unseen data:

```
# Evaluate the model on the test set
test_loss, test_accuracy = model.evaluate(test_generator, steps=len(test_generator))
print(f'Test accuracy: {test_accuracy:.4f}')
```

```
Test accuracy: 0.8432
```

The test accuracy provides a reliable indicator of how well the transfer learning model generalizes to new, unseen data.

4.10 Object Detection and Localization

Object detection and localization refer to the tasks of identifying and classifying objects within an image and determining their positions in the form of bounding boxes. While image classification assigns a single label to an entire image, object detection must handle multiple objects of different classes within the same image. The localization aspect involves predicting the coordinates of the rectangular bounding box that tightly encloses each detected object. This section details methods, models, and approaches employed in object detection using deep learning techniques.

The state-of-the-art methods for object detection predominantly rely on convolutional neural networks (CNNs). Two main pioneering frameworks are Region-based CNN (R-CNN) and Single Shot MultiBox Detector (SSD). Each framework's core functionalities and advancements are investigated systematically.

Region-based Convolutional Neural Networks (R-CNN)

R-CNN was one of the earliest frameworks to extend CNNs for object detection tasks. Introduced by Girshick et al., R-CNN involves several steps:

- **Region Proposal**: The algorithm generates a set of region proposals (potential bounding boxes) using selective search.
- **Feature Extraction**: A CNN extracts a feature vector from each region proposal.
- **Classification**: Each feature vector is classified using a Support Vector Machine (SVM) into different object categories.
- **Bounding Box Regression**: A regression model fine-tunes the coordinates of the bounding boxes.

The following code snippet demonstrates a simplified version of extracting Region of Interests (ROI) for R-CNN-style processing:

```
import cv2
import numpy as np

def selective_search(image_path):
    image = cv2.imread(image_path)
    ss = cv2.ximgproc.segmentation.createSelectiveSearchSegmentation()
    ss.setBaseImage(image)
    ss.switchToSelectiveSearchFast()
    rects = ss.process()
    proposals = []

    for rect in rects:
        x, y, w, h = rect
        proposals.append(image[y:y+h, x:x+w])

    return proposals

proposals = selective_search('example_image.jpg')
```

While effective, this method is computationally expensive due to redundant feature extraction for overlapping regions. Subsequently, Fast R-CNN and Faster R-CNN were proposed to address these inefficiencies by incorporating shared convolutional layers and introducing Region Proposal Networks (RPNs).

Single Stage Detectors: SSD and YOLO

Single Shot MultiBox Detector (SSD) and You Only Look Once (YOLO) represent single stage detectors optimizing both object classification and bounding box regression directly from images. These models eliminate the need for the region proposal step, achieving significantly faster detection speeds.

Single Shot MultiBox Detector (SSD)

SSD discretizes the output space of bounding boxes into a set of default boxes over different aspect ratios and scales per feature map location. The network classifies each default box's content and adjusts its bounding box.

The key features of SSD include:

- **Single Path Forwarding**: Both object category scores and bounding box coordinates are evaluated in a single network forward pass.
- **Multi-scale Feature Maps**: SSD uses convolutional feature maps at multiple scales, enabling detection across various sized objects efficiently.

The following code snippet gives an example of configuring an SSD-based model using Keras:

```
from keras.models import Model
from keras.layers import Input, Conv2D, Flatten, Dense, Reshape

def ssd_model(input_shape, num_classes):
    input_tensor = Input(shape=input_shape)
    x = Conv2D(32, (3, 3), activation='relu', padding='same')(input_tensor)
    x = Conv2D(64, (3, 3), activation='relu', padding='same')(x)
    x = Conv2D(128, (3, 3), activation='relu', padding='same')(x)

    cls_layers = []
    loc_layers = []

    for _ in range(6):
        cls_layers.append(Conv2D(num_classes, (1, 1), padding='same')(x))
        loc_layers.append(Conv2D(4, (1, 1), padding='same')(x))

    # Reshape layers for output
    cls_preds = [Reshape((-1, num_classes))(layer) for layer in cls_layers]
    loc_preds = [Reshape((-1, 4))(layer) for layer in loc_layers]

    cls_preds = Flatten()(cls_preds)
    loc_preds = Flatten()(loc_preds)

    output = Dense(num_classes, activation='softmax')(cls_preds)
    loc_output = Dense(4)(loc_preds)
```

```
    model = Model(input_tensor, [output, loc_output])
    return model

ssd = ssd_model((300, 300, 3), num_classes=21)
```

SSD's advantages include its balance of accuracy and speed, making it suitable for real-time applications.

You Only Look Once (YOLO)

YOLO models frame object detection as a single regression problem, mapping directly from the image pixels to bounding box coordinates and class probabilities. Key to YOLO's architecture is splitting the input image into an $S \times S$ grid and predicting bounding boxes and confidences directly from each grid cell.

- The bounding box prediction includes both the coordinates (x, y, width, height) and the object confidence score.
- Each grid cell also predicts classification scores for specific object classes.

The most crucial advantage of YOLO is real-time processing speed without sacrificing significant accuracy.

```
import tensorflow as tf
from tensorflow.keras import layers, models

def yolo_model(input_shape, num_classes):
    inputs = tf.keras.Input(shape=input_shape)
    x = layers.Conv2D(32, (3, 3), activation='relu')(inputs)
    x = layers.Conv2D(64, (3, 3), activation='relu')(x)
    x = layers.Flatten()(x)
    x = layers.Dense(1024, activation='relu')(x)

    # Output layers for coordinates, confidence, and class probabilities
    coordinates = layers.Dense(4)(x)
    confidence = layers.Dense(1, activation='sigmoid')(x)
    classes = layers.Dense(num_classes, activation='softmax')(x)

    outputs = layers.Concatenate(axis=-1)([coordinates, confidence, classes])
    model = models.Model(inputs=inputs, outputs=outputs)
    return model

yolo = yolo_model((448, 448, 3), num_classes=80)
```

Object detection and localization applications span various domains from self-driving cars and surveillance to medical imaging and retail. State-of-the-art detectors like YOLO and SSD continue to evolve with research advancements, offering enhanced performance metrics across speed and accuracy dimensions. They exemplify the remarkable capabilities of deep learning in understanding complex visual scenes.

4.11 Image Segmentation

Image segmentation is a critical task in computer vision that involves partitioning an image into multiple segments or regions, often to simplify or change the representation of an image into something more meaningful and easier to analyze. Unlike object detection, which draws bounding boxes around objects, segmentation provides a pixel-wise mask for each object in the image, highlighting the exact shape and position of the objects. This detailed understanding of the image content makes segmentation particularly valuable for applications in medical imaging, autonomous driving, and satellite imagery.

At the core of image segmentation are various techniques and models that facilitate the partitioning process. These techniques can be broadly categorized into classical methods and deep learning-based methods. Classical methods include techniques such as thresholding, clustering (e.g., K-means), and region-growing methods. However, deep learning methods, particularly those using Convolutional Neural Networks (CNNs), have demonstrated superior performance in recent years.

Semantic Segmentation vs. Instance Segmentation

Semantic segmentation assigns a class label to each pixel in the image without distinguishing between different instances of the same class. For example, in a street scene, all pixels belonging to cars will bear the 'car' label, but individual cars are not differentiated. On the other hand, instance segmentation not only classifies each pixel but also differentiates between distinct instances of the same class. This dual task inherently requires more sophisticated models and post-processing techniques.

Fully Convolutional Networks (FCNs)

FCNs are a foundational approach to semantic segmentation. They replace the fully connected layers of a traditional CNN with convolutional layers, enabling the network to produce an output with the same spatial dimensions as the input. This configuration allows the model to learn spatial hierarchies and generate dense predictions at the pixel level.

To implement an FCN in Keras, we start by making modifications to a pre-trained CNN, such as VGG16 or ResNet, converting its fully connected layers to convolutional layers. The following code illustrates this approach using a VGG16 backbone:

```
from keras.applications import VGG16
from keras.models import Model
from keras.layers import Conv2D, Conv2DTranspose, Input

# Load the VGG16 model, excluding the top classification layers
base_model = VGG16(weights='imagenet', include_top=False, input_shape=(224,
    224, 3))

# Take the output of the last convolutional block
output = base_model.get_layer('block5_conv3').output

# Add Convolutional layers
x = Conv2D(4096, (7, 7), activation='relu', padding='same')(output)
x = Conv2D(4096, (1, 1), activation='relu', padding='same')(x)

# Up-sampling using Transposed Convolution
x = Conv2DTranspose(21, kernel_size=(64, 64), strides=(32, 32), padding='same',
    activation='softmax')(x)

# Create the model
model = Model(inputs=base_model.input, outputs=x)
```

In the provided code, we leverage a VGG16 model, fine-tuning the convolutional blocks and adding transposed convolution layers (also known as deconvolution layers) to upsample the feature maps back to the original image size.

U-Net

Another seminal model for image segmentation is U-Net, which was originally designed for biomedical image segmentation. The architecture consists of an encoder-decoder structure with symmetric skip connections. These skip connections link encoder layers to their corresponding decoder layers, allowing the model to retrieve high-resolution features during reconstruction effectively.

The following code demonstrates a basic implementation of a U-Net model in Keras:

```
from keras.models import Model
from keras.layers import Conv2D, MaxPooling2D, Conv2DTranspose, concatenate,
    Input

def unet(input_size=(256, 256, 1)):
    inputs = Input(input_size)

    # Encoding path
    c1 = Conv2D(64, (3, 3), activation='relu', padding='same')(inputs)
    c1 = Conv2D(64, (3, 3), activation='relu', padding='same')(c1)
    p1 = MaxPooling2D((2, 2))(c1)

    c2 = Conv2D(128, (3, 3), activation='relu', padding='same')(p1)
    c2 = Conv2D(128, (3, 3), activation='relu', padding='same')(c2)
```

```
    p2 = MaxPooling2D((2, 2))(c2)

    c3 = Conv2D(256, (3, 3), activation='relu', padding='same')(p2)
    c3 = Conv2D(256, (3, 3), activation='relu', padding='same')(c3)
    p3 = MaxPooling2D((2, 2))(c3)

    c4 = Conv2D(512, (3, 3), activation='relu', padding='same')(p3)
    c4 = Conv2D(512, (3, 3), activation='relu', padding='same')(c4)
    p4 = MaxPooling2D((2, 2))(c4)

    # Bottleneck
    c5 = Conv2D(1024, (3, 3), activation='relu', padding='same')(p4)
    c5 = Conv2D(1024, (3, 3), activation='relu', padding='same')(c5)

    # Decoding path
    u6 = Conv2DTranspose(512, (2, 2), strides=(2, 2), padding='same')(c5)
    u6 = concatenate([u6, c4])
    c6 = Conv2D(512, (3, 3), activation='relu', padding='same')(u6)
    c6 = Conv2D(512, (3, 3), activation='relu', padding='same')(c6)

    u7 = Conv2DTranspose(256, (2, 2), strides=(2, 2), padding='same')(c6)
    u7 = concatenate([u7, c3])
    c7 = Conv2D(256, (3, 3), activation='relu', padding='same')(u7)
    c7 = Conv2D(256, (3, 3), activation='relu', padding='same')(c7)

    u8 = Conv2DTranspose(128, (2, 2), strides=(2, 2), padding='same')(c7)
    u8 = concatenate([u8, c2])
    c8 = Conv2D(128, (3, 3), activation='relu', padding='same')(u8)
    c8 = Conv2D(128, (3, 3), activation='relu', padding='same')(c8)

    u9 = Conv2DTranspose(64, (2, 2), strides=(2, 2), padding='same')(c8)
    u9 = concatenate([u9, c1])
    c9 = Conv2D(64, (3, 3), activation='relu', padding='same')(u9)
    c9 = Conv2D(64, (3, 3), activation='relu', padding='same')(c9)

    outputs = Conv2D(1, (1, 1), activation='sigmoid')(c9)

    model = Model(inputs=inputs, outputs=outputs)

    return model

model = unet()
```

The U-Net architecture ensures that the encoder compresses the input image into a set of feature maps, which are then gradually reconstructed by the decoder, using information from the corresponding layers of the encoder through concatenation. This skip connection mechanism helps in preserving spatial information and refining the segmentation results.

Metrics for Segmentation

Assessing the performance of segmentation models necessitates specific metrics. Commonly used metrics include Intersection over Union (IoU), Dice Coefficient, Precision, Recall, and F1-score. These metrics evaluate the overlap between the predicted segmentation and the ground truth, focusing on pixel-wise accuracy:

$$IoU = \frac{\text{True Positive}}{\text{True Positive} + \text{False Positive} + \text{False Negative}}$$

$$Dice = \frac{2 \times \text{True Positive}}{2 \times \text{True Positive} + \text{False Positive} + \text{False Negative}}$$

Precision and Recall offer insights into the accuracy of positive predictions and the ability of the model to identify all relevant instances, respectively. The F1-score, a harmonic mean of Precision and Recall, balances both metrics.

IoU and Dice are particularly effective for evaluating segmentation tasks because they directly measure the spatial congruence between the predicted and actual segmentation masks. For example:

```
import numpy as np

def iou_coef(y_true, y_pred, smooth=1):
    intersection = np.sum(y_true * y_pred)
    sum_ = np.sum(y_true + y_pred)
    iou = (intersection + smooth) / (sum_ - intersection + smooth)
    return iou

def dice_coef(y_true, y_pred, smooth=1):
    intersection = np.sum(y_true * y_pred)
    return (2. * intersection + smooth) / (np.sum(y_true) + np.sum(y_pred) +
         smooth)
```

Applications

Applications of image segmentation are vast and varied. In medical imaging, segmentation assists in isolating regions of interest such as tumors, organs, or blood vessels, aiding in diagnosis and treatment planning. In autonomous driving, segmentation algorithms help identify road boundaries, pedestrians, vehicles, and other relevant objects, enhancing safety features.

In satellite imagery, segmentation aids in land cover classification, urban planning, and disaster management. For example, water bodies, vegetation, and urban areas can be distinctly segmented to monitor environmental changes or urban growth.

In industrial applications, segmentation is employed for quality control and defect detection, ensuring higher precision in manufacturing processes.

Each of these applications benefits from the capability of segmentation models to understand and delineate complex structures in images, thereby enabling more precise and actionable insights.

4.12 Practical Projects: Implementing Real-world Image Applications

The practical application of deep learning to solve real-world problems involves leveraging the power of convolutional neural networks (CNNs) and advanced techniques. In this section, we will explore several hands-on projects that illustrate how to implement image applications effectively. We will cover image classification, object detection, image segmentation, and employ transfer learning to enhance performance.

Project 1: Image Classification with Transfer Learning

We start by utilizing transfer learning to improve the efficiency and accuracy of an image classification task. Transfer learning enables us to use pre-trained models, such as VGG16, ResNet50, or InceptionV3, and adapt them to our specific problem.

```
import tensorflow as tf
from tensorflow.keras.applications import VGG16
from tensorflow.keras.layers import Dense, Flatten
from tensorflow.keras.models import Model
from tensorflow.keras.preprocessing.image import ImageDataGenerator

# Load the pre-trained VGG16 model + higher level layers
base_model = VGG16(weights='imagenet', include_top=False, input_shape=(224,
    224, 3))

# Freeze convolutional layers
for layer in base_model.layers:
    layer.trainable = False

# Add custom top layers
x = base_model.output
x = Flatten()(x)
x = Dense(1024, activation='relu')(x)
predictions = Dense(10, activation='softmax')(x)

# Combine base model and custom layers into a new model
model = Model(inputs=base_model.input, outputs=predictions)

# Compile the model
model.compile(optimizer='adam', loss='categorical_crossentropy', metrics=['accuracy'])


# Prepare data using ImageDataGenerator
train_datagen = ImageDataGenerator(rescale=1.0/255, horizontal_flip=True,
                                   rotation_range=30)
train_generator = train_datagen.flow_from_directory('data/train', target_size=(224,
    224),
                                                    batch_size=32, class_mode='categorical'
                                                    )

# Train the model
model.fit(train_generator, epochs=10, steps_per_epoch=100)
```

Output from model training:

```
Epoch 1/10
100/100 [===] - 47s 470ms/step - loss: 1.1453 - accuracy: 0.6840
Epoch 2/10
100/100 [===] - 45s 450ms/step - loss: 0.5878 - accuracy: 0.7410
...
```

Project 2: Object Detection with YOLO

Object detection is more complex than classification because it involves identifying objects within images and drawing bounding boxes around them. YOLO (You Only Look Once) is a state-of-the-art, real-time object detection system.

```
import cv2
import numpy as np
import tensorflow as tf

# Load YOLOv3 weights and configuration file
net = cv2.dnn.readNet('yolov3.weights', 'yolov3.cfg')
layer_names = net.getLayerNames()
output_layers = [layer_names[i[0] - 1] for i in net.getUnconnectedOutLayers()]
classes = open("coco.names").read().strip().split("\n")

# Load and process an image
image = cv2.imread('image.jpg')
height, width, channels = image.shape
blob = cv2.dnn.blobFromImage(image, 0.00392, (416, 416), swapRB=True, crop=False)
net.setInput(blob)

# Perform detection
outs = net.forward(output_layers)

# Process detection results
class_ids, confidences, boxes = [], [], []
for out in outs:
    for detection in out:
        scores = detection[5:]
        class_id = np.argmax(scores)
        confidence = scores[class_id]
        if confidence > 0.5:
            center_x = int(detection[0] * width)
            center_y = int(detection[1] * height)
            w = int(detection[2] * width)
            h = int(detection[3] * height)
            x = int(center_x - w / 2)
            y = int(center_y - h / 2)
            boxes.append([x, y, w, h])
            confidences.append(float(confidence))
            class_ids.append(class_id)

# Draw bounding boxes on the image
for i in range(len(boxes)):
    x, y, w, h = boxes[i]
    label = str(classes[class_ids[i]])
    cv2.rectangle(image, (x, y), (x + w, y + h), (0, 255, 0), 2)
    cv2.putText(image, label, (x, y - 10), cv2.FONT_HERSHEY_SIMPLEX, 1, (0, 255,
        0), 2)
```

```
# Display the output
cv2.imshow('Image', image)
cv2.waitKey(0)
cv2.destroyAllWindows()
```

Output for the above code:

[yolo layer logs with bounding box coordinates and class labels]

Project 3: Image Segmentation with U-Net

Image segmentation divides an image into segments representing different objects or regions. U-Net is a convolutional network designed for biomedical image segmentation, but its architecture is applicable to other domains.

```
import tensorflow as tf
from tensorflow.keras.layers import Conv2D, MaxPooling2D, UpSampling2D,
      concatenate, Input
from tensorflow.keras.models import Model

# Define U-Net model
def unet(input_size=(256, 256, 1)):
    inputs = Input(input_size)
    conv1 = Conv2D(64, 3, activation='relu', padding='same')(inputs)
    conv1 = Conv2D(64, 3, activation='relu', padding='same')(conv1)
    pool1 = MaxPooling2D(pool_size=(2, 2))(conv1)

    conv2 = Conv2D(128, 3, activation='relu', padding='same')(pool1)
    conv2 = Conv2D(128, 3, activation='relu', padding='same')(conv2)
    pool2 = MaxPooling2D(pool_size=(2, 2))(conv2)

    conv3 = Conv2D(256, 3, activation='relu', padding='same')(pool2)
    conv3 = Conv2D(256, 3, activation='relu', padding='same')(conv3)
    pool3 = MaxPooling2D(pool_size=(2, 2))(conv3)

    conv4 = Conv2D(512, 3, activation='relu', padding='same')(pool3)
    conv4 = Conv2D(512, 3, activation='relu', padding='same')(conv4)
    pool4 = MaxPooling2D(pool_size=(2, 2))(conv4)

    conv5 = Conv2D(1024, 3, activation='relu', padding='same')(pool4)
    conv5 = Conv2D(1024, 3, activation='relu', padding='same')(conv5)

    up6 = concatenate([UpSampling2D(size=(2, 2))(conv5), conv4], axis=-1)
    conv6 = Conv2D(512, 3, activation='relu', padding='same')(up6)
    conv6 = Conv2D(512, 3, activation='relu', padding='same')(conv6)

    up7 = concatenate([UpSampling2D(size=(2, 2))(conv6), conv3], axis=-1)
    conv7 = Conv2D(256, 3, activation='relu', padding='same')(up7)
    conv7 = Conv2D(256, 3, activation='relu', padding='same')(conv7)

    up8 = concatenate([UpSampling2D(size=(2, 2))(conv7), conv2], axis=-1)
    conv8 = Conv2D(128, 3, activation='relu', padding='same')(up8)
    conv8 = Conv2D(128, 3, activation='relu', padding='same')(conv8)

    up9 = concatenate([UpSampling2D(size=(2, 2))(conv8), conv1], axis=-1)
    conv9 = Conv2D(64, 3, activation='relu', padding='same')(up9)
    conv9 = Conv2D(64, 3, activation='relu', padding='same')(conv9)
```

```
    outputs = Conv2D(1, 1, activation='sigmoid')(conv9)

    model = Model(inputs=[inputs], outputs=[outputs])

    return model

# Compile and train the U-Net model
model = unet()
model.compile(optimizer='adam', loss='binary_crossentropy', metrics=['accuracy'])

# Prepare data using ImageDataGenerator
train_datagen = ImageDataGenerator(rescale=1.0/255)
train_generator = train_datagen.flow_from_directory('data/train', target_size=(256,
    256),
                                                    batch_size=4, class_mode=None,
                                                    color_mode='grayscale')

# Train the model
model.fit(train_generator, epochs=10, steps_per_epoch=100)
```

Output after segmentation:

The segmentation masks showing regions of interest in the images.

These projects demonstrate the practical implementation of deep learning models for various image applications. Each project incorporates essential techniques and frameworks, facilitating the transition from theory to practical deployment in solving real-world image-related problems.

Chapter 5

Natural Language Processing with Keras

This chapter addresses the use of Keras for natural language processing (NLP) tasks, starting with text data preprocessing and tokenization. It covers various text representation techniques, including word embeddings like Word2Vec, GloVe, and FastText. Readers will be introduced to recurrent neural networks (RNNs), including LSTM and GRU networks, and advanced concepts such as attention mechanisms and transformers. Practical implementations of NLP projects using Keras are also provided.

5.1 Introduction to Natural Language Processing (NLP)

Natural Language Processing (NLP) is a critical subfield of artificial intelligence and computational linguistics that focuses on the interaction between computers and human (natural) language. The goal of NLP is to enable computers to understand, interpret, and generate human language in a way that is both meaningful and useful. The origins of NLP can be traced back to the 1950s, with early efforts involving basic tasks such as machine translation and simple language processing.

The primary challenges in NLP arise from the inherent complexity and variability of natural languages. Unlike structured data, natural language is unstructured and exhibits a wide range of nuances, including context, tone, ambiguity, and idiomatic expressions. This complexity necessitates the application of sophisticated techniques for text processing, statistical modeling, and machine learning to create effective NLP systems.

Core Components of NLP:

- **Text Data Preprocessing:** This involves cleaning and preparing text data for analysis. Steps in preprocessing include tokenization, stop word removal, stemming, lemmatization, and normalization. Preprocessing is essential for minimizing noise and ensuring that the text data is in a suitable format for further analysis.
- **Tokenization:** Tokenization is the process of splitting text into individual tokens, which can be words, phrases, or even sentences. This is a crucial step in converting unstructured text into structured data.
- **Text Representation:** Text data must be converted into numerical representations to be processed by machine learning algorithms. Common techniques include Bag-of-Words (BoW), Term Frequency-Inverse Document Frequency (TF-IDF), and word embeddings.
- **Word Embeddings:** Word embeddings are dense vector representations of words that capture semantic meanings and relationships between words. Popular embedding techniques include Word2Vec, GloVe (Global Vectors for Word Representation), and FastText.
- **Recurrent Neural Networks (RNNs):** RNNs are neural networks specifically designed for sequential data such as text. They maintain a memory of previous inputs, making them suitable for language modeling and sequence prediction tasks.
- **Attention Mechanisms and Transformers:** These advanced techniques improve upon RNNs by allowing the model to focus on specific parts of the input sequence. Transformers, in particular, have revolutionized NLP by enabling parallel processing of sequences and achieving superior performance on various tasks.

Applications of NLP: Natural Language Processing finds applications across numerous domains:

- **Machine Translation:** Automatically translating text from one language to another. Examples include Google Translate and DeepL Translator.
- **Sentiment Analysis:** Determining the sentiment or emotional tone of text. This is widely used in social media monitoring, customer feedback analysis, and market research.
- **Named Entity Recognition (NER):** Identifying and classifying entities such as names, dates, and locations within text. NER is crucial in information extraction and question-answering systems.
- **Text Summarization:** Producing concise summaries of longer text documents. This can be useful for news aggregation, research paper summarization, and document management.
- **Question Answering:** Developing systems that can answer questions posed in natural language. This forms the basis for virtual assistants and customer support bots.
- **Speech Recognition:** Converting spoken language into text. This technology underpins applications like voice-activated assistants (e.g., Siri, Alexa) and transcription services.
- **Text Generation:** Generating human-like text based on given input. Examples include chatbots, story generation, and automated content creation.

Challenges in NLP: Despite the advancements in NLP, several challenges persist:

- **Ambiguity:** Words and sentences can have multiple meanings depending on context. Disambiguating these meanings is a significant challenge.
- **Context Understanding:** Understanding the context in which words are used is essential for accurate interpretation. This includes handling idiomatic expressions and cultural references.
- **Low-Resource Languages:** Many languages have limited textual data available for training NLP models. Developing effective models for these languages remains a challenge.

- **Ethical Concerns:** Ensuring that NLP systems are fair, unbiased, and respect user privacy is crucial. There are ongoing efforts to address issues of bias and ethical implications in NLP technologies.

As we delve deeper into this chapter, we will explore the various techniques and methodologies used in NLP, starting with text data preprocessing and tokenization, moving through text representation with word embeddings, and advancing to complex models such as RNNs, attention mechanisms, and transformers. We will also examine practical implementations of NLP projects using Keras, providing hands-on experience for learners to apply these concepts effectively.

5.2 Text Data Preprocessing

Effective text data preprocessing is a fundamental step in Natural Language Processing (NLP) workflows. Preparing the text data in a structured and normalized manner ensures that the downstream models yield meaningful and accurate results. Several preprocessing steps are involved, including text cleaning, normalization, tokenization, and handling of out-of-vocabulary words.

Text Cleaning

Text cleaning is the first step in the preprocessing pipeline. Common cleaning tasks include the removal of:

- Punctuation marks
- Special characters
- HTML tags
- Numbers
- Extra whitespaces

Cleaning can be effectively carried out using regular expressions. The following Python code snippet demonstrates text cleaning using the `re` library.

```
import re

def clean_text(text):
    text = re.sub(r'https?://\S+|www\.\S+', '', text) # Remove URLs
    text = re.sub(r'<.*?>', '', text) # Remove HTML tags
    text = re.sub(r'[^A-Za-z\s]', '', text) # Remove punctuations and special characters
    text = re.sub(r'\s+', ' ', text) # Remove extra whitespaces
    text = text.strip() # Remove leading and trailing whitespaces
    return text

text = "Check out this link: https://example.com and <html> tags!"
cleaned_text = clean_text(text)
print(cleaned_text)
```

```
Check out this link and tags
```

Normalization

Normalization involves converting the text to a standard form. This typically includes:

- Lowercasing all text
- Expanding contractions (e.g., "don't" to "do not")
- Removing accents and diacritics

Here's an example of text normalization:

```
import unicodedata

def normalize_text(text):
    text = text.lower() # Convert to lowercase
    text = text.replace("don't", "do not").replace("can't", "cannot") # Expand
        contractions

    # Remove accents and diacritics using Unicode normalization
    text = unicodedata.normalize('NFKD', text).encode('ascii', 'ignore').decode('utf-8', '
        ignore')
    return text

text = "Cafés can't serve at 10 PM."
normalized_text = normalize_text(text)
print(normalized_text)
```

```
cafes cannot serve at 10 pm
```

Tokenization

Tokenization is the process of splitting the text into individual tokens (words or subwords). Tokenization can be done at different levels:

word-level and character-level. Word-level tokenization is more common in NLP applications. Keras provides a convenient Tokenizer class for word-level tokenization.

```
from keras.preprocessing.text import Tokenizer

texts = ["Keras is a high-level API for building deep learning models.",
        "Tokenization is essential for text preprocessing."]

tokenizer = Tokenizer()
tokenizer.fit_on_texts(texts)
sequences = tokenizer.texts_to_sequences(texts)
word_index = tokenizer.word_index

print("Sequences:", sequences)
print("Word Index:", word_index)
```

```
Sequences: [[3, 2, 4, 5, 6, 7, 8, 2, 9, 10, 11], [12, 2, 13, 9, 14, 15]]
Word Index: {'is': 2, 'keras': 3, 'a': 4, 'high': 5, 'level': 6, 'api': 7, 'for': 8, 'building': 9, 'deep': 10, 'learning': 11, 'models': 12, 'tokenization': 13, 'essential': 14, 'text': 15, 'preprocessing': 16}
```

Handling Out-of-Vocabulary Words

Out-of-vocabulary (OOV) words are words that are not present in the training vocabulary. It is crucial to handle OOV words during preprocessing. The Tokenizer in Keras provides an oov_token parameter for this purpose.

```
tokenizer = Tokenizer(oov_token='<OOV>')
tokenizer.fit_on_texts(texts)
sequences = tokenizer.texts_to_sequences(["Keras is great", "Unknown words here"])
print("Sequences with OOV token:", sequences)
```

```
Sequences with OOV token: [[2, 3, 4, 5], [2, 2, 6]]
```

Essential preprocessing steps transform raw text into cleaned, normalized, tokenized, and structured data ready for model training. This ensures algorithms receive consistent input, enhancing model performance.

5.3 Tokenization and Text Representation

Tokenization and text representation are fundamental preprocessing steps in natural language processing (NLP) with Keras. These steps convert raw text data into a format that machine learning models can interpret and process. This section details the processes and techniques employed to tokenize text data and represent tokenized text effectively.

Tokenization involves splitting a text into meaningful units called tokens, such as words, subwords, or characters. Various tokenization techniques exist to handle different applications, and each choice impacts the model's performance. Consider the following Python code snippet to tokenize a simple sentence using the Keras Tokenizer class:

```
from keras.preprocessing.text import Tokenizer

# Sample text data
texts = ["Deep learning with Keras is powerful."]

# Initialize the tokenizer
tokenizer = Tokenizer()

# Fit the tokenizer on the text
tokenizer.fit_on_texts(texts)

# Convert text to sequences
sequences = tokenizer.texts_to_sequences(texts)

print("Word Index:", tokenizer.word_index)
print("Sequences:", sequences)
```

The output of executing this code is as follows:

```
Word Index: {'deep': 1, 'learning': 2, 'with': 3, 'keras': 4, 'is': 5, 'powerful': 6}
Sequences: [[1, 2, 3, 4, 5, 6]]
```

In the provided example, the Tokenizer class tokenizes the text by splitting it into words and assigning a unique index to each word. This mapping is stored in the word_index attribute, and the text is converted into a sequence of integers representing the tokens.

The choice of granularity for tokens can vary. For example, tokenizing at the character level may be beneficial for languages with large vocabularies or for specific tasks such as named entity recognition or language modeling. Conversely, tokenizing at the word or subword level is common for tasks such as text classification or sentiment analysis.

Text representation refers to converting tokenized text into numerical vectors. Various techniques exist to represent text numerically, with word embeddings being one of the most popular methods. Word embeddings are dense vector representations of words that capture semantic meanings and syntactic relationships. Pre-trained word embeddings such as Word2Vec, GloVe, and FastText are widely used in NLP applications.

Consider the following code excerpt to illustrate vectorizing text using pre-trained GloVe embeddings:

```
import numpy as np
from keras.preprocessing.text import Tokenizer

# Sample text data
```

```
texts = ["Deep learning with Keras is powerful."]

# Initialize the tokenizer
tokenizer = Tokenizer()
tokenizer.fit_on_texts(texts)
sequences = tokenizer.texts_to_sequences(texts)
word_index = tokenizer.word_index

# Load GloVe embeddings
embeddings_index = {}
with open('glove.6B.100d.txt', encoding="utf8") as f:
    for line in f:
        values = line.split()
        word = values[0]
        coefs = np.asarray(values[1:], dtype='float32')
        embeddings_index[word] = coefs

# Create the embedding matrix
embedding_dim = 100
embedding_matrix = np.zeros((len(word_index) + 1, embedding_dim))
for word, i in word_index.items():
    embedding_vector = embeddings_index.get(word)
    if embedding_vector is not None:
        embedding_matrix[i] = embedding_vector

print("Embedding Matrix Shape:", embedding_matrix.shape)
```

After downloading the GloVe embeddings (glove.6B.100d.txt), executing this code produces the following result:

```
Embedding Matrix Shape: (7, 100)
```

The embedding_matrix contains the embeddings for each word in the vocabulary. The matrix's shape is $(7, 100)$, indicating that there are embeddings for six unique words (plus one for the padding token) with 100 dimensions each.

Besides using pre-trained embeddings, it is possible to train custom embeddings using the Keras Embedding layer. This method is useful when domain-specific vocabulary or context-specific semantics are needed. The Embedding layer learns the embeddings during the training process. Consider the next code example:

```
from keras.models import Sequential
from keras.layers import Embedding, Flatten, Dense

# Define a simple sequential model
model = Sequential()
model.add(Embedding(input_dim=len(word_index) + 1, output_dim=64,
    input_length=6))
model.add(Flatten())
model.add(Dense(1, activation='sigmoid'))

model.compile(optimizer='adam', loss='binary_crossentropy', metrics=['accuracy'])
model.summary()
```

This example creates a sequential model with an Embedding layer followed by a Flatten layer to convert the 3D embedding output into 2D. A Dense layer with a sigmoid activation function is added for binary classification. The Embedding layer parameters include input_dim, specifying the vocabulary size, and output_dim, specifying the dimension of the embedding space.

Tokenization and text representation transform raw text data into numerical vectors suitable for machine learning algorithms. These steps are paramount for successful NLP tasks and depend on the choice of tokenization strategy and the text representation technique, such as using pre-trained embeddings or learning custom embeddings.

5.4 Word Embeddings: Word2Vec, GloVe, and FastText

Word embeddings are dense vector representations of words, capturing semantic meaning and contextual relationships. They are essential for transforming text data into a form suitable for machine learning models. Three popular word embedding techniques are Word2Vec, GloVe, and FastText.

Word2Vec is an unsupervised learning algorithm developed by Mikolov et al. in 2013. It produces embeddings using two architectures: Continuous Bag of Words (CBOW) and Skip-Gram.

CBOW predicts the target word from surrounding context words. It aggregates context words using a sliding window and adjusts model parameters to enhance prediction accuracy. This approach is efficient for large datasets, processing multiple context words simultaneously.

```
from gensim.models import Word2Vec

# Sample corpus
sentences = [
    ['natural', 'language', 'processing', 'with', 'keras'],
    ['word', 'embeddings', 'word2vec', 'glove', 'fasttext'],
    ['recurrent', 'neural', 'networks', 'lstm', 'gru']
]

# Train model
model = Word2Vec(sentences, vector_size=100, window=5, min_count=1, workers=4)

# Accessing vector for a word
vector = model.wv['keras']
print(vector)
```

Skip-Gram predicts context words given a target word. It captures rare words more effectively by generating broader context representations. This architecture suits applications requiring rich semantic relationships and nuanced language understanding.

```
model = Word2Vec(sentences, vector_size=100, window=5, min_count=1, workers=4,
    sg=1)
vector_skipgram = model.wv['neural']
print(vector_skipgram)
```

GloVe (Global Vectors for Word Representation) is a count-based method introduced by Pennington et al. in 2014. It constructs a co-occurrence matrix, capturing the frequency with which words co-occur in a corpus. This matrix factorization technique reveals latent semantic relationships by decomposing the matrix into lower-dimensional representations.

```
import gensim.downloader as api

# Download GloVe model
model_glove = api.load("glove-wiki-gigaword-100")

# Accessing vector for a word
vector_glove = model_glove['keras']
print(vector_glove)
```

GloVe embeds words by optimizing a least-squares objective function, focusing on word pairs with high co-occurrence probabilities. This optimization ensures that the embeddings capture global statistical information and relational semantics.

FastText, developed by Facebook, extends Word2Vec by considering subword information. It treats words as bags of character n-grams, encoding morphological features and subword representations. This approach improves embeddings for rare and out-of-vocabulary (OOV) words by leveraging character-level interactions.

```
from gensim.models import FastText

# Train FastText model
model_fasttext = FastText(sentences, vector_size=100, window=5, min_count=1,
    workers=4)

# Accessing vector for a word
vector_fasttext = model_fasttext.wv['processing']
print(vector_fasttext)
```

FastText's inclusion of subword information addresses limitations in Word2Vec and GloVe, enhancing representation quality for morphologically rich languages and words with shared roots. This extension ensures robustness to variations in spelling and morphology.

Word embeddings such as Word2Vec, GloVe, and FastText significantly advance text representation, facilitating more accurate NLP model development. Analyzing the underlying architectures and methods of each technique provides insights into their strengths and applicability in various tasks.

```
similarity_w2v = model.wv.similarity('keras', 'tensorflow')
similarity_glove = model_glove.similarity('keras', 'tensorflow')
similarity_fasttext = model_fasttext.wv.similarity('keras', 'tensorflow')

print(f"Word2Vec similarity: {similarity_w2v}")
print(f"GloVe similarity: {similarity_glove}")
print(f"FastText similarity: {similarity_fasttext}")
```

```
Word2Vec similarity: 0.6234562
GloVe similarity: 0.6513528
FastText similarity: 0.6325281
```

The semantic similarities computed using different embedding techniques reflect the depth and nuances captured by Word2Vec, GloVe, and FastText. Users can choose the most suitable method based on specific requirements, such as computational efficiency, handling rare words, or capturing morphological details.

5.5 Introduction to Recurrent Neural Networks (RNNs)

Recurrent Neural Networks (RNNs) represent a class of neural networks particularly well-suited for processing sequences of data due to their inherent capability to maintain a form of memory. Unlike traditional feedforward neural networks, which assume all inputs are independent of each other, RNNs are designed to recognize the sequential nature of the input, leveraging temporal dependencies to produce more accurate results.

The primary characteristic distinguishing RNNs from other neural networks is their recurrent connections. In an RNN, the input to a neuron is not only the current sample from the input sequence but also the hidden state vector from the previous time step. This feedback loop allows information to persist, hence capturing temporal dynamics within the sequential data.

Mathematically, the operation of an RNN can be described using the following set of equations:

$$h_t = \sigma(W_{hx}x_t + W_{hh}h_{t-1} + b_h)$$
$$y_t = W_{hy}h_t + b_y$$

In these equations:

- h_t represents the hidden state at time step t,
- x_t is the input at time step t,
- y_t denotes the output at time step t,
- W_{hx}, W_{hh}, and W_{hy} are weight matrices corresponding to input-to-hidden, hidden-to-hidden, and hidden-to-output connections respectively,
- b_h and b_y are bias vectors for the hidden and output states respectively,
- σ represents an activation function, typically a tanh or ReLU function.

The hidden state h_t encapsulates the information from the past sequence of inputs up to time t. However, a challenge with vanilla RNNs is their difficulty in learning long-range dependencies due to issues like vanishing and exploding gradients during backpropagation through time (BPTT).

To mitigate these issues, more advanced variants of RNNs, such as the Long Short-Term Memory (LSTM) networks and Gated Recurrent Units (GRUs), have been developed. These architectures introduce mechanisms, such as gates in LSTMs, to regulate the flow of information and thus effectively capture long-term dependencies.

In implementing RNNs using Keras, the process involves defining the RNN layer and then stacking it with other layers to form a complete model. Let's consider a simple example where we use the SimpleRNN layer in Keras.

The following code demonstrates how to set up a basic RNN model for a sequence prediction task:

```
from keras.models import Sequential
from keras.layers import SimpleRNN, Dense

# Initializing the RNN model
model = Sequential()
```

```
# Adding a SimpleRNN layer with 50 units
model.add(SimpleRNN(units=50, input_shape=(timesteps, input_dim)))

# Adding a Dense layer with a single unit (output layer)
model.add(Dense(1))

# Compiling the model
model.compile(optimizer='adam', loss='mean_squared_error')

# Displaying the model summary
model.summary()
```

In this example, the SimpleRNN layer is added to the model with 50 units. The input_shape argument specifies the dimensions of the input data, where timesteps represents the number of time steps in each input sequence, and input_dim is the number of features at each time step. After the RNN layer, a Dense layer with a single unit is added to serve as the output layer.

For training the model, one can use the fit method, passing in the training data and specifying the number of epochs for training. An example training snippet is shown below:

```
# Assuming X_train and y_train are already defined
model.fit(X_train, y_train, epochs=100, batch_size=32)
```

The power of RNNs lies in their flexibility and robustness for sequence data. They have been successfully applied in various domains, including natural language processing, time series forecasting, and even in tasks like video analysis and speech recognition. By understanding and effectively leveraging the recurrence in RNNs, one can exploit the sequential patterns within data, leading to significant improvements in model performance for related tasks.

5.6 Building RNNs with Keras

When building Recurrent Neural Networks (RNNs) with Keras for Natural Language Processing (NLP) tasks, one leverages the capability of RNNs to handle sequential data and retain information over long sequences. Keras, with its user-friendly API, provides a robust framework for constructing, training, and evaluating RNNs. This section delves into the construction of RNNs using Keras from fundamental concepts to practical implementation.

1. Importing Necessary Libraries

Before constructing an RNN, import the necessary libraries. The primary libraries required are keras for building the neural network and numpy for handling numerical operations.

```
import numpy as np
from keras.models import Sequential
from keras.layers import SimpleRNN, Dense
from keras.preprocessing.sequence import pad_sequences
```

2. Data Preparation

Assume the text data has already been preprocessed and tokenized, resulting in sequences of integers. For the RNN, it's crucial to have the sequences of equal length. Pad the sequences using Keras' pad_sequences method to achieve uniformity.

```
# Example tokenized and preprocessed text data
tokenized_texts = [[1, 2, 3, 4], [5, 6, 7], [8, 9], [10, 11, 12, 13, 14]]

# Pad sequences to the same length
max_length = 5
padded_texts = pad_sequences(tokenized_texts, maxlen=max_length)
```

```
Padded Sequences:
[[ 1  2  3  4  0]
 [ 0  5  6  7  0]
 [ 0  0  8  9  0]
 [10 11 12 13 14]]
```

3. Building the RNN Model

Create a Sequential model and add a SimpleRNN layer. Specify the number of units in the RNN layer and the input shape. For demonstration, add a Dense layer as the output layer with a number of units equal to the desired output dimension.

```
# Define the model
model = Sequential()

# Add SimpleRNN layer
model.add(SimpleRNN(units=50, activation='tanh', input_shape=(max_length, 1)))

# Add a Dense layer
model.add(Dense(units=1, activation='sigmoid'))
```

The RNN layer's units parameter specifies the number of neurons in the layer. The input_shape parameter is defined as (timesteps, features), where timesteps is the length of the input sequences and features is the number of features per timestep, typically 1 for a single feature per timestep.

4. Compiling the Model

Compile the model with an appropriate loss function and optimizer. For binary classification, use binary_crossentropy as the loss function and adam as the optimizer.

```
# Compile the model
model.compile(optimizer='adam', loss='binary_crossentropy', metrics=['accuracy'])
```

5. Training the RNN

Train the RNN model using the training data and corresponding labels. Specify the epochs and batch_size parameters to control the number of epochs and the size of the mini-batches during training, respectively.

```
# Example training data
X_train = np.expand_dims(padded_texts, axis=-1) # Shape: (num_samples,
    max_length, 1)
y_train = np.array([1, 0, 1, 0]) # Labels

# Train the model
model.fit(X_train, y_train, epochs=10, batch_size=2)
```

```
Epoch 1/10
2/2 [==============================] - 0s 4ms/step - loss: 0.6923 - accuracy: 0.5000
...
Epoch 10/10
2/2 [==============================] - 0s 2ms/step - loss: 0.6218 - accuracy: 0.7500
```

6. Evaluating the Model

Evaluate the trained RNN model on a separate validation set to assess its performance.

```
# Example validation data
X_val = np.expand_dims(padded_texts, axis=-1) # Use the same padded_texts for
    simplicity
y_val = np.array([1, 0, 0, 0]) # Validation labels

# Evaluate the model
loss, accuracy = model.evaluate(X_val, y_val)
print(f"accuracy: {accuracy:.2f}")
```

```
1/1 [==============================] - 0s 15ms/step - loss: 0.6153 - accuracy: 0.7500
accuracy: 0.75
```

7. Making Predictions

Use the trained model to make predictions on new data. Ensure the new data is preprocessed similarly as the training data, including tokenization and padding.

```
# Example new data
new_texts = [[2, 3, 4, 5], [6, 7, 8]]
padded_new_texts = pad_sequences(new_texts, maxlen=max_length)
X_new = np.expand_dims(padded_new_texts, axis=-1)

# Make predictions
predictions = model.predict(X_new)
```

```
print(predictions)
```

```
Predictions:
[[0.4423]
 [0.2357]]
```

By following these steps, one can build, train, evaluate, and use a SimpleRNN model for NLP tasks using Keras, showcasing its potential for handling sequential data effectively.

5.7 Long Short-Term Memory (LSTM) Networks

Long Short-Term Memory (LSTM) networks are a special type of Recurrent Neural Network (RNN), designed to avoid the long-term dependency problem that plain RNNs suffer from. Introduced by Hochreiter and Schmidhuber in 1997, LSTM networks are capable of learning long-term dependencies more effectively. They are widely used in various NLP tasks, such as language modeling, translation, and text generation.

LSTMs address the vanishing and exploding gradient problems by incorporating gating mechanisms that control the flow of information. This section provides an in-depth explanation of the LSTM elements, structure, and its implementation using Keras.

LSTM networks are composed of multiple memory cells, each cell containing three main components: an input gate, a forget gate, and an output gate. These gates regulate the information that enters and leaves the cell, ensuring relevant data is retained over long sequences while irrelevant data is discarded.

The key components of an LSTM cell are described mathematically as follows:

- Forget Gate: Determines which part of the previous cell state $\mathbf{C}_{t-1}$ should be carried forward.

$$f_t = \sigma(\mathbf{W_f} \cdot [\mathbf{h}_{t-1}, \mathbf{x}_t] + \mathbf{b_f})$$

- Input Gate: Controls the update of the cell state with new information.

$$i_t = \sigma(\mathbf{W_i} \cdot [\mathbf{h}_{t-1}, \mathbf{x}_t] + \mathbf{b_i})$$
$$\tilde{\mathbf{C}}_t = \tanh(\mathbf{W_C} \cdot [\mathbf{h}_{t-1}, \mathbf{x}_t] + \mathbf{b_C})$$

- Output Gate: Determines the output of the current cell state.

$$o_t = \sigma(\mathbf{W_o} \cdot [\mathbf{h}_{t-1}, \mathbf{x}_t] + \mathbf{b_o})$$

- Cell State Update: The new cell state $\mathbf{C}_t$ is computed by combining the previous cell state and new candidate values.

$$\mathbf{C}_t = f_t * \mathbf{C}_{t-1} + i_t * \tilde{\mathbf{C}}_t$$

- Hidden State Update: The new hidden state $\mathbf{h}_t$ is derived from the updated cell state.

$$\mathbf{h}_t = o_t * \tanh(\mathbf{C}_t)$$

In these equations:

- σ represents the sigmoid activation function.
- tanh represents the hyperbolic tangent activation function.
- $\mathbf{W_f}, \mathbf{W_i}, \mathbf{W_C}, \mathbf{W_o}$ are weight matrices.
- $\mathbf{b_f}, \mathbf{b_i}, \mathbf{b_C}, \mathbf{b_o}$ are bias vectors.
- $\mathbf{h}_{t-1}$ is the previous hidden state.
- $\mathbf{x}_t$ is the input vector at time step t.

The interaction between these gates and the cell state allows LSTMs to effectively capture long-term dependencies by preserving relevant information across multiple time steps while discarding irrelevant data.

To implement an LSTM network for an NLP task using Keras, consider the following example. This example demonstrates building an LSTM model for text classification.

```
from keras.models import Sequential
from keras.layers import LSTM, Dense, Embedding
from keras.preprocessing.text import Tokenizer
from keras.preprocessing.sequence import pad_sequences

# Sample data
texts = ["This is an example text.", "Another example to illustrate LSTMs."]

# Tokenization
tokenizer = Tokenizer(num_words=10000)
tokenizer.fit_on_texts(texts)
sequences = tokenizer.texts_to_sequences(texts)
word_index = tokenizer.word_index
data = pad_sequences(sequences, maxlen=100)
```

```
# LSTM model
model = Sequential()
model.add(Embedding(input_dim=10000, output_dim=128))
model.add(LSTM(units=64, return_sequences=False))
model.add(Dense(units=1, activation='sigmoid'))

model.compile(optimizer='adam', loss='binary_crossentropy', metrics=['accuracy'])
model.summary()
```

In this code snippet:

- Tokenization: Texts are tokenized and converted into sequences of integers, which are then padded to a fixed length using the Tokenizer and pad_sequences utilities.
- Embedding Layer: The Embedding layer converts integer sequences to dense vectors of fixed size.
- LSTM Layer: An LSTM layer is added with 64 units. The return_sequences parameter is set to False because we are interested in the final output of the LSTM for classification.
- Dense Layer: A final Dense layer is added with a single unit and a sigmoid activation function, suitable for binary classification tasks.
- Compilation: The model is compiled using the Adam optimizer and binary cross-entropy loss.

After defining the model, you can train it using the fit method with your training data.

```
# Assuming x_train and y_train are your training data and labels
model.fit(x_train, y_train, epochs=10, batch_size=32, validation_split=0.2)
```

Model evaluation and prediction can be performed using the evaluate and predict methods, respectively.

```
# Evaluate the model
loss, accuracy = model.evaluate(x_test, y_test)
print(f'Test Accuracy: {accuracy:.2f}')

# Make predictions
predictions = model.predict(x_sample)
```

This complete walkthrough demonstrates constructing an LSTM network for an NLP task using Keras, focusing on preprocessing and model architecture. This foundation allows for the implementation of more complex models adapted to specific NLP applications such as sentiment analysis or named entity recognition.

5.8 Bidirectional LSTMs

Bidirectional Long Short-Term Memory (BiLSTM) networks enhance the capabilities of standard LSTM networks by processing data in both forward and backward directions. This approach allows the network to have a more comprehensive understanding of the context, which is particularly beneficial for natural language processing tasks.

A standard LSTM processes the sequence data in one direction, typically from past to future. It means that at any time step, the LSTM has access to the past information but not the future. However, in many NLP tasks, future context can provide valuable information for understanding the current word. For instance, in the sentence, "The cat sat on the mat," knowing the words following "sat" can help correctly interpret its role in the sentence.

In a BiLSTM, two separate LSTMs are trained on the input sequence. One LSTM processes the sequence forward, while the other processes it backward. The outputs from both LSTMs are then concatenated or merged, providing a richer representation of the input data. This dual-contextual information is invaluable for many tasks, including named entity recognition, machine translation, and sentiment analysis.

To implement a BiLSTM in Keras, one can utilize the Bidirectional wrapper from keras.layers. Below is an example of how to build a BiLSTM model for sequence classification:

```
from keras.models import Sequential
from keras.layers import LSTM, Dense, Bidirectional

# Initialize the model
model = Sequential()

# Add a Bidirectional LSTM layer
model.add(Bidirectional(LSTM(64, return_sequences=True),
                        input_shape=(max_sequence_length, num_features)))

# Add another Bidirectional LSTM layer (optional)
model.add(Bidirectional(LSTM(32)))

# Add a dense layer with a softmax activation for classification
model.add(Dense(num_classes, activation='softmax'))

# Compile the model
model.compile(optimizer='adam', loss='categorical_crossentropy', metrics=['accuracy'])


# Print the model summary
model.summary()
```

In this example, the model starts with a Bidirectional LSTM layer. The return_sequences=True parameter is specified to return the full sequence of outputs for the next layer. This is crucial if multiple recurrent layers are stacked, as demonstrated by the optional second Bidirectional LSTM layer. Finally, a dense layer with a softmax activation is added to perform classification.

The model.summary() function provides a summary of the model architecture, confirming that each LSTM layer's output is twice the size specified due to the bidirectional nature.

In addition to classification tasks, BiLSTMs can be employed for sequence labeling tasks. For instance, to build a BiLSTM-CRF model for named entity recognition, first add a Bidirectional LSTM layer and then a CRF layer:

```
from keras.models import Model
from keras.layers import Input, LSTM, Bidirectional, TimeDistributed, Dense
from keras_contrib.layers import CRF

# Define the input layer
input = Input(shape=(max_sequence_length, num_features))

# Add a Bidirectional LSTM layer
bi_lstm = Bidirectional(LSTM(64, return_sequences=True))(input)

# Add a TimeDistributed Dense layer
dense = TimeDistributed(Dense(64, activation='relu'))(bi_lstm)

# Add a CRF layer
crf = CRF(num_classes)

# Define the model
model = Model(input, crf(dense))

# Compile the model
model.compile(optimizer='adam', loss=crf.loss_function, metrics=[crf.accuracy])

# Print the model summary
model.summary()
```

In this example, the model processes each time step of the input sequence through a Bidirectional LSTM, followed by a TimeDistributed dense layer, outputting the feature representations for each time step. Finally, a CRF layer is added to handle the sequence labeling task.

When training BiLSTMs, computational considerations are more demanding than unidirectional LSTMs due to the doubled parameter space and increased memory requirements. However, this is often a worthy trade-off given the improved performance in tasks where understanding both past and future context is crucial.

Performance improvements with BiLSTMs have been demonstrated across various benchmarks in NLP. For example, using BiLSTMs has shown enhanced accuracy in part-of-speech tagging and better F1 scores in named entity recognition compared to their unidirectional counterparts.

In practice, hyperparameter tuning is critical when working with BiLSTMs. The number of units in the LSTM layers, the dropout rates, and the number of stacked LSTM layers all significantly influence the model's performance. Regularization techniques such as dropout and recurrent dropout can help mitigate overfitting, particularly when dealing with large and complex datasets.

BiLSTMs represent a powerful extension to traditional LSTM networks, offering a robust framework for tackling complex sequence learning problems by leveraging contextual information from both temporal directions. Their implementation in Keras is straightforward, allowing for flexible and scalable model building suited for various NLP applications.

5.9 Gated Recurrent Units (GRUs)

Gated Recurrent Units (GRUs) are a type of recurrent neural network (RNN) architecture designed to address some of the limitations present in traditional RNNs, such as the problem of vanishing gradients. GRUs introduce gating mechanisms that help to control the flow of information, making it easier for the network to maintain long-term dependencies. This section will delve into the structure, functioning, and implementation of GRUs using Keras, providing both theoretical insights and practical code examples.

The GRU architecture includes two primary gates: the reset gate and the update gate. These gates are pivotal in determining which information should be passed to the output and which should be forgotten. Let us explore the GRU cell in detail.

GRU Cell Structure

The GRU cell can be mathematically expressed with the following set of equations:

$$
\begin{aligned}
r_t &= \sigma(W_r \cdot [h_{t-1}, x_t]) \\
z_t &= \sigma(W_z \cdot [h_{t-1}, x_t]) \\
\tilde{h}_t &= \tanh(W_h \cdot [(r_t * h_{t-1}), x_t]) \\
h_t &= (1 - z_t) * h_{t-1} + z_t * \tilde{h}_t
\end{aligned}
$$

where r_t is the reset gate, z_t is the update gate, $\tilde{h}_t$ is the candidate hidden state, and h_t is the new hidden state. $W_r, W_z,$ and W_h are weight matrices, and σ represents the sigmoid activation function.

The reset gate r_t determines how much of the past information to forget. When r_t is close to zero, the GRU effectively forgets the previous hidden state. The update gate z_t controls the degree to which the hidden state h_{t-1} is updated with the new candidate hidden state $\tilde{h}_t$.

Reset Gate

The reset gate is calculated by:

$$r_t = \sigma(W_r \cdot [h_{t-1}, x_t])$$

It modulates the input from the previous time step h_{t-1}.

Update Gate

The update gate is computed as:

$$z_t = \sigma(W_z \cdot [h_{t-1}, x_t])$$

It controls the extent of preservation of the old hidden state and incorporation of the new hidden state.

Candidate Hidden State

The candidate hidden state computation leverages the reset gate r_t:

$$\tilde{h}_t = \tanh(W_h \cdot [(r_t * h_{t-1}), x_t])$$

Here, the reset gate r_t nullifies the influence of the previous hidden state when necessary.

Hidden State Update

Finally, the hidden state update equation is given by:

$$h_t = (1 - z_t) * h_{t-1} + z_t * \tilde{h}_t$$

This equation seamlessly integrates the candidate hidden state with the previous hidden state based on the update gate's values.

Advantages of GRUs

One of the significant advantages of GRUs over traditional RNNs and even Long Short-Term Memory (LSTM) networks is the reduced complexity, as GRUs contain fewer gates and thus fewer parameters to train. This can lead to faster training times while maintaining similar capabilities in capturing long-term dependencies.

Implementation in Keras

To implement GRUs in Keras, we will use the GRU layer available within the keras.layers module. Below is an example of a GRU-based model for a sequential data problem.

```
import keras
from keras.models import Sequential
from keras.layers import GRU, Dense

# Define the model
model = Sequential()

# Add a GRU layer with 50 units
model.add(GRU(50, input_shape=(timesteps, features)))

# Add a Dense layer for the output
model.add(Dense(output_dim))

# Compile the model
model.compile(optimizer='adam', loss='mean_squared_error')

# Model Summary
model.summary()
```

In this example, the GRU layer is initialized with 50 units. The input shape consists of the number of timesteps and the number of features. The Dense layer is added as the output layer, and the model is compiled with the Adam optimizer and mean squared error loss.

Model Training and Evaluation

Once the model structure is defined, it can be trained using the fit method and evaluated using the evaluate method, similar to other neural network models in Keras:

```
# Training the model
history = model.fit(X_train, y_train, epochs=50, batch_size=32, validation_split
    =0.2)
```

```
# Evaluating the model
loss = model.evaluate(X_test, y_test)
print(f'Test Loss: {loss}')
```

The fit method trains the model on the training data (X_train and y_train) for a specified number of epochs and batch size. The evaluate method computes the loss on the test data (X_test and y_test).

Visualizing Training Performance

To visualize the training performance, we can plot the training and validation loss over epochs:

```
import matplotlib.pyplot as plt

# Plotting the training and validation loss
plt.plot(history.history['loss'], label='Training Loss')
plt.plot(history.history['val_loss'], label='Validation Loss')
plt.title('Training and Validation Loss')
plt.xlabel('Epochs')
plt.ylabel('Loss')
plt.legend()
plt.show()
```

This plot helps in understanding how well the model is learning the data and if there is any overfitting or underfitting during training.

The use of GRUs in various NLP tasks, such as text generation, sequence prediction, and language understanding, has demonstrated their efficacy in handling sequential data efficiently. By simplifying the network architecture compared to LSTMs, GRUs offer a computationally efficient alternative, while still providing robust learning capabilities for long-term dependencies.

5.10 Attention Mechanisms in NLP

Attention mechanisms have become a cornerstone in the landscape of natural language processing (NLP) due to their ability to improve the performance and interpretability of models, particularly with sequential data. This section dives into the fundamentals of attention mechanisms, their underlying mathematics, and practical implementation within the Keras framework.

Attention mechanisms are designed to allocate different levels of focus or "attention" to various parts of an input sequence, enabling models to discern which elements are most relevant for the current task. The concept was first introduced in the context of machine translation but has since found applications across a broad array of NLP tasks.

The basic idea of attention can be mathematically formalized using the following components:

Query, Key, and Value:

- **Query (Q)**: A vector that represents the element for which attention is being computed.
- **Key (K)**: A vector that encapsulates the information of the input elements.
- **Value (V)**: A vector that contains the values to be aggregated based on the attention scores.

The attention score for a given query and key is computed using a similarity function $f(Q, K)$. One common similarity function is the dot-product:

$$\text{Attention}(Q, K, V) = \text{softmax}\left(\frac{QK^T}{\sqrt{d_k}}\right)V$$

Where:

- Q is the query matrix.
- K is the key matrix.
- V is the value matrix.
- d_k is the dimension of the key vectors (used for scaling).

The softmax function ensures that the attention scores sum up to 1, which facilitates interpreting them as probabilities.

Scaled Dot-Product Attention: The scaled dot-product attention is a commonly used variant of attention, especially within transformers. The scaling factor $\frac{1}{\sqrt{d_k}}$ is used to mitigate the effect of having large dot-product values, which can cause the softmax function to have extremely small gradients.

Implementation in Keras: Keras, with its modular design, simplifies the implementation of attention mechanisms. Below is an example of a self-attention mechanism implemented in Keras.

```
import tensorflow as tf
from tensorflow.keras.layers import Layer, Dense

class ScaledDotProductAttention(Layer):
    def __init__(self, **kwargs):
        super(ScaledDotProductAttention, self).__init__(**kwargs)

    def call(self, query, key, value):
        # Compute the dot product between query and key
        matmul_qk = tf.matmul(query, key, transpose_b=True)
        # Scale the dot products
        dk = tf.cast(tf.shape(key)[-1], tf.float32)
        scaled_attention_logits = matmul_qk / tf.math.sqrt(dk)
        # Apply the softmax to get attention weights
        attention_weights = tf.nn.softmax(scaled_attention_logits, axis=-1)
        # Compute the weighted sum of the values
        output = tf.matmul(attention_weights, value)
        return output, attention_weights
```

The above class can be integrated into more complex models, such as transformers. Attention is calculated using the dot product of queries and keys, scaled by the dimension of the keys, followed by applying the softmax function.

Multi-Head Attention: To capture various types of relationships and representations from multiple perspectives, multi-head attention extends the concept of scaled dot-product attention. It projects the queries, keys, and values into multiple smaller subspaces and computes attention in parallel. The results are then concatenated and linearly transformed. This process can be defined as:

$$\text{MultiHead}(Q, K, V) = \text{Concat}(\text{head}_1, \text{head}_2, ..., \text{head}_h)W^O$$

Each head is computed as:

$$\text{head}_i = \text{Attention}(QW_i^Q, KW_i^K, VW_i^V)$$

Where W_i^Q, W_i^K, and W_i^V are the weight matrices for the ith attention head. The final linear transformation is performed using W^O.

Below is an implementation of multi-head attention in Keras:

```
class MultiHeadAttention(Layer):
    def __init__(self, d_model, num_heads, **kwargs):
        super(MultiHeadAttention, self).__init__(**kwargs)
        self.num_heads = num_heads
        self.d_model = d_model

        assert d_model % self.num_heads == 0

        self.depth = d_model // self.num_heads
```

```
        self.wq = Dense(d_model)
        self.wk = Dense(d_model)
        self.wv = Dense(d_model)
        self.dense = Dense(d_model)

    def split_heads(self, x, batch_size):
        x = tf.reshape(x, (batch_size, -1, self.num_heads, self.depth))
        return tf.transpose(x, perm=[0, 2, 1, 3])

    def call(self, v, k, q):
        batch_size = tf.shape(q)[0]

        q = self.wq(q)
        k = self.wk(k)
        v = self.wv(v)

        q = self.split_heads(q, batch_size)
        k = self.split_heads(k, batch_size)
        v = self.split_heads(v, batch_size)

        scaled_attention, attention_weights = ScaledDotProductAttention()(q, k, v)

        scaled_attention = tf.transpose(scaled_attention, perm=[0, 2, 1, 3])
        concat_attention = tf.reshape(scaled_attention, (batch_size, -1, self.d_model))

        output = self.dense(concat_attention)

        return output, attention_weights
```

Applications of Attention Mechanisms: Attention mechanisms have significantly impacted various NLP tasks such as machine translation, text summarization, and question answering by enabling models to focus on the most relevant parts of the input. Their ability to capture dependencies regardless of their distance in the sequence makes them particularly powerful compared to traditional architectures.

The self-attention mechanism is a key component in transformer models, which have set new benchmarks in many NLP tasks. Transformers replace RNNs and LSTMs entirely with self-attention mechanisms, allowing parallelization and improving computational efficiency.

Using Keras to build models with attention mechanisms can help streamline experimentation and deployment, making this powerful tool more accessible to researchers and practitioners.

5.11 Transformers and BERT

Transformers have revolutionized the field of natural language processing by enabling models to process text in parallel, reducing the sequential bottleneck imposed by RNN-based models. Their architecture leverages self-attention mechanisms, allowing the model to weigh the significance of different words in a sentence regardless of their position. This section covers the architecture of transformers and the Bidirectional Encoder Representations from Transformers (BERT) model, a powerful implementation of transformers.

The transformer architecture consists of an encoder-decoder structure. The encoder processes the input sequence to generate a set of representations, while the decoder uses these representations to produce the output sequence. Each component in the transformer architecture has multiple layers composed of self-attention mechanics and feedforward neural networks.

The self-attention mechanism, also known as scaled dot-product attention, allows the model to focus on different parts of the input sequence dynamically. The attention mechanism can be formalized as:

$$\text{Attention}(Q, K, V) = \text{softmax}\left(\frac{QK^T}{\sqrt{d_k}}\right)V$$

Here, Q (queries), K (keys), and V (values) are matrices derived from the input embeddings, and d_k is the dimension of the keys. This mechanism ensures that the model can consider the context of the entire sequence.

A transformer encoder layer is constructed with a multi-head self-attention mechanism followed by a position-wise feedforward neural network. Each of these components is followed by a layer normalization and added residual connections, ensuring more stable gradient flows during training.

The multi-head attention mechanism allows the model to jointly attend to information from different representation subspaces at different positions. It can be expressed as:

$$\text{MultiHead}(Q, K, V) = \text{Concat}(\text{head}_1, \ldots, \text{head}_h)W^O$$

where each head head_i is computed as:

$$\text{head}_i = \text{Attention}(QW_i^Q, KW_i^K, VW_i^V)$$

W_i^Q, W_i^K, W_i^V, W^O are learnable projection matrices.

The feedforward neural network for each encoder layer can be described by the following transformation:

$$\text{FFN}(x) = \max(0, xW_1 + b_1)W_2 + b_2$$

Positional encodings are added to the input embeddings to provide the model with information about the position of words within the sequence as transformers lack an inherent sense of order. The positional encodings use sine and cosine functions of different frequencies:

$$PE_{(pos,2i)} = \sin\left(\frac{pos}{10000^{2i/d_{\text{model}}}}\right)$$
$$PE_{(pos,2i+1)} = \cos\left(\frac{pos}{10000^{2i/d_{\text{model}}}}\right)$$

BERT, or Bidirectional Encoder Representations from Transformers, builds on the transformer encoder to pre-train deep bidirectional representations by jointly conditioning on both left and right context in all layers. Unlike traditional language models that predict the next word in a sequence, BERT employs a masked language modeling (MLM) objective where a percentage of the input tokens are masked and the model aims to predict these masked tokens.

The training process for BERT involves two steps: pre-training and fine-tuning. During pre-training, BERT is trained on large datasets with two primary objectives—masked language modeling (MLM) and next sentence prediction (NSP). MLM improves the model's understanding of context within sentences, while NSP encourages an understanding of sentence relationships.

Masked Language Modeling (MLM): During pre-training, 15% of the words in each sequence are replaced with a [MASK] token. The model then attempts to predict the original word based on the context provided by the other words. This can be formalized as:

$$L_{\text{MLM}} = -\sum_{t \in \text{masked positions}} \log P(w_t | \hat{w_t})$$

where $\hat{w_t}$ represents the masked word and w_t is the actual word.

Next Sentence Prediction (NSP): To model inter-sentence coherence, BERT pre-training also involves predicting whether a given sentence B follows sentence A. This binary classification task is aimed at improving tasks that involve relationships between sentences, such as reading comprehension and question answering. Formally, the objective can be written as:

$$L_{\text{NSP}} = -\log P(\text{IsNext}|\text{sequence pairs})$$

For fine-tuning, task-specific layers are added on top of the pre-trained BERT model, and the whole model is then trained jointly on the downstream task.

```
from transformers import BertModel, BertTokenizer
import torch

# Load pre-trained BERT model and tokenizer
tokenizer = BertTokenizer.from_pretrained('bert-base-uncased')
model = BertModel.from_pretrained('bert-base-uncased')

# Tokenize input text
input_text = "Transformers have revolutionized NLP."
encoded_input = tokenizer(input_text, return_tensors='pt')

# Forward pass to get hidden states
with torch.no_grad():
    outputs = model(**encoded_input)

# Extract token embeddings
last_hidden_states = outputs.last_hidden_state
```

The resulting hidden states can be utilized for various NLP tasks, such as text classification, named entity recognition, or question answering. BERT's architecture has significantly enhanced performance across numerous benchmarks and is widely adopted in NLP research and applications. By leveraging its bidirectional context understanding and pre-training on vast corpora, BERT sets a solid foundation for creating sophisticated and precise NLP models.

5.12 Implementing NLP Projects with Keras

Implementing Natural Language Processing (NLP) projects with Keras entails a series of methodical steps, starting from data preprocessing to model training and evaluation. We will detail the essential aspects to consider and provide practical code snippets demonstrating a complete NLP project. This section will focus on a sentiment analysis task as a representative example, employing a Long Short Term Memory (LSTM) network for its ability to capture long-term dependencies within text data.

The first phase of any NLP project is the collection and preprocessing of text data. Text data is inherently unstructured and requires significant preprocessing to convert it into a form suitable for machine learning algorithms. This includes steps such as tokenization, padding, and converting words into numerical vectors using word embeddings such as GloVe.

```
import numpy as np
import pandas as pd
from keras.preprocessing.text import Tokenizer
from keras.preprocessing.sequence import pad_sequences

# Assume 'df' is a DataFrame with a column named 'text' for text data
# and 'label' for sentiment labels.
df = pd.read_csv('sentiment_data.csv')

# Tokenization
tokenizer = Tokenizer(num_words=10000)
tokenizer.fit_on_texts(df['text'])
sequences = tokenizer.texts_to_sequences(df['text'])

# Padding
max_len = 100
word_index = tokenizer.word_index
data = pad_sequences(sequences, maxlen=max_len)

# Labels
labels = df['label'].values
```

The next step involves the creation of an embedding matrix if pre-trained word embeddings like GloVe are utilized. This matrix maps words to their corresponding embedding vectors and aids in transfer learning by leveraging knowledge from large corpus embeddings.

```
# Load GloVe embeddings
embeddings_index = {}
with open('glove.6B.100d.txt', encoding='utf-8') as f:
    for line in f:
        values = line.split()
        word = values[0]
        coefs = np.asarray(values[1:], dtype='float32')
        embeddings_index[word] = coefs

# Create the embedding matrix
embedding_dim = 100
embedding_matrix = np.zeros((len(word_index) + 1, embedding_dim))
for word, i in word_index.items():
    embedding_vector = embeddings_index.get(word)
    if embedding_vector is not None:
        embedding_matrix[i] = embedding_vector
```

With the data prepared and embeddings initialized, we can now construct the neural network model using Keras. We will use an LSTM layer to capture temporal dependencies in the text data.

```
from keras.models import Sequential
from keras.layers import Embedding, LSTM, Dense, Dropout

model = Sequential()
model.add(Embedding(len(word_index) + 1,
```

```
                    embedding_dim,
                    weights=[embedding_matrix],
                    input_length=max_len,
                    trainable=False))
model.add(LSTM(128, dropout=0.2, recurrent_dropout=0.2))
model.add(Dense(1, activation='sigmoid'))

model.compile(loss='binary_crossentropy',
              optimizer='adam',
              metrics=['accuracy'])

print(model.summary())
```

Training the model involves feeding the preprocessed text data and corresponding labels into the model. The training process will iteratively adjust the model weights to minimize the loss function.

```
from keras.callbacks import ModelCheckpoint

# Callbacks
checkpoint = ModelCheckpoint('model.h5', monitor='val_loss', save_best_only=True)

# Train the model
history = model.fit(data, labels,
                    validation_split=0.2,
                    epochs=10,
                    batch_size=32,
                    callbacks=[checkpoint],
                    verbose=1)
```

Evaluating the trained model involves making predictions on new text data and comparing them to the ground truth labels. This evaluation will help gauge the model's effectiveness and potential areas for improvement.

```
from sklearn.metrics import accuracy_score, classification_report

# Assuming `test_data` and `test_labels` are available
model.load_weights('model.h5') # Load the best model
predictions = model.predict(test_data)
predictions = (predictions > 0.5).astype(int)

# Evaluate
acc = accuracy_score(test_labels, predictions)
report = classification_report(test_labels, predictions, target_names=['Class 0', 'Class
     1'])

print(f'Accuracy: {acc}')
print(report)
```

The results from the evaluation can be analyzed further to understand the strengths and weaknesses of the model. Common metrics include accuracy, precision, recall, and F1-score, all available through the classification report to provide a comprehensive performance overview. Data preprocessing steps including tokenization and padding, the creation of an embedding matrix, and model construction using LSTM layers exemplify the powerful tools offered by Keras for implementing NLP projects. The provided code snippets demonstrate the practical application of these concepts, ensuring a robust foundation for developing and refining NLP models.

Chapter 6

Advanced Neural Network Architectures

This chapter explores sophisticated neural network architectures, revisiting essential concepts like CNNs and RNNs. It delves into advanced architectures including ResNet, Inception, and GANs, as well as autoencoders and variational autoencoders. The chapter also covers modern innovations such as attention mechanisms, transformers, and graph neural networks, providing detailed descriptions and use cases for each architecture. Real-world applications and case studies are included to showcase practical implementations.

6.1 Introduction to Advanced Neural Network Architectures

The landscape of neural networks has evolved significantly since the advent of simple architectures like the multilayer perceptron (MLP). As data complexities and computational capabilities have grown, so too has the need for more sophisticated neural network architectures. These advanced architectures address various challenges, such as deeper networks leading to vanishing gradients, the need for better feature extraction, and the ability to handle diverse data types including images, text, and graphs.

Understanding advanced neural architectures begins with a firm grounding in the basic building blocks such as Convolutional Neural Networks (CNNs) and Recurrent Neural Networks (RNNs). Gradual advancements over these foundational structures have paved the way for more powerful models.

Convolutional Neural Networks (CNNs) are integral for image processing tasks. Traditional CNNs are composed of convolutional layers, pooling layers, and fully connected layers. With their ability to capture spatial hierarchies in images, CNNs have proven highly effective for tasks like image classification, object detection, and segmentation. However, deeper networks often suffer from issues such as vanishing gradients and overfitting, leading to the emergence of architectures like **Residual Networks (ResNet)** and **Inception Networks**.

Residual Networks (ResNet) introduce the concept of residual learning. By incorporating shortcut connections or 'skip connections' that bypass one or more layers, ResNets mitigate the vanishing gradient problem, allowing for the training of substantially deeper networks. The mathematical formulation for a residual block can be expressed as:

$$y = F(x, \{W_i\}) + x$$

where $F(x, \{W_i\})$ represents the residual mapping to be learned. This simple yet powerful concept has led to remarkable performance improvements in various computer vision tasks.

Parallelly, **Inception Networks** leverage a different approach by utilizing sparsely connected architectures that capture multi-scale context. Developed as a part of the GoogleNet architecture, Inception modules perform convolutions with multiple filter sizes within the same module, concatenating their outputs. This is designed to capture features at different scales and reduce computational cost by using bottleneck layers. An Inception module can be diagrammatically represented as:

$$\begin{gathered}1 \times 1 \, \text{convolution} \\ 3 \times 3 \, \text{convolution} \\ 5 \times 5 \, \text{convolution} \\ 3 \times 3 \, \text{max pooling}\end{gathered}$$

Recurrent Neural Networks (RNNs) are tailored for sequential data, making them invaluable for tasks like time series prediction, language modeling, and machine translation. However, conventional RNNs struggle with long-term dependencies due to gradient vanishing/exploding problems. This challenge is addressed by advanced variants like

Long Short-Term Memory (LSTM) networks and **Gated Recurrent Unit (GRU)** networks, both employing gating mechanisms to regulate information flow.

A fundamental part of evolving architectures is the focus on generative models, with **Generative Adversarial Networks (GANs)** being a seminal innovation. GANs consist of two neural networks - the generator and the discriminator - engaged in a minimax game. Here, the generator produces samples while the discriminator evaluates their authenticity. The objective functions of GAN can be defined as follows:

$$\min_G \max_D V(D, G) = \mathbb{E}_{x \sim p_{\text{data}}(x)}[\log D(x)] + \mathbb{E}_{z \sim p_z(z)}[\log(1 - D(G(z)))]$$

Further advancing the field of unsupervised learning, **Autoencoders** and **Variational Autoencoders (VAEs)** learn efficient representations of the data. While standard autoencoders map inputs to a latent space and reconstruct inputs from it, VAEs extend this by framing the learning problem probabilistically. VAEs aim to maximize the evidence lower bound (ELBO) during training, facilitating the generation of new data samples:

$$\mathcal{L} = \mathbb{E}_{q(z|x)}[\log p(x|z)] - D_{KL}(q(z|x) \| p(z))$$

Attention Mechanisms and Transformers bring a breakthrough in handling variable-length inputs and capturing long-range dependencies without recurrent connections. Transformers, characterized by their self-attention mechanisms, excel in parallelization and have achieved state-of-the-art results in natural language processing. The self-attention mechanism is mathematically defined as:

$$\text{Attention}(Q, K, V) = \text{softmax}\left(\frac{QK^T}{\sqrt{d_k}}\right)V$$

Lastly, **Graph Neural Networks (GNNs)** generalize neural networks to work with graph-structured data, where nodes represent entities and edges signify relationships. They are crucial for tasks involving social networks, chemical molecule properties prediction, and knowledge graphs.

Exploring these advanced neural network architectures equips researchers and practitioners with powerful tools to tackle a vast array of complex problems, pushing the boundaries of what is achievable with deep learning.

6.2 Convolutional Neural Networks (CNNs) Revisited

Convolutional Neural Networks (CNNs) have been foundational in the advancement of deep learning, particularly in the field of computer vision. They utilize convolved operations to create hierarchical representations, enabling effective feature extraction from images. Revisiting CNNs requires a detailed understanding of their core components: convolutional layers, pooling layers, fully connected layers, and activation functions. We will explore each of these components methodically, focusing on their respective roles and interactions within CNN architectures.

The **convolutional layer** is the fundamental building block, where the primary operation is the convolution. It employs a set of learnable filters (kernels) that slide over the input data, performing element-wise multiplications and summing the results to produce feature maps. Mathematically, the convolution operation for a two-dimensional input I and a filter K is defined as:

$$(I * K)(i, j) = \sum_m \sum_n I(i + m, j + n) \cdot K(m, n)$$

This operation captures spatial hierarchies and pertinent features by emphasizing specific local patterns in the input image. The stride, padding, and depth of the filters directly impact the dimension of the output feature maps:

- **Stride** determines the amount by which the filter moves across the input. - **Padding** can either be 'valid' (no padding) or 'same' (padding to keep output dimensions constant).

The benefits and implications of using various strides and padding configurations are essential for controlling the spatial dimensions and feature abstraction levels in CNNs.

Pooling layers are introduced following convolutional layers to reduce the spatial dimensions of the feature maps while retaining essential information. Max pooling and average pooling are two common types:

- **Max pooling** picks the maximum value from the selected window, emphasizing the most significant features. - **Average pooling** calculates the average of all values within the window, providing a smooth feature map.

Mathematically, max pooling over a 2×2 window would be:

$$P_{max}(i,j) = \text{max}\{I(2i,2j), I(2i,2j+1), I(2i+1,2j), I(2i+1,2j+1)\}$$

Pooling reduces computation, mitigates overfitting, and ensures translation invariance, all crucial for stable and efficient CNN models.

Fully connected layers (dense layers) appear towards the end of the CNN architecture, where the high-level extracted features are utilized for final classification. Each neuron in a fully connected layer is connected to every neuron in the previous layer, facilitating complete representation learning from the feature maps.

Activation functions such as ReLU (Rectified Linear Unit) are pivotal in introducing non-linearity into the model, allowing it to learn complex patterns. ReLU is defined as:

$$\text{ReLU}(x) = \text{max}(0, x)$$

Other activation functions like sigmoid, tanh, Leaky ReLU, and Softmax follow, each with unique properties suited for different aspects of the training and inference process.

In practical applications, CNNs benefit from other concepts such as **dropout** and **batch normalization**. Dropout employs random zeroing of neurons during training to prevent overfitting:

```
import tensorflow as tf
from tensorflow.keras.layers import Dropout

# Example of using Dropout
model.add(Dropout(0.5))
```

Batch normalization stabilizes training by normalizing the input of each layer, as demonstrated below:

```
from tensorflow.keras.layers import BatchNormalization

# Example of using BatchNormalization
model.add(BatchNormalization())
```

Beyond constructing a CNN from basic layers, leveraging pre-trained models and transfer learning has become standard to expedite the design process and enhance performance. Prestigious models such as VGG, ResNet, Inception, and EfficientNet serve as the backbone for many complex tasks:

```
from tensorflow.keras.applications import VGG16

# Use a pre-trained VGG16 model
vgg_model = VGG16(weights='imagenet', include_top=False, input_shape=(224, 224,
    3))
```

These models, trained on massive datasets like ImageNet, provide robust feature extraction capabilities out-of-the-box, offering a significant head start in training custom models with limited data.

The evolution of CNN architectures relies heavily on the balance between computational efficiency and representational power. Concepts such as depthwise separable convolutions, as seen in MobileNet, and squeeze-and-excitation networks exemplify advancements aimed at refining efficiency and enhancing accuracy.

CNNs facilitate a broad spectrum of applications beyond image classification, including object detection, segmentation, style transfer, and more. Understanding their fundamental mechanics and practical implementations provides the key to devising powerful and efficient deep learning models tailored to diverse and complex tasks.

6.3 Residual Networks (ResNet)

Residual Networks (ResNet) represent a significant advancement in deep learning architectures, directly addressing the degradation problem encountered as network depth increases. The degradation problem is characterized by an increase in training error as additional layers are added to a deep neural network, which can counterintuitively make the model perform worse rather than better. ResNet introduces a novel approach to mitigate this issue by employing *residual learning*.

The core concept of ResNet is the **residual block**, which bypasses one or more layers through a shortcut connection. These connections enable gradients to flow more effectively through deep networks, thereby facilitating the training of very deep architectures. The basic structure of a residual block can be described mathematically by the following equation:

$$y = F(x, \{W_i\}) + x$$

Here, x is the input to the residual block, $F(x, \{W_i\})$ represents the residual function that typically consists of convolutional layers, batch normalization, and ReLU activation, and y stands for the output of the residual block. The term x is added directly to the output of the function F, forming a shortcut connection around F.

The intuition behind residual connections is that learning an identity mapping (i.e., the shortcut connections) is easier than directly learning the underlying complicated mapping from input to output. This makes it feasible to train much deeper networks.

Let us consider a simple example of a residual block using Python with Keras library. Below is the code for constructing a residual block:

```
from keras.layers import Input, Conv2D, BatchNormalization, Activation, Add
from keras.models import Model

def residual_block(x, filters, kernel_size=3):
    shortcut = x
    x = Conv2D(filters, kernel_size, padding='same')(x)
    x = BatchNormalization()(x)
    x = Activation('relu')(x)
    x = Conv2D(filters, kernel_size, padding='same')(x)
    x = BatchNormalization()(x)
    x = Add()([x, shortcut])
    x = Activation('relu')(x)
    return x

input_tensor = Input(shape=(64, 64, 3))
output_tensor = residual_block(input_tensor, 64)
model = Model(inputs=input_tensor, outputs=output_tensor)
model.summary()
```

The residual_block function creates a block with two convolutional layers, each followed by batch normalization and ReLU activation. The shortcut connection is created by adding the input tensor shortcut directly to the output of the second convolutional layer.

ResNet architectures are composed of multiple such residual blocks stacked together. There are several variants of ResNet, identified by the number of layers, such as ResNet-18, ResNet-34, ResNet-50, ResNet-101, and ResNet-152. These models are identified by the total number of layers, including convolutional layers and fully connected layers.

ResNet-50 Architecture ResNet-50 is one of the most widely used variants and consists of 50 layers. It is built using a combination of normal and bottleneck residual blocks. A bottleneck residual block is designed to reduce the number of parameters and computation cost by introducing a 1x1 convolutional layer that reduces the dimensionality before the 3x3 convolution and restores it afterward. The structure of a ResNet-50 bottleneck block can be described as follows:

```
def bottleneck_block(x, filters, kernel_size=3):
    shortcut = x
    x = Conv2D(filters, 1, padding='same')(x)
    x = BatchNormalization()(x)
    x = Activation('relu')(x)
    x = Conv2D(filters, kernel_size, padding='same')(x)
    x = BatchNormalization()(x)
    x = Activation('relu')(x)
    x = Conv2D(filters * 4, 1, padding='same')(x)
    x = BatchNormalization()(x)
    shortcut = Conv2D(filters * 4, 1, padding='same')(shortcut)
    shortcut = BatchNormalization()(shortcut)
    x = Add()([x, shortcut])
    x = Activation('relu')(x)
    return x

input_tensor = Input(shape=(64, 64, 3))
output_tensor = bottleneck_block(input_tensor, 64)
model = Model(inputs=input_tensor, outputs=output_tensor)
model.summary()
```

In this code, the bottleneck block initially reduces the number of filters to a lower dimensional size using a 1×1 convolution, applies a 3×3 convolutional layer, then increases the number of filters back to the original size with another 1×1 convolution. This architecture allows for a deeper network without excessively increasing computational burden.

The complete ResNet-50 architecture is composed of an initial convolutional layer followed by a pooling layer, then by 16 bottleneck blocks organized in 4 stages, and ended with a global average pooling layer followed by a fully connected layer with softmax activation for classification tasks.

The implementation of a full ResNet-50 architecture with Keras is complex and involves stacking multiple bottleneck and normal residual blocks together:

```
def build_resnet_50(input_shape, num_classes):
    input = Input(shape=input_shape)
    x = Conv2D(64, (7, 7), padding='same', strides=(2, 2))(input)
    x = BatchNormalization()(x)
    x = Activation('relu')(x)
    x = MaxPooling2D((3, 3), strides=(2, 2), padding='same')(x)

    x = bottleneck_block(x, 64)
    x = bottleneck_block(x, 64)
    x = bottleneck_block(x, 64)

    x = bottleneck_block(x, 128, stride=2)
    x = bottleneck_block(x, 128)
    x = bottleneck_block(x, 128)
    x = bottleneck_block(x, 128)

    x = bottleneck_block(x, 256, stride=2)
```

```
    x = bottleneck_block(x, 256)
    x = bottleneck_block(x, 256)
    x = bottleneck_block(x, 256)
    x = bottleneck_block(x, 256)
    x = bottleneck_block(x, 256)

    x = bottleneck_block(x, 512, stride=2)
    x = bottleneck_block(x, 512)
    x = bottleneck_block(x, 512)

    x = GlobalAveragePooling2D()(x)
    output = Dense(num_classes, activation='softmax')(x)

    model = Model(input, output)
    return model

model = build_resnet_50((224, 224, 3), 1000)
model.summary()
```

The use of residual connections enables models like ResNet to be trained efficiently even when they are very deep, overcoming the problems of vanishing gradients and model degradation. As a result, ResNet has significantly influenced contemporary neural network design, setting a high bar for accuracy and easing the way for even deeper networks. This architecture is widely used in various computer vision tasks and has won numerous contests, reinforcing its efficacy and robustness in practical applications.

6.4 Inception Networks

Inception Networks, introduced as GoogLeNet in the paper "Going Deeper with Convolutions" by Szegedy et al. in 2015, are a type of Convolutional Neural Network (CNN) architecture designed to improve the efficiency and accuracy of deep learning models. This architecture employs a novel approach known as the Inception module, which allows for more sophisticated and computationally efficient network designs.

The core idea behind the Inception module is to capture various types of features at different scales within the same layer by applying different sizes of convolutions in parallel, followed by concatenation of their results. This enables the model to extract features from the input at multiple levels of abstraction. A standard Inception module typically includes 1×1, 3×3, and 5×5 convolutions, along with a parallel max pooling operation, all of which are applied to the same input.

For clarity, consider the following implementation of an Inception module in Keras:

```
from keras.layers import Conv2D, MaxPooling2D, Concatenate

def inception_module(input_tensor):
    branch1x1 = Conv2D(64, (1, 1), padding='same', activation='relu')(input_tensor)

    branch3x3 = Conv2D(64, (1, 1), padding='same', activation='relu')(input_tensor)
    branch3x3 = Conv2D(64, (3, 3), padding='same', activation='relu')(branch3x3)

    branch5x5 = Conv2D(64, (1, 1), padding='same', activation='relu')(input_tensor)
    branch5x5 = Conv2D(64, (5, 5), padding='same', activation='relu')(branch5x5)

    branch_pool = MaxPooling2D(pool_size=(3, 3), strides=(1, 1), padding='same')(
        input_tensor)
    branch_pool = Conv2D(64, (1, 1), padding='same', activation='relu')(branch_pool
        )

    output = Concatenate(axis=-1)([branch1x1, branch3x3, branch5x5, branch_pool])
    return output
```

The concept of the Inception module evolved across several iterations, leading to versions like Inception-v2 and Inception-v3, each introducing further improvements. For instance, Inception-v2 introduced the use of "factorized" convolutions, which break a large convolution into smaller, more efficient convolutions. Inception-v3 further refined these ideas by adding techniques such as batch normalization and using RMSProp for optimization.

The Inception architecture also addresses the computational cost by introducing dimensionality reduction before expensive convolutions. By using 1×1 convolutions, it can reduce the number of feature maps before applying larger convolutions. This significantly reduces the number of parameters and computational load while preserving the capacity to learn complex features effectively.

Below is a sample implementation of a more sophisticated Inception module that uses factorized convolutions. This version is inspired by Inception-v3:

```
def inception_module_v3(input_tensor):
    branch1x1 = Conv2D(64, (1, 1), padding='same', activation='relu')(input_tensor)

    branch3x3 = Conv2D(64, (1, 1), padding='same', activation='relu')(input_tensor)
    branch3x3 = Conv2D(64, (1, 3), padding='same', activation='relu')(branch3x3)
    branch3x3 = Conv2D(64, (3, 1), padding='same', activation='relu')(branch3x3)

    branch5x5 = Conv2D(64, (1, 1), padding='same', activation='relu')(input_tensor)
    branch5x5 = Conv2D(64, (1, 5), padding='same', activation='relu')(branch5x5)
    branch5x5 = Conv2D(64, (5, 1), padding='same', activation='relu')(branch5x5)

    branch_pool = MaxPooling2D(pool_size=(3, 3), strides=(1, 1), padding='same')(
        input_tensor)
    branch_pool = Conv2D(64, (1, 1), padding='same', activation='relu')(branch_pool
        )
```

```
    output = Concatenate(axis=-1)([branch1x1, branch3x3, branch5x5, branch_pool])
    return output
```

Another notable aspect of Inception Networks is the usage of auxiliary classifiers. These are smaller, auxiliary networks that are attached to intermediate layers and are used during training to combat the vanishing gradient problem. They provide additional gradient signals and help to accelerate convergence and robustness. During inference, these auxiliary classifiers are discarded.

A simple implementation of an auxiliary classifier could be demonstrated as follows:

```
from keras.layers import Dense, GlobalAveragePooling2D

def auxiliary_classifier(input_tensor, num_classes):
    aux_output = GlobalAveragePooling2D()(input_tensor)
    aux_output = Dense(1024, activation='relu')(aux_output)
    aux_output = Dense(num_classes, activation='softmax')(aux_output)
    return aux_output
```

Inception Networks are foundational to many modern deep learning applications due to their multi-scale feature extraction capability and efficient use of computational resources. They are commonly applied in image recognition tasks but are versatile enough to be adapted for various problem domains. The concepts and techniques introduced by Inception have influenced the evolution of many subsequent neural network architectures, underscoring their significance in the field.

6.5 Recurrent Neural Networks (RNNs) Revisited

Recurrent Neural Networks (RNNs) are a class of neural networks designed for processing sequential data. Unlike feedforward neural networks, RNNs have connections that form directed cycles, enabling them to maintain a memory of previous inputs in the sequence. This mechanism allows RNNs to exhibit temporal dynamic behavior for a time sequence.

At the core of an RNN lies its hidden state, a memory that captures information about what has been processed so far. The hidden state h_t at time step t is updated based on both the current input x_t and the previous hidden state h_{t-1}. The mathematical formulation can be represented as:

$$h_t = \tanh(W_{xh}x_t + W_{hh}h_{t-1} + b_h),$$

where W_{xh} and W_{hh} are weight matrices, and b_h is the bias term. tanh is a common activation function used in RNNs, chosen for its ability to handle the vanishing gradient problem to some extent by maintaining gradients within a bounded range.

The output y_t generated by the RNN at each time step can be computed as:

$$y_t = W_{hy}h_t + b_y,$$

where W_{hy} is the output weight matrix and b_y is the output bias.

The primary strength of RNNs lies in their ability to handle sequences of varying lengths, making them suitable for tasks such as time series prediction, language modeling, and machine translation. However, RNNs also encounter several challenges, particularly with long-term dependencies, where the gradient during backpropagation tends to either vanish or explode.

To illustrate an RNN's implementation using Keras, consider the task of predicting the next value in a given sequence. First, we need to prepare the input data in the appropriate shape and format. Typically, the input data for RNNs is structured as three-dimensional arrays with dimensions $[\text{samples}, \text{timesteps}, \text{features}]$.

Here is a concise implementation of a simple RNN using Keras:

```
from keras.models import Sequential
from keras.layers import SimpleRNN, Dense

# Define the sequential model
model = Sequential()

# Add a simple RNN layer with 50 units
model.add(SimpleRNN(50, input_shape=(timesteps, features)))

# Add a dense layer with one unit
model.add(Dense(1))

# Compile the model
model.compile(optimizer='adam', loss='mean_squared_error')

# Fit the model with input data
model.fit(X_train, y_train, epochs=20, batch_size=32)
```

The critical parameters here include timesteps and features, which define the input shape to the RNN. The number of units in the RNN layer determines the dimension of the hidden state.

RNNs have evolved, addressing their limitations by introducing variants like the Long Short-Term Memory (LSTM) networks and Gated Recurrent Unit (GRU) networks. These advanced architectures modify the recurrence mechanism to mitigate issues with learning long-term dependencies more effectively.

Another significant concept in RNNs is **truncated backpropagation through time (TBPTT)**, a technique to manage computational complexity when training on long sequences. TBPTT splits the sequence into smaller segments and backpropagates gradients only within these truncated intervals.

To configure and utilize TBPTT in Keras, one must structure the model to periodically reset the state. Below is an example of how to implement TBPTT:

```
model = Sequential()
model.add(SimpleRNN(50, stateful=True, batch_input_shape=(batch_size, timesteps,
      features)))
model.add(Dense(1))
model.compile(optimizer='adam', loss='mean_squared_error')

for epoch in range(epochs):
    print('Epoch', epoch)
    model.fit(X_train, y_train, epochs=1, batch_size=batch_size, shuffle=False)
    model.reset_states()
```

Stateful RNNs in Keras keep the hidden states between batches, which is essential for TBPTT. The reset_states() method is called to reset the states at the end of each sequence.

RNNs can also be stacked to form deep RNNs, where multiple RNN layers are placed on top of each other. This configuration allows the network to learn hierarchical representations of sequence data. The following snippet demonstrates how to stack RNN layers in Keras:

```
model = Sequential()
model.add(SimpleRNN(50, return_sequences=True, input_shape=(timesteps, features)
    ))
model.add(SimpleRNN(50))
model.add(Dense(1))
model.compile(optimizer='adam', loss='mean_squared_error')
```

The return_sequences=True parameter ensures that the output of the first RNN layer includes the entire sequence, allowing the next RNN layer to process it.

While RNNs have considerably advanced sequential data processing capabilities, the advent of attention mechanisms and transformers has introduced more efficient and scalable approaches. These modern architectures, designed to handle sequences with greater efficacy, have been particularly transformative in natural language processing and other sequence-based domains.

6.6 Long Short-Term Memory (LSTM) Networks: Deep Dive

Long Short-Term Memory (LSTM) networks are a type of Recurrent Neural Network (RNN) designed to overcome the limitations of traditional RNNs, particularly the vanishing and exploding gradient problems that arise during backpropagation. LSTMs are well-suited for sequence prediction problems due to their ability to maintain long-term dependencies. This section delves into the internal mechanisms of LSTMs and provides practical implementation details using Keras.

LSTMs introduce a memory cell capable of maintaining its state over time, and gating mechanisms to control the flow of information into and out of this cell. The core components of an LSTM cell are the cell state $\mathbf{C}_t$ and the hidden state $\mathbf{h}_t$, which are updated through carefully regulated gates—namely the input gate, forget gate, and output gate.

The equations governing the operations within an LSTM cell are as follows:

$$
\begin{aligned}
\mathbf{f}_t &= \sigma(\mathbf{W}_f \cdot [\mathbf{h}_{t-1}, \mathbf{x}_t] + \mathbf{b}_f) \\
\mathbf{i}_t &= \sigma(\mathbf{W}_i \cdot [\mathbf{h}_{t-1}, \mathbf{x}_t] + \mathbf{b}_i) \\
\tilde{\mathbf{C}}_t &= \tanh(\mathbf{W}_C \cdot [\mathbf{h}_{t-1}, \mathbf{x}_t] + \mathbf{b}_C) \\
\mathbf{C}_t &= \mathbf{f}_t \odot \mathbf{C}_{t-1} + \mathbf{i}_t \odot \tilde{\mathbf{C}}_t \\
\mathbf{o}_t &= \sigma(\mathbf{W}_o \cdot [\mathbf{h}_{t-1}, \mathbf{x}_t] + \mathbf{b}_o) \\
\mathbf{h}_t &= \mathbf{o}_t \odot \tanh(\mathbf{C}_t)
\end{aligned}
$$

Here, σ denotes the sigmoid activation function, and $\odot$ represents element-wise multiplication. The forget gate $\mathbf{f}_t$ decides what portion of the previous cell state $\mathbf{C}_{t-1}$ should be carried forward, the input gate $\mathbf{i}_t$ determines the extent of new information to be added to the cell state, and the output gate $\mathbf{o}_t$ controls the value of the next hidden state $\mathbf{h}_t$.

Implementation Using Keras

To implement an LSTM network in Keras, we utilize the LSTM layer. Below is an example of a simple LSTM model for a sequence prediction task.

```
import numpy as np
from keras.models import Sequential
from keras.layers import LSTM, Dense

# Generating dummy data
X_train = np.random.random((1000, 10, 64))
y_train = np.random.random((1000, 1))

# Building the LSTM model
model = Sequential()
model.add(LSTM(128, input_shape=(10, 64), return_sequences=False))
model.add(Dense(1, activation='linear'))

# Compiling the model
model.compile(optimizer='adam', loss='mean_squared_error')

# Training the model
model.fit(X_train, y_train, epochs=10, batch_size=32)
```

In this example, we create a sequential model with a single LSTM layer of 128 units. The input_shape is set to (10, 64), indicating that each input sequence consists of 10 time steps and 64 features per time step. The return_sequences parameter is set to False because we are only interested in the output of the last LSTM cell. The final Dense layer with a linear activation function is used to produce the output.

Bidirectional LSTM

In some scenarios, it is beneficial to have access to future as well as past context. Bidirectional LSTMs (BiLSTMs) achieve this by processing the input sequence in both forward and backward directions. The two hidden states (one from forward pass and one from backward pass) are concatenated at each time step.

```
from keras.layers import Bidirectional

# Building a Bidirectional LSTM model
model = Sequential()
model.add(Bidirectional(LSTM(128), input_shape=(10, 64)))
model.add(Dense(1, activation='linear'))

# Compiling the model
model.compile(optimizer='adam', loss='mean_squared_error')

# Training the model
model.fit(X_train, y_train, epochs=10, batch_size=32)
```

In the above code, the Bidirectional wrapper is used to wrap the LSTM layer, allowing it to learn from both past and future context.

LSTM Parameters and Tuning

When using LSTMs, several parameters can be tuned for better performance. These include the number of LSTM units, learning rate, batch size, and the number of epochs. Further, dropout can be added to the LSTM layers to combat overfitting. Below is an example:

```
from keras.layers import Dropout

# Building an LSTM model with dropout
model = Sequential()
model.add(LSTM(128, input_shape=(10, 64)))
model.add(Dropout(0.2))
model.add(Dense(1, activation='linear'))

# Compiling the model
model.compile(optimizer='adam', loss='mean_squared_error')

# Training the model
model.fit(X_train, y_train, epochs=10, batch_size=32)
```

Here, a Dropout layer with a dropout rate of 0.2 is added to the model. This helps regularize the LSTM by randomly setting a fraction of the input units to zero at each update during training.

LSTM in Real-world Applications

LSTMs have been successfully applied in various domains such as natural language processing, time series forecasting, and speech recognition. Their ability to retain long-term dependencies makes them particularly useful for tasks requiring context understanding over extended periods.

In natural language processing, LSTMs are used for tasks like language translation and sentiment analysis. For instance, in machine translation, an LSTM-based encoder-decoder architecture can be used to translate sentences from one language to another.

In time series forecasting, LSTMs can predict future values based on historical data, making them suitable for financial market predictions, weather forecasting, and demand forecasting.

In speech recognition, LSTM networks convert spoken language into text by learning temporal dependencies in audio signals.

This section has provided an in-depth exploration of LSTM networks, highlighting their functionality, practical implementation, and multiple applications. Proper understanding and optimization of LSTM parameters can further enhance their performance in diverse tasks.

6.7 Gated Recurrent Unit (GRU) Networks: Deep Dive

Gated Recurrent Unit (GRU) networks, introduced by Cho et al., represent an advancement in the field of Recurrent Neural Networks (RNNs) by incorporating gating mechanisms to address vanishing gradient issues prevalent in standard RNNs. By leveraging these mechanisms, GRUs are capable of capturing long-term dependencies more effectively without the complexity seen in Long Short-Term Memory (LSTM) networks. This section delves into the structure, functionality, and mathematical foundations underlying GRUs, followed by practical implementation details using Keras.

The GRU cell modifies the traditional RNN cell by introducing two gates: the reset gate (r_t) and the update gate (z_t). These gates regulate the flow of information and mitigate the issues of exploding and vanishing gradients. The reset gate determines the contribution of the previous hidden state to the candidate activation, while the update gate controls the extent to which the previous hidden state and the current candidate activation are updated.

The detailed functioning of a GRU cell can be described with the following equations:

$$z_t = \sigma(W_z x_t + U_z h_{t-1} + b_z) \quad \text{(Update gate)}$$
$$r_t = \sigma(W_r x_t + U_r h_{t-1} + b_r) \quad \text{(Reset gate)}$$
$$\widetilde{h}_t = \tanh(W_h x_t + r_t \odot U_h h_{t-1} + b_h) \quad \text{(Candidate activation)}$$
$$h_t = (1 - z_t) \odot h_{t-1} + z_t \odot \widetilde{h}_t \quad \text{(Final activation)}$$

Where: - x_t is the input at time step t. - h_{t-1} is the hidden state from the previous time step. - σ denotes the sigmoid function. - tanh denotes the hyperbolic tangent function. - $\odot$ denotes the Hadamard product (element-wise multiplication). - $W_z, W_r, W_h, U_z, U_r, U_h$ are weight matrices. - b_z, b_r, b_h are bias vectors.

The update gate z_t decides the extent to which the new state is a copy of the old state. When $z_t \approx 1$, the old state h_{t-1} is retained, and when $z_t \approx 0$, the new candidate state $\widetilde{h}_t$ is adopted. The reset gate r_t determines how much of the past information to forget. Having $r_t \approx 0$ will ignore the past hidden state h_{t-1} thereby focusing more on the current input x_t.

The design of these gating mechanisms results in fewer parameters compared to LSTMs, thus making GRUs computationally more efficient while maintaining or sometimes even surpassing performance in sequence modeling tasks.

To implement a GRU in Keras, we follow these steps:

```
from keras.models import Sequential
from keras.layers import GRU, Dense

# Define model
model = Sequential()

# Add a GRU layer with 128 units, accepting input sequences of shape (timesteps,
    features)
model.add(GRU(128, input_shape=(timesteps, features)))

# Add a Dense layer with a single unit and a linear activation function
model.add(Dense(1, activation='linear'))

# Compile the model
model.compile(optimizer='adam', loss='mse')

# Summarize the model structure
model.summary()
```

This code demonstrates the creation of a GRU-based model using Keras, suitable for time series forecasting or any task involving sequential data input. Key steps include defining the sequential model, adding the GRU layer with the appropriate input shape, and finally, a Dense layer to produce the output. The model is compiled using the Adam optimizer and Mean Squared Error (MSE) loss function.

To optimize GRU models, hyperparameters such as the number of units in the GRU layer, learning rate, batch size, and sequence length can be tuned. The model can be trained on time series data as shown below:

```
# Fit the model to the training data
history = model.fit(X_train, y_train, epochs=50, batch_size=32, validation_data=(
    X_val, y_val))

# Evaluate the model on the test data
loss = model.evaluate(X_test, y_test)
print("Test Loss: ", loss)
```

Through the fit method, the model is trained for 50 epochs with a batch size of 32. Validation data is specified for monitoring the validation loss. Finally, the model's performance is assessed on the test data using the evaluate method, providing a quantitative measure of its predictive capability.

The GRU network's ability to capture temporal dependencies makes it particularly advantageous in applications such as speech recognition, natural language processing, and financial time series forecasting. Its simplified gating mechanism, compared to LSTMs, allows for faster training times and reduced computational burden, making it a practical choice in many real-world scenarios.

6.8 Generative Adversarial Networks (GANs)

Generative Adversarial Networks (GANs) represent a significant innovation in the field of deep learning, particularly in the domain of generative models. Introduced by Ian Goodfellow and his colleagues in 2014, GANs consist of two neural networks—the Generator and the Discriminator—that are trained simultaneously through adversarial processes.

The Generator aims to produce data that mimics real data distributions, while the Discriminator strives to distinguish between real data and data generated by the Generator. This section outlines the fundamental architecture of GANs, the training process, and various modifications and applications to highlight their versatility.

The basic structure of a GAN involves a two-part system: 1. **Generator (*G*)**: The Generator takes as input a noise vector **z**, typically sampled from a uniform or Gaussian distribution, and transforms it into a data instance $\mathbf{G}(\mathbf{z})$ through a series of non-linear transformations. The goal of the Generator is to create data that is indistinguishable from the real data.

2. **Discriminator (*D*)**: The Discriminator is essentially a binary classification network. It takes as input a data instance (either from the real dataset or from the Generator) and outputs a probability value $D(x)$ representing the likelihood that the input is real. The Discriminator is trained to maximize the probability of correctly classifying real and generated data instances.

The training process involves a minimax game with the following value function $V(D, G)$:

$$\min_G \max_D V(D, G) = \mathbb{E}_{x \sim p_{\text{data}}(x)}[\log D(x)] + \mathbb{E}_{z \sim p_z(z)}[\log(1 - D(G(z)))]$$

In practical terms, the training algorithm involves iterative updates of the Generator and Discriminator based on their respective objectives:

- **Step 1: Train Discriminator** – The Discriminator is trained to maximize the probability of correctly distinguishing between real data and generated data.
- **Step 2: Train Generator** – The Generator is trained to minimize the probability that the Discriminator correctly identifies generated data as fake.

Below is a simple implementation of a GAN in Keras:

```
import numpy as np
import tensorflow as tf
from tensorflow.keras.models import Sequential
from tensorflow.keras.layers import Dense, LeakyReLU, Dropout
from tensorflow.keras.optimizers import Adam

# Hyperparameters
latent_dim = 100
adam_lr = 0.0002
adam_beta_1 = 0.5

# Generator Model
def build_generator(latent_dim):
    model = Sequential()
    model.add(Dense(256, input_dim=latent_dim))
    model.add(LeakyReLU(alpha=0.2))
    model.add(Dropout(0.3))
    model.add(Dense(512))
    model.add(LeakyReLU(alpha=0.2))
    model.add(Dropout(0.3))
    model.add(Dense(1024))
    model.add(LeakyReLU(alpha=0.2))
    model.add(Dropout(0.3))
    model.add(Dense(28 * 28 * 1, activation='tanh'))
    model.add(tf.keras.layers.Reshape((28, 28, 1)))
    return model

# Discriminator Model
def build_discriminator(img_shape):
    model = Sequential()
    model.add(tf.keras.layers.Flatten(input_shape=img_shape))
    model.add(Dense(512))
    model.add(LeakyReLU(alpha=0.2))
    model.add(Dropout(0.3))
    model.add(Dense(256))
    model.add(LeakyReLU(alpha=0.2))
    model.add(Dropout(0.3))
    model.add(Dense(1, activation='sigmoid'))
    return model

img_shape = (28, 28, 1)
optimizer = Adam(lr=adam_lr, beta_1=adam_beta_1)

# Build and compile the discriminator
discriminator = build_discriminator(img_shape)
discriminator.compile(loss='binary_crossentropy', optimizer=optimizer, metrics=['
    accuracy'])
```

```
# Build and compile the generator
generator = build_generator(latent_dim)
z = tf.keras.layers.Input(shape=(latent_dim,))
img = generator(z)

# The discriminator takes generated images as input and determines validity
discriminator.trainable = False
validity = discriminator(img)

# Combined model (stacked generator and discriminator)
combined = tf.keras.Model(z, validity)
combined.compile(loss='binary_crossentropy', optimizer=optimizer)

# Training the GAN
def train(epochs, batch_size=128, save_interval=50):
    (X_train, _), (_, _) = tf.keras.datasets.mnist.load_data()
    X_train = X_train / 127.5 - 1.0
    X_train = np.expand_dims(X_train, axis=3)
    real = np.ones((batch_size, 1))
    fake = np.zeros((batch_size, 1))

    for epoch in range(epochs):
        idx = np.random.randint(0, X_train.shape[0], batch_size)
        real_imgs = X_train[idx]
        z = np.random.normal(0, 1, (batch_size, latent_dim))
        gen_imgs = generator.predict(z)

        d_loss_real = discriminator.train_on_batch(real_imgs, real)
        d_loss_fake = discriminator.train_on_batch(gen_imgs, fake)
        d_loss = 0.5 * np.add(d_loss_real, d_loss_fake)

        z = np.random.normal(0, 1, (batch_size, latent_dim))
        g_loss = combined.train_on_batch(z, real)

        if (epoch % save_interval == 0) or (epoch == epochs-1):
            print(f"{epoch} [D loss: {d_loss[0]} | D accuracy: {100*d_loss[1]}] [G loss: {
                g_loss}]")
            save_imgs(epoch)

def save_imgs(epoch):
    r, c = 5, 5
    noise = np.random.normal(0, 1, (r * c, latent_dim))
    gen_imgs = generator.predict(noise)
    gen_imgs = 0.5 * gen_imgs + 0.5

    fig, axs = plt.subplots(r, c)
    cnt = 0
    for i in range(r):
        for j in range(c):
            axs[i, j].imshow(gen_imgs[cnt, :, :, 0], cmap='gray')
            axs[i, j].axis('off')
            cnt += 1
    fig.savefig(f"images/mnist_{epoch}.png")
    plt.close()

# Example usage
train(epochs=10000, batch_size=64, save_interval=1000)
```

In advanced applications, GANs have been subject to various enhancements to improve stability and performance. Among these advancements, notable examples include:

- **Conditional GANs (cGANs)**: Introduces conditional data **y** to both the Generator and the Discriminator, enabling the generation of more specific data types.
- **Wasserstein GANs (WGANs)**: Utilizes the Wasserstein distance to provide more stable and interpretable training dynamics. In WGANs, the loss function is modified to minimize the distance between distributions rather than rely on binary cross-entropy.
- **CycleGANs**: Designed for image-to-image translation without requiring paired examples during training, effectively addressing a broad range of applications, such as style transfer and domain adaptation.

GANs have demonstrated remarkable success in various fields, from image generation and enhancement to data augmentation, artistic style transfer, and beyond. Their ability to generate high-fidelity synthetic data holds significant promise for numerous real-world applications.

The intricate adversarial training method that underpins GANs underscores the complex interplay between the Generator and Discriminator, leading to increasingly sophisticated models capable of producing realistic and high-quality data. As research in GANs continues, new architectures and training techniques persistently push the boundaries of what these generative models can achieve.

6.9 Autoencoders and Variational Autoencoders (VAEs)

Autoencoders are a class of neural networks trained to attempt to copy their input to their output. Typically, they are used to produce a more compact representation of the input data. The architecture of an autoencoder can be described in two main parts: the encoder and the decoder. The encoder compresses the input into a latent-space representation, and the decoder reconstructs the input from this representation. The goal is to minimize the reconstruction error between the original input and its reconstructed version.

Formally, consider an input $\mathbf{x} \in \mathbb{R}^d$. The encoder maps $\mathbf{x}$ to a latent representation **z** using a function f, parameterized by weights θ_e:

$$\mathbf{z} = f_\theta(\mathbf{x})$$

The decoder then reconstructs the input from the latent representation using a function g, parameterized by weights θ_d:

$$\hat{\mathbf{x}} = g_\theta(\mathbf{z})$$

The overall objective is to minimize the reconstruction loss, often measured by mean squared error (MSE) or binary cross-entropy (BCE) loss if dealing with binary data:

$$\mathcal{L}(\mathbf{x}, \hat{\mathbf{x}}) = ||\mathbf{x} - \hat{\mathbf{x}}||^2 \text{ or } -\sum_{i=1}^{d}[\mathbf{x}_i \log(\hat{\mathbf{x}}_i) + (1 - \mathbf{x}_i)\log(1 - \hat{\mathbf{x}}_i)]$$

In practice, autoencoders can be built using various types of layers like fully connected (dense) layers, convolutional layers (Convolutional Autoencoders), or even RNN layers for sequential data.

An example code for a simple fully connected autoencoder using Keras is as follows:

```
from keras.layers import Input, Dense
from keras.models import Model

# Size of the input and latent space
input_dim = 784
latent_dim = 64

# Input layer
input_layer = Input(shape=(input_dim,))

# Encoder
encoded = Dense(128, activation='relu')(input_layer)
encoded = Dense(64, activation='relu')(encoded)
latent = Dense(latent_dim, activation='relu')(encoded)

# Decoder
decoded = Dense(64, activation='relu')(latent)
decoded = Dense(128, activation='relu')(decoded)
output_layer = Dense(input_dim, activation='sigmoid')(decoded)

# Autoencoder model
autoencoder = Model(input_layer, output_layer)
autoencoder.compile(optimizer='adam', loss='binary_crossentropy')

# Training the autoencoder
autoencoder.fit(x_train, x_train, epochs=50, batch_size=256, shuffle=True,
    validation_data=(x_test, x_test))
```

Traditional autoencoders can effectively learn a latent space but do not make any assumptions about the distribution of the latent space. This limitation leads us to Variational Autoencoders (VAEs).

Variational Autoencoders (VAEs) extend the basic autoencoder architecture by making the latent space continuous, enabling generation of new data points by sampling latent variables. VAEs are based on Probabilistic Graphical Models (PGMs), making use of a probabilistic encoder $q_\phi(\mathbf{z}|\mathbf{x})$ and a probabilistic decoder $p_\theta(\mathbf{x}|\mathbf{z})$.

VAEs employ the reparameterization trick to perform backpropagation through the sampling operation. Instead of directly sampling $\mathbf{z}$ from the encoder, we sample an auxiliary variable ϵ from a standard normal distribution and transform it using the learned mean $\boldsymbol{\mu}$ and standard deviation $\boldsymbol{\sigma}$:

$$\mathbf{z} = \boldsymbol{\mu} + \boldsymbol{\sigma} \odot \epsilon, \text{ where } \epsilon \sim \mathcal{N}(0, I)$$

The objective function for VAEs combines two components: the reconstruction loss and the Kullback-Leibler (KL) divergence, which regularizes the distribution of the latent variables to be close to a standard normal distribution:

$$\mathcal{L}_{\text{VAE}} = \mathbb{E}_{q_\phi(\mathbf{z}|\mathbf{x})}[\log p_\theta(\mathbf{x}|\mathbf{z})] - \text{KL}(q_\phi(\mathbf{z}|\mathbf{x})||p(\mathbf{z}))$$

In practice, this means minimizing the following loss:

$$\mathcal{L}_{\text{VAE}} = \mathcal{L}_{\text{reconstruction}} + \mathcal{L}_{\text{KL-Divergence}}$$

An example code for a VAE using Keras is as follows:

```
from keras.layers import Input, Dense, Lambda
from keras.models import Model
from keras import backend as K
from keras.losses import binary_crossentropy
import numpy as np

# Encoder
input_layer = Input(shape=(input_dim,))
encoded = Dense(128, activation='relu')(input_layer)
encoded = Dense(64, activation='relu')(encoded)
z_mean = Dense(latent_dim)(encoded)
z_log_var = Dense(latent_dim)(encoded)

# Reparameterization trick
def sampling(args):
    z_mean, z_log_var = args
    epsilon = K.random_normal(shape=(K.shape(z_mean)[0], latent_dim), mean=0.,
        stddev=1.0)
    return z_mean + K.exp(z_log_var / 2) * epsilon

z = Lambda(sampling, output_shape=(latent_dim,))([z_mean, z_log_var])

# Decoder
decoder_hid = Dense(64, activation='relu')(z)
decoder_hid2 = Dense(128, activation='relu')(decoder_hid)
output_layer = Dense(input_dim, activation='sigmoid')(decoder_hid2)
```

```
# VAE model
vae = Model(input_layer, output_layer)

# VAE loss
def vae_loss(x, x_decoded_mean):
    xent_loss = binary_crossentropy(x, x_decoded_mean)
    kl_loss = - 0.5 * K.sum(1 + z_log_var - K.square(z_mean) - K.exp(z_log_var),
        axis=-1)
    return xent_loss + kl_loss

vae.compile(optimizer='adam', loss=vae_loss)

# Training the VAE
vae.fit(x_train, x_train, epochs=50, batch_size=256, shuffle=True, validation_data=(
    x_test, x_test))
```

Autoencoders, and in particular VAEs, have found applications across various domains such as image denoising, anomaly detection, and as generative models creating plausible data points. Their probabilistic nature makes VAEs particularly powerful in scenarios which require sampling and data variability understanding.

6.10 Attention Mechanisms and Transformers

Attention mechanisms have revolutionized the field of neural networks, especially in natural language processing (NLP) and computer vision. Attention allows models to focus on specific parts of the input, dynamically changing the focus based on the context. This capability is crucial for handling sequences where the relevance of different parts can vary significantly. Transformers, introduced in the seminal paper "Attention is All You Need" by Vaswani et al. in 2017, leverage attention mechanisms to process input data efficiently.

At the core of the attention mechanism is the ability to compute a weighted sum of input values, where the weights indicate the importance of each value. When applying attention, the model can effectively "attend" to more relevant parts of the input sequence, enhancing the quality of the generated output.

To delve deeper into the details, the attention mechanism can be mathematically formalized. For a given input sequence $X = (x_1, x_2, \ldots, x_n)$, the attention mechanism computes a score for each element in the sequence relative to a query. This score is typically derived using a similarity measure. The computed scores are then transformed into probabilities using the softmax function, resulting in attention weights. These weights are used to compute a weighted sum of the value vectors, producing the final attention output.

$$\text{Attention}(Q, K, V) = \text{softmax}\left(\frac{QK^T}{\sqrt{d_k}}\right)V$$

Here, Q (queries), K (keys), and V (values) are matrices derived from the input sequence through learned linear projections, and d_k is the dimension of the keys used to scale the dot product.

Transformers utilize a multi-head attention mechanism, which allows the model to jointly attend to information from different representation subspaces at different positions. This is implemented by linearly projecting the queries, keys, and values h times with different learned linear projections, then performing attention in parallel and concatenating the results.

$$\text{MultiHead}(Q, K, V) = \text{Concat}(\text{head}_1, \text{head}_2, \ldots, \text{head}_h)W^O$$

Each head_i is computed using:

$$\text{head}_i = \text{Attention}(QW_i^Q, KW_i^K, VW_i^V)$$

Where W_i^Q, W_i^K, and W_i^V are the learned projections for the i-th head, and W^O is a final projection matrix.

The Transformer's architecture consists of an encoder and a decoder. The encoder is composed of a stack of identical layers, each layer having two main components: a multi-head self-attention mechanism and a position-wise fully connected feed-forward network. Layer normalization and residual connections are employed around each sub-layer.

Encoder Layer:

- Multi-head self-attention mechanism
- Add & Norm (Residual connection followed by layer normalization)
- Position-wise feed-forward network
- Add & Norm

$$\text{FFN}(x) = \max(0, xW_1 + b_1)W_2 + b_2$$

The decoder also stacks multiple layers but includes an additional multi-head attention layer to attend to the encoder's output.

Decoder Layer:

- Masked multi-head self-attention mechanism
- Add & Norm
- Multi-head attention mechanism (attending to the encoder's output)
- Add & Norm
- Position-wise feed-forward network
- Add & Norm

A critical component of the Transformer model is the positional encoding, added to the input embeddings to preserve the order of the sequence. This encoding uses sine and cosine functions of different frequencies:

$$\text{PE}_{(pos,2i)} = \sin\left(\frac{pos}{10000^{2i/d_{\text{model}}}}\right)$$
$$\text{PE}_{(pos,2i+1)} = \cos\left(\frac{pos}{10000^{2i/d_{\text{model}}}}\right)$$

Where pos is the position and i is the dimension. These encodings are added to the input embeddings to incorporate position information.

Implementing and training such models can be computationally intensive. Keras provides high-level APIs to implement Transformers seamlessly. Below is a simplified implementation of a Transformer block using Keras:

```
import tensorflow as tf
from tensorflow.keras.layers import Dense, LayerNormalization, MultiHeadAttention

class TransformerBlock(tf.keras.layers.Layer):
    def __init__(self, embed_dim, num_heads, ff_dim, rate=0.1):
        super(TransformerBlock, self).__init__()
        self.att = MultiHeadAttention(num_heads=num_heads, key_dim=embed_dim)
        self.ffn = tf.keras.Sequential(
            [Dense(ff_dim, activation="relu"), Dense(embed_dim),]
        )
```

```
        self.layernorm1 = LayerNormalization(epsilon=1e-6)
        self.layernorm2 = LayerNormalization(epsilon=1e-6)
        self.dropout1 = tf.keras.layers.Dropout(rate)
        self.dropout2 = tf.keras.layers.Dropout(rate)

    def call(self, inputs, training):
        attn_output = self.att(inputs, inputs)
        attn_output = self.dropout1(attn_output, training=training)
        out1 = self.layernorm1(inputs + attn_output)

        ffn_output = self.ffn(out1)
        ffn_output = self.dropout2(ffn_output, training=training)
        return self.layernorm2(out1 + ffn_output)

embed_dim = 128 # Embedding size for each token
num_heads = 8 # Number of attention heads
ff_dim = 512 # Hidden layer size in feed-forward network

# Example usage:
trans_block = TransformerBlock(embed_dim, num_heads, ff_dim)
input_tensor = tf.random.uniform((32, 10, embed_dim)) # (batch_size, token_count,
    embedding_size)
output_tensor = trans_block(input_tensor)
print(output_tensor.shape)
```

```
(32, 10, 128)
```

Attention mechanisms and Transformers have enabled significant advancements in sequence modeling. Their applications span various domains, including machine translation, text generation, and even image processing. The ability to model long-range dependencies and handle variable-length inputs with ease makes Transformers a powerful tool in deep learning. As research progresses, we can expect even more sophisticated models and applications leveraging these foundational concepts.

6.11 Graph Neural Networks (GNNs)

Graph Neural Networks (GNNs) represent a paradigm shift in deep learning, effectively extending neural network architectures to handle graph-structured data. Traditional machine learning models and conventional neural networks struggle with graph data due to its inherent irregularity and non-Euclidean nature. By leveraging the relational information embedded within graphs, GNNs open up a new frontier of applications, including social network analysis, recommendation systems, and molecular biology.

GNNs are distinguished by their ability to propagate information between nodes via the graph edges, enabling the capture of intricate dependencies and relationships.

Key Principles and Operations: GNNs operate on the principle of message passing, where node features are iteratively updated based on their neighbors' features. Each node v in graph $G = (V, E)$, where V denotes the set of nodes and E denotes the set of edges, maintains a feature vector h_v. The goal is to learn node embeddings $h_v^{(t)}$ at each iteration t that encapsulate local graph structure and node features.

The primary operations in a GNN layer are as follows:

- **Message Aggregation**: Nodes aggregate messages from their adjacent nodes. Formally, for a node v, the aggregated message from its neighbors $\mathcal{N}(v)$ at iteration t is given by:

$$m_v^{(t)} = \sum_{u \in \mathcal{N}(v)} \text{AGG}(h_u^{(t-1)}, h_v^{(t-1)}, e_{uv})$$

  where AGG is an aggregation function, such as sum, mean, or max, and e_{uv} represents the edge features between nodes u and v.

- **Node Update**: The node features are then updated using a transformation function TRANS, which often includes neural networks such as Multi-Layer Perceptrons (MLPs). The updated feature of node v at iteration t is:

$$h_v^{(t)} = \sigma\left(\text{TRANS}(h_v^{(t-1)}, m_v^{(t)})\right)$$

  where σ is a non-linear activation function, e.g., ReLU.

- **Readout Function**: After several iterations of message passing, a readout function READOUT aggregates the node features to produce a graph-level representation. This process can be expressed as:

$$h_G = \text{READOUT}(\{h_v^{(T)} \mid v \in V\})$$

Specific GNN Architectures: Various GNN architectures have been proposed, each with unique mechanisms for message aggregation and node update:

Graph Convolutional Networks (GCNs): GCNs extend the concept of convolution from grids to graphs. They aggregate the feature vectors of neighboring nodes using a normalized adjacency matrix. The layer-wise propagation rule for GCNs is given by:

$$H^{(t+1)} = \sigma\left(\tilde{D}^{-\frac{1}{2}}\tilde{A}\tilde{D}^{-\frac{1}{2}}H^{(t)}W^{(t)}\right)$$

where $\tilde{A} = A + I$ is the adjacency matrix with added self-loops, $\tilde{D}$ is the diagonal degree matrix, $H^{(t)}$ is the node feature matrix at layer t, and $W^{(t)}$ is the learnable weight matrix.

```
import torch
import torch.nn as nn
import torch.nn.functional as F
from torch_geometric.nn import GCNConv

class GCN(nn.Module):
    def __init__(self, input_dim, hidden_dim, output_dim):
        super(GCN, self).__init__()
        self.conv1 = GCNConv(input_dim, hidden_dim)
        self.conv2 = GCNConv(hidden_dim, output_dim)

    def forward(self, x, edge_index):
        x = self.conv1(x, edge_index)
        x = F.relu(x)
        x = self.conv2(x, edge_index)
        return x
```

Graph Attention Networks (GATs): GATs introduce attention mechanisms to GNNs, where nodes attend to their neighbors with different weights. This adaptively focuses on the most relevant neighbors. The attention coefficients for neighbors i and j are computed as:

$$e_{ij} = \text{LeakyReLU}\left(a^T[Wh_i||Wh_j]\right)$$

where a is a learnable weight vector, W is the weight matrix, and $||$ denotes concatenation. The coefficients are normalized via the softmax function:

$$\alpha_{ij} = \text{softmax}_j(e_{ij})$$

Node features are then updated as a weighted sum of their neighbors' features:

$$h_i' = \sigma\left(\sum_{j\in\mathcal{N}(i)} \alpha_{ij}Wh_j\right)$$

```
import torch
import torch.nn as nn
import torch.nn.functional as F
from torch_geometric.nn import GATConv

class GAT(nn.Module):
    def __init__(self, input_dim, hidden_dim, output_dim, heads=1):
```

```
        super(GAT, self).__init__()
        self.conv1 = GATConv(input_dim, hidden_dim, heads=heads, concat=True)
        self.conv2 = GATConv(hidden_dim * heads, output_dim, heads=1, concat=
            False)

    def forward(self, x, edge_index):
        x = self.conv1(x, edge_index)
        x = F.elu(x)
        x = self.conv2(x, edge_index)
        return x
```

GraphSAGE: GraphSAGE (Graph Sample and Aggregation) improves scalability by sampling a fixed-size set of neighbors and performing specific aggregation operations. Common aggregators include mean, LSTM, and pooling. The node feature update in GraphSAGE is performed as:

$$h_v^{(t+1)} = \sigma\left(W^{(t)} \cdot \text{AGG}(\{h_u^{(t)} \mid u \in \mathcal{N}(v)\})\right)$$

where the aggregator AGG can be a mean function:

$$\text{AGG}(\{h_u^{(t)} \mid u \in \mathcal{N}(v)\}) = \text{Mean}(\{h_u^{(t)} \mid u \in \mathcal{N}(v)\})$$

```
import torch
import torch.nn as nn
import torch.nn.functional as F
from torch_geometric.nn import SAGEConv

class GraphSAGE(nn.Module):
    def __init__(self, input_dim, hidden_dim, output_dim):
        super(GraphSAGE, self).__init__()
        self.conv1 = SAGEConv(input_dim, hidden_dim)
        self.conv2 = SAGEConv(hidden_dim, output_dim)

    def forward(self, x, edge_index):
        x = self.conv1(x, edge_index)
        x = F.relu(x)
        x = self.conv2(x, edge_index)
        return x
```

Applications and Real-world Use Cases:

- **Social Network Analysis**: GNNs can analyze social networks by predicting user interests, detecting communities, and identifying influential users.
- **Recommendation Systems**: By modeling users and items as nodes, GNNs enhance personalized recommendations through better understanding user-item interactions.
- **Knowledge Graphs**: In knowledge graphs, GNNs capture complex relationships between entities, improving tasks like entity recognition and link prediction.

- **Molecular Chemistry**: GNNs predict molecular properties by modeling atoms as nodes and bonds as edges, aiding in drug discovery and material science.
- **Traffic Prediction**: In traffic networks, GNNs analyze and predict traffic flow by considering road intersections as nodes and routes as edges.

The versatility and power of Graph Neural Networks continue to expand as research in this domain evolves. GNNs provide a robust framework for leveraging the rich relational structure inherent in graph data, unlocking new insights and capabilities across various fields.

6.12 Case Studies of Advanced Neural Networks in Real-world Applications

The practical application of advanced neural network architectures extends beyond theoretical constructs and academic exercises into impactful real-world scenarios. In this section, we explore various case studies illustrating the deployment of state-of-the-art neural networks in diverse fields, emphasizing the direct benefits and innovative solutions they bring.

Medical Imaging and Diagnosis with Convolutional Neural Networks (CNNs)

Medical imaging presents a critical area wherein convolutional neural networks (CNNs) have demonstrated exceptional efficacy. Leveraging the hierarchical structure of CNNs, models trained on large-scale, annotated datasets can achieve remarkable diagnostic accuracy, often surpassing human experts.

In a pioneering study, a deep CNN was utilized to detect diabetic retinopathy in retinal images. The dataset comprised tens of thousands of annotated retinal images, labeled for varying severity of the condition. The CNN architecture was designed with multiple convolutional layers, pooling layers, and fully connected layers culminating in a softmax output layer for classification.

```
import keras
from keras.models import Sequential
from keras.layers import Conv2D, MaxPooling2D, Dense, Flatten, Dropout

model = Sequential()
```

```
model.add(Conv2D(32, kernel_size=(3, 3), activation='relu', input_shape=(256, 256,
    3)))
model.add(MaxPooling2D(pool_size=(2, 2)))
model.add(Conv2D(64, kernel_size=(3, 3), activation='relu'))
model.add(MaxPooling2D(pool_size=(2, 2)))
model.add(Conv2D(128, kernel_size=(3, 3), activation='relu'))
model.add(MaxPooling2D(pool_size=(2, 2)))
model.add(Flatten())
model.add(Dense(128, activation='relu'))
model.add(Dropout(0.5))
model.add(Dense(5, activation='softmax'))

model.compile(optimizer='adam', loss='categorical_crossentropy', metrics=['accuracy'])

model.fit(training_data, training_labels, validation_data=(validation_data,
    validation_labels), epochs=10)
```

The trained model achieved significant accuracy, enabling timely diagnosis and management of diabetic retinopathy, illustrating CNN's potential in medical diagnostics.

Natural Language Processing with Transformer Networks

Transformers have revolutionized natural language processing (NLP) through their attention mechanisms, enabling efficient handling of long-range dependencies in text. The BERT (Bidirectional Encoder Representations from Transformers) model exemplifies this innovation's impact.

In a comprehensive case study, BERT was fine-tuned for sentiment analysis on the IMDB movie review dataset. The architecture consists of bidirectional transformers pre-trained on a vast corpus of text, with fine-tuning performed using labeled sentiment data. The model's attention layers enable it to grasp nuanced contextual relationships within text sequences.

```
from transformers import BertTokenizer, BertForSequenceClassification, Trainer,
    TrainingArguments

tokenizer = BertTokenizer.from_pretrained('bert-base-uncased')
model = BertForSequenceClassification.from_pretrained('bert-base-uncased')

train_encodings = tokenizer(train_texts, truncation=True, padding=True)
val_encodings = tokenizer(val_texts, truncation=True, padding=True)

train_dataset = tf.data.Dataset.from_tensor_slices((train_encodings['input_ids'],
    train_labels))
val_dataset = tf.data.Dataset.from_tensor_slices((val_encodings['input_ids'],
    val_labels))

training_args = TrainingArguments(
    output_dir='./results',
    num_train_epochs=3,
    per_device_train_batch_size=16,
    per_device_eval_batch_size=64,
    warmup_steps=500,
```

```
    weight_decay=0.01,
    logging_dir='./logs',
)

trainer = Trainer(
    model=model,
    args=training_args,
    train_dataset=train_dataset,
    eval_dataset=val_dataset
)

trainer.train()
```

Upon evaluation, the fine-tuned model exhibited a high degree of accuracy in classifying reviews as positive or negative. Such implementations underscore Transformer-based models' prowess in enhancing NLP applications.

Generative Adversarial Networks (GANs) in Image Synthesis

Generative Adversarial Networks (GANs) have redefined image synthesis, enabling the creation of high-fidelity synthetic images that are virtually indistinguishable from real images. The architecture comprises a generator and a discriminator in a min-max game, progressively refining the generator's output quality.

An illustrative example is GANs used for generating high-resolution human faces. The training involves a dataset of real human face images, with the generator learning to create realistic images and the discriminator distinguishing real from fake. The Progressive Growing of GANs (ProGAN) methodology resulted in highly detailed images.

```
import torch
import torch.nn as nn

class Generator(nn.Module):
    def __init__(self):
        super(Generator, self).__init__()
        self.main = nn.Sequential(
            nn.ConvTranspose2d(100, 512, 4, 1, 0, bias=False),
            nn.BatchNorm2d(512),
            nn.ReLU(True),
            nn.ConvTranspose2d(512, 256, 4, 2, 1, bias=False),
            nn.BatchNorm2d(256),
            nn.ReLU(True),
            nn.ConvTranspose2d(256, 128, 4, 2, 1, bias=False),
            nn.BatchNorm2d(128),
            nn.ReLU(True),
            nn.ConvTranspose2d(128, 64, 4, 2, 1, bias=False),
            nn.BatchNorm2d(64),
            nn.ReLU(True),
            nn.ConvTranspose2d(64, 3, 4, 2, 1, bias=False),
            nn.Tanh()
        )

    def forward(self, input):
```

```
        return self.main(input)

class Discriminator(nn.Module):
    def __init__(self):
        super(Discriminator, self).__init__()
        self.main = nn.Sequential(
            nn.Conv2d(3, 64, 4, 2, 1, bias=False),
            nn.LeakyReLU(0.2, inplace=True),
            nn.Conv2d(64, 128, 4, 2, 1, bias=False),
            nn.BatchNorm2d(128),
            nn.LeakyReLU(0.2, inplace=True),
            nn.Conv2d(128, 256, 4, 2, 1, bias=False),
            nn.BatchNorm2d(256),
            nn.LeakyReLU(0.2, inplace=True),
            nn.Conv2d(256, 512, 4, 2, 1, bias=False),
            nn.BatchNorm2d(512),
            nn.LeakyReLU(0.2, inplace=True),
            nn.Conv2d(512, 1, 4, 1, 0, bias=False),
            nn.Sigmoid()
        )

    def forward(self, input):
        return self.main(input)

# Training loop

# Initialize models, optimizers, loss function etc

for epoch in range(num_epochs):
    for i, data in enumerate(dataloader, 0):
        # Update Discriminator
        # Update Generator
        pass
```

The synthetic images generated by the ProGAN model demonstrated superior resolution and realism, showcasing the unprecedented creative potential of GAN-based architectures.

These case studies not only highlight the versatility and power of advanced neural networks across various domains but also provide concrete examples underlining the applicability of sophisticated architectures such as CNNs, Transformers, and GANs in solving real-world problems.

Chapter 7

Training Neural Networks

This chapter focuses on the methodologies for training neural networks, encompassing the training loop, optimizer selection, and learning rate scheduling. It addresses issues of overfitting and underfitting, and introduces techniques to mitigate them, such as batch normalization and regularization. Gradient descent variants, performance monitoring, and strategies for handling imbalanced datasets are also discussed. Advanced topics include distributing training across multiple GPUs and debugging training-related issues.

7.1 Introduction to Training Neural Networks

Training neural networks involves a series of meticulously designed steps aimed at minimizing the error between predicted outputs and actual targets. This process is rooted in optimizing the neural network parameters - often referred to as weights and biases - using algorithms that adjust these parameters iteratively based on the gradients of a defined loss function. Understanding this fundamental mechanism is critical for effectively developing and deploying neural networks.

The training process begins with the initialization of the network parameters. This step is important as the initial values can significantly influence the training dynamics. Common initialization techniques include Xavier initialization and He initialization, which are designed to prevent issues related to vanishing or exploding gradients.

Once the parameters are initialized, the heart of the training process - the training loop - commences. This loop consists of three core components: the forward pass, the backward pass, and the parameter update step. During the forward pass, inputs are propagated through the network layers, processed by the activation functions, and finally, the predictions are produced. The predictions are then compared to the true labels using a loss function, which quantifies the error in the predictions.

Key loss functions include Mean Squared Error (MSE), Cross-Entropy Loss, and Hinge Loss, depending on the nature of the problem (regression, classification, etc.). For instance, in a binary classification problem, the Binary Cross-Entropy loss is often used, which is defined as follows:

$$L(y, \hat{y}) = -\frac{1}{N} \sum_{i=1}^{N} [y_i \log(\hat{y}_i) + (1 - y_i) \log(1 - \hat{y}_i)]$$

where y is the true label, $\hat{y}$ is the predicted probability, and N is the number of samples.

Following the forward pass, the backward pass involves calculating the gradients of the loss function with respect to each parameter using the chain rule of calculus, a process known as backpropagation. The gradients indicate the direction and rate of change of the loss function with respect to each parameter.

Next, an optimization algorithm, such as Stochastic Gradient Descent (SGD) or Adam, updates the network parameters in the opposite direction of the gradients to minimize the loss function. The general update rule for a parameter θ at the t-th step using gradient descent can be expressed as:

$$\theta_t = \theta_{t-1} - \eta \nabla_\theta L(\theta)$$

where η is the learning rate, and $\nabla_\theta L(\theta)$ is the gradient of the loss function with respect to the parameter θ.

The learning rate η is a crucial hyperparameter and determines the step size during each iteration of the parameter update. Poor choice of learning rate can lead to suboptimal training – too high a learning rate may result in overshooting the minima, while too low a learning rate may cause slow convergence.

Training progresses iteratively, cycling through the entire dataset multiple times, a process referred to as epochs. Within each epoch, the dataset is typically divided into mini-batches, allowing for computational efficiency and faster convergence. This process is known as mini-batch gradient descent, and it provides a good compromise between the robustness of stochastic gradient descent and the stability of batch gradient descent.

Monitoring tools, such as validation loss and metrics, are used to assess the network's generalization capability to new data. This helps to avoid overfitting, which occurs when the network learns the training data too well, including its noise, but fails to perform well on unseen data. Techniques like early stopping, where training is halted once the performance on a validation set starts to degrade, are employed to mitigate such issues.

Regularization methods, including L2 regularization (weight decay) and dropout, are also introduced to enhance model generalization by adding a penalty to the loss function or randomly omitting units during training, respectively.

The entire process of training a neural network, from initialization to optimization, is a blend of mathematical rigor and practical engineering. Careful tuning of hyperparameters, selection of appropriate loss functions, and utilization of regularization techniques collaboratively ensure effective training and robust models.

```
from keras.models import Sequential
from keras.layers import Dense
from keras.optimizers import SGD

# Initialize the neural network
model = Sequential()

# Adding layers to the network
model.add(Dense(units=64, activation='relu', input_dim=100))
model.add(Dense(units=10, activation='softmax'))

# Compile the model with optimizer and loss function
model.compile(loss='categorical_crossentropy',
              optimizer=SGD(learning_rate=0.01),
              metrics=['accuracy'])

# Summary of the model
model.summary()

# Fitting the model
model.fit(x_train, y_train, epochs=10, batch_size=32, validation_data=(x_val, y_val
    ))
```

```
# Sample output
Epoch 1/10
...
Train on 1000 samples, validate on 200 samples
1000/1000 [==============================] - 0s - loss: 0.6000 - accuracy: 0.8500 - val_loss: 0.5000 - val_accuracy: 0.8700
...
Epoch 10/10
1000/1000 [==============================] - 0s - loss: 0.2100 - accuracy: 0.9300 - val_loss: 0.3100 - val_accuracy: 0.9000
```

This comprehensive understanding of the training process lays a solid foundation for exploring more advanced topics in the subsequent sections. As the journey through training neural networks continues, concepts such as optimizer selection, learning rate scheduling, and techniques for handling specific training challenges will be elaborated upon, enhancing the depth of understanding and practical proficiency.

7.2 The Training Loop: Forward and Backward Pass

The training loop is the core mechanism through which a neural network learns from data. It involves two main stages: the forward pass and the backward pass. These stages are iterated over the dataset for a specified number of epochs or until convergence criteria are met.

During the forward pass, the input data is passed through the network layer by layer until the final output is produced. Each layer applies an affine transformation (linear combination of weights and inputs), optionally followed by a non-linear activation function. The output of one layer becomes the input to the next, propagating the signal forward through the network. The goal of the forward pass is to compute the predicted outputs for a given input.

To illustrate the forward pass, consider a simple neural network with an input layer, one hidden layer, and an output layer. Let $\mathbf{x}$ be the input vector, $\mathbf{W}_1$ and $\mathbf{W}_2$ be the weight matrices for the hidden and output layers respectively, $\mathbf{b}_1$ and $\mathbf{b}_2$ be the bias vectors, and ϕ be the activation function:

$$\mathbf{h} = \phi(\mathbf{W}_1\mathbf{x} + \mathbf{b}_1)$$

$$\mathbf{y} = \mathbf{W}_2\mathbf{h} + \mathbf{b}_2$$

Here, $\mathbf{h}$ represents the hidden layer output, and $\mathbf{y}$ represents the final output of the network. The activation function ϕ, commonly chosen as ReLU (Rectified Linear Unit), Sigmoid, or Tanh, introduces non-linearity, allowing the network to learn complex representations.

Once the forward pass is complete and the predictions are obtained, the loss function $L(\mathbf{y}, \mathbf{y}_{\text{true}})$ evaluates the error between the predicted outputs $\mathbf{y}$ and the true labels $\mathbf{y}_{\text{true}}$. Popular loss functions include Mean Squared Error (MSE) for regression tasks and Cross-Entropy Loss for classification tasks.

The backward pass, also known as backpropagation, computes the gradients of the loss function with respect to the network weights. These gradients indicate the direction and magnitude of change needed in the weights to reduce the loss. The backward pass leverages the chain rule of calculus to propagate the gradients from the output layer back to the input layer.

To see this in action, we compute the gradient of the loss L with respect to the weights $\mathbf{W}_2$ and $\mathbf{W}_1$:

$$\frac{\partial L}{\partial \mathbf{W}_2} = \frac{\partial L}{\partial \mathbf{y}} \cdot \frac{\partial \mathbf{y}}{\partial \mathbf{W}_2}$$

$$\frac{\partial \mathbf{y}}{\partial \mathbf{W}_2} = \mathbf{h}$$

$$\frac{\partial L}{\partial \mathbf{W}_2} = \frac{\partial L}{\partial \mathbf{y}} \cdot \mathbf{h}^\top$$

$$\frac{\partial L}{\partial \mathbf{W}_1} = \left(\frac{\partial L}{\partial \mathbf{y}} \cdot \mathbf{W}_2^\top \cdot \frac{\partial \mathbf{h}}{\partial \mathbf{z}_1}\right) \cdot \mathbf{x}^\top$$

Where $\mathbf{z}_1 = \mathbf{W}_1\mathbf{x} + \mathbf{b}_1$ and $\frac{\partial \mathbf{h}}{\partial \mathbf{z}_1}$ is the gradient of the activation function.

Keras, a high-level neural network API, simplifies the process of defining and training neural networks. The forward and backward passes are abstracted away, allowing practitioners to focus on model architecture and hyperparameter tuning.

Below is an example training loop using Keras:

```
import numpy as np
import keras
from keras.models import Sequential
from keras.layers import Dense

# Generate dummy dataset
x_train = np.random.random((1000, 20))
y_train = keras.utils.to_categorical(np.random.randint(10, size=(1000, 1)),
        num_classes=10)

# Define the model
```

```
model = Sequential()
model.add(Dense(64, activation='relu', input_dim=20))
model.add(Dense(10, activation='softmax'))

# Compile the model
model.compile(loss='categorical_crossentropy',
              optimizer='sgd',
              metrics=['accuracy'])

# Train the model
model.fit(x_train, y_train, epochs=10, batch_size=32)
```

Here, the training loop is implicitly handled by the fit method. The forward pass involves computing predictions, and the backward pass calculates gradients and updates weights using the chosen optimizer, in this case, stochastic gradient descent (SGD).

A key aspect to ensure efficient training is to monitor and debug the training process. Observing the loss and accuracy metrics across epochs provides insights into the model's learning progress and potential issues. When training plateaus or diverges, it might indicate problems such as inappropriate learning rates, insufficient model capacity, or data-related issues requiring investigation.

To exemplify a forward and backward pass without Keras abstraction, consider the following:

```
import numpy as np

# Initialize weights
W1 = np.random.rand(20, 64)
b1 = np.random.rand(64)
W2 = np.random.rand(64, 10)
b2 = np.random.rand(10)

# Define the ReLU activation function
def relu(x):
    return np.maximum(0, x)

# Forward pass
def forward_pass(x):
    z1 = np.dot(x, W1) + b1
    h = relu(z1)
    z2 = np.dot(h, W2) + b2
    y = softmax(z2)
    return y, h, z1

# Backward pass
def backward_pass(x, y_true, y_pred, h, z1):
    global W1, W2, b1, b2
    dz2 = y_pred - y_true
    dW2 = np.dot(h.T, dz2)
    db2 = np.sum(dz2, axis=0)
    dh = np.dot(dz2, W2.T)
    dz1 = dh * (z1 > 0)
    dW1 = np.dot(x.T, dz1)
    db1 = np.sum(dz1, axis=0)
```

```
    # Update weights
    W1 -= learning_rate * dW1
    W2 -= learning_rate * dW2
    b1 -= learning_rate * db1
    b2 -= learning_rate * db2

# Training loop
for epoch in range(epochs):
    for i in range(len(x_train)):
        y_pred, h, z1 = forward_pass(x_train[i])
        backward_pass(x_train[i], y_train[i], y_pred, h, z1)
```

In this example, the forward and backward passes are explicitly defined, demonstrating manual gradient computation and weight update processes.

Understanding these mechanics ensures that one can customize and optimize the training process, crucial for advanced neural network development and deployment.

7.3 Choosing the Right Optimizer

Selecting an appropriate optimizer is a critical step in training neural networks effectively. Optimizers are algorithms or methods used to update the weights of the network model to minimize the loss function. The choice of optimizer significantly affects the speed and quality of the training process. This section will delve into the characteristics, functionalities, and application scenarios of commonly used optimizers: Stochastic Gradient Descent (SGD), Momentum, Nesterov Accelerated Gradient (NAG), Adagrad, Adadelta, RMSprop, and Adam.

Stochastic Gradient Descent (SGD) is a fundamental optimization algorithm. It updates the weights using the gradient of the loss function concerning the weights. The update rule for SGD is given by:

$$\theta_{t+1} = \theta_t - \eta \nabla_\theta J(\theta_t)$$

Here, θ_t represents the model parameters at iteration t, η is the learning rate, and $\nabla_\theta J(\theta_t)$ is the gradient of the loss function J at θ_t. Despite the simplicity of SGD, it can converge slowly and may get stuck in local minima or saddle points.

To address the limitations of vanilla SGD, **Momentum** is introduced. Momentum helps accelerate gradients vectors in the right directions, leading to faster converging. The update rule for momentum-based SGD is:

$$v_{t+1} = \gamma v_t + \eta \nabla_\theta J(\theta_t)$$
$$\theta_{t+1} = \theta_t - v_{t+1}$$

In these equations, v_t denotes the velocity vector and γ is the momentum term, typically set to a value such as 0.9. Momentum effectively dampens oscillations.

An extension to Momentum is the **Nesterov Accelerated Gradient (NAG)**, which anticipates the future position of the parameters to calculate the gradient more accurately. The update rule for NAG is:

$$v_{t+1} = \gamma v_t + \eta \nabla_\theta J(\theta_t - \gamma v_t)$$
$$\theta_{t+1} = \theta_t - v_{t+1}$$

NAG provides a more responsive update, reducing the risk of being misguided by the current momentum alone.

Adagrad adapts the learning rate to the parameters, performing smaller updates (i.e., using lower learning rates) for parameters associated with frequently occurring features, and larger updates for parameters associated with infrequent features. Its update rule is expressed as:

$$\theta_{t+1} = \theta_t - \frac{\eta}{\sqrt{G_{t,t} + \epsilon}} \nabla_\theta J(\theta_t)$$

Where $G_{t,t}$ is a diagonal matrix where each diagonal element i, i is the sum of the squares of the gradients w.r.t. θ_i up to time step t, and ϵ is a small smoothing term to prevent division by zero.

Adadelta is an extension of Adagrad that aims to reduce its aggressive, monotonically decreasing learning rate. The update rule for Adadelta is:

$$E[g^2]_t = \rho E[g^2]_{t-1} + (1-\rho) g_t^2$$
$$\Delta\theta_t = -\frac{\sqrt{E[\Delta\theta^2]_{t-1} + \epsilon}}{\sqrt{E[g^2]_t + \epsilon}} g_t$$
$$E[\Delta\theta^2]_t = \rho E[\Delta\theta^2]_{t-1} + (1-\rho)(\Delta\theta_t)^2$$

Where $E[g^2]_t$ and $E[\Delta\theta^2]_t$ are moving averages of the squared gradient and squared parameter updates, respectively.

RMSprop also aims to resolve the diminishing learning rates of Adagrad. The RMSprop update rule is:

$$E[g^2]_t = \rho E[g^2]_{t-1} + (1-\rho)g_t^2$$
$$\theta_{t+1} = \theta_t - \frac{\eta}{\sqrt{E[g^2]_t + \epsilon}} g_t$$

RMSprop maintains a moving average of the squared gradients, with ρ typically set to 0.9.

The **Adam** (Adaptive Moment Estimation) optimizer combines the advantages of both RMSprop and Momentum. It maintains two moving averages of the gradient: the mean and the uncentered variance. The update rules for Adam are:

$$m_t = \beta_1 m_{t-1} + (1-\beta_1)g_t$$
$$v_t = \beta_2 v_{t-1} + (1-\beta_2)g_t^2$$
$$\hat{m}_t = \frac{m_t}{1-\beta_1^t}$$
$$\hat{v}_t = \frac{v_t}{1-\beta_2^t}$$
$$\theta_{t+1} = \theta_t - \frac{\eta \hat{m}_t}{\sqrt{\hat{v}_t} + \epsilon}$$

Here, m_t and v_t are the first moment (mean) and the second moment (uncentered variance), respectively, while $\hat{m}_t$ and $\hat{v}_t$ are their bias-corrected estimates.

The choice between these optimizers often depends on the specific problem and neural network architecture. SGD is useful for large-scale and sparse data, while Momentum and NAG are preferred for faster convergence when facing steep and narrow ravines on the loss surface. Adagrad is beneficial for dealing with sparse data and feature engineering, whereas RMSprop and Adam are favored for their adaptive learning rates and overall robustness in handling different types of data and models.

Choosing the right optimizer involves understanding these nuances and experimenting to see which algorithm works best for your specific use case. Here is an example of how to implement these optimizers in Keras:

```
from keras.optimizers import SGD, Adam, RMSprop

# Define the model
model = Sequential()
model.add(Dense(units=64, activation='relu', input_dim=100))
model.add(Dense(units=10, activation='softmax'))

# Different optimizer configurations
sgd = SGD(learning_rate=0.01, momentum=0.9)
adam = Adam(learning_rate=0.001)
rmsprop = RMSprop(learning_rate=0.001)

# Compile the model with different optimizers
model.compile(optimizer=sgd, loss='categorical_crossentropy', metrics=['accuracy'])
model.compile(optimizer=adam, loss='categorical_crossentropy', metrics=['accuracy'])
model.compile(optimizer=rmsprop, loss='categorical_crossentropy', metrics=['accuracy'
    ])

# Train the model
model.fit(x_train, y_train, epochs=10, batch_size=32)
```

The outputs from such training processes can typically be logged as follows:

```
Epoch 1/10
1875/1875 [==============================] - 5s 2ms/step - loss: 0.6724 - accuracy: 0.8123
Epoch 2/10
1875/1875 [==============================] - 3s 2ms/step - loss: 0.2126 - accuracy: 0.9373
...
```

This will provide a continuous insight into the optimizer's performance, convergence speed, and how well it's helping the network to generalize on the training data.

7.4 Learning Rate Schedulers

Learning rate schedulers play a crucial role in the training of neural networks, functioning as mechanisms to adaptively adjust the learning rate during the training process. The learning rate (η) is a hyperparameter that significantly impacts the convergence and performance of the training algorithm. A poorly chosen fixed learning rate can lead to suboptimal convergence behavior. Hence, learning rate schedulers are employed to dynamically modify the learning rate, ensuring efficient and stable convergence.

Several strategies are available for scheduling the learning rate, each with its own advantages and use cases. Here, we delve into the most prominent types of learning rate schedulers: step decay, exponential decay, and adaptive learning rates.

Step Decay

Step decay involves reducing the learning rate by a constant factor after a predefined number of epochs. This method allows the network to train rapidly at the beginning with a relatively high learning rate and fine-tune the weights with a smaller learning rate towards the end of training. The learning rate η_t at epoch t can be defined as:

$$\eta_t = \eta_0 \times \text{drop}^{\left\lfloor \frac{t}{\text{epochs\_drop}} \right\rfloor}$$

where:

- η_0 is the initial learning rate.
- drop is the factor by which the learning rate is reduced (e.g., 0.5).
- epochs_drop is the frequency (in epochs) with which the learning rate is reduced.

For example, if $\eta_0 = 0.1$, drop $= 0.5$, and epochs_drop $= 10$, the learning rate would be halved every 10 epochs.

Exponential Decay

Exponential decay decreases the learning rate exponentially over epochs. This method is smooth compared to step decay and continuously reduces the learning rate, which can be beneficial for a stable convergence. The learning rate η_t at epoch t is governed by:

$$\eta_t = \eta_0 \times e^{-\text{decay\_rate} \times t}$$

where:

- η_0 is the initial learning rate.
- decay_rate is the rate at which the learning rate decays over epochs.

If $\eta_0 = 0.1$ and decay_rate $= 0.01$, the learning rate would exponentially decrease according to the specified decay rate.

Adaptive Learning Rates

Adaptive learning rate schedulers adjust the learning rate based on the performance of the model on the validation dataset. The most common adaptive learning rate techniques include ReduceLROnPlateau and LearningRateScheduler in Keras.

- **ReduceLROnPlateau:** This scheduler reduces the learning rate when a monitored metric (e.g., validation loss) stops improving. It dynamically adapts the learning rate to fluctuate across training epochs, aiming to achieve a balance between rapid training and precise convergence. An example usage is:

```
from keras.callbacks import ReduceLROnPlateau

reduce_lr = ReduceLROnPlateau(monitor='val_loss', factor=0.2,
                              patience=5, min_lr=0.001)
model.fit(X_train, y_train, epochs=50, validation_data=(X_val, y_val),
          callbacks=[reduce_lr])
```

- **LearningRateScheduler:** This scheduler allows for custom learning rate adjustments via a user-defined function that specifies the learning rate for each epoch. It provides robust control over the learning rate schedule. Here is an example:

```
from keras.callbacks import LearningRateScheduler

def scheduler(epoch, lr):
    if epoch < 10:
        return lr
    else:
        return lr * tf.math.exp(-0.1)

lr_scheduler = LearningRateScheduler(scheduler)
model.fit(X_train, y_train, epochs=50, validation_data=(X_val, y_val),
          callbacks=[lr_scheduler])
```

Utilizing appropriate learning rate schedulers can profoundly impact the efficiency and effectiveness of training neural networks. Choosing the right scheduler requires consideration of the specific problem, neural network architecture, and empirical performance across different training scenarios.

The integration of learning rate schedulers into the training process ensures adaptive control over the learning rate, promoting optimal convergence and improved model performance. By carefully selecting and configuring these schedulers, we can address the challenges posed by fixed learning rates and achieve superior training outcomes.

7.5 Understanding Overfitting and Underfitting

The phenomena of overfitting and underfitting are indicative of a model's performance relative to the data it has been exposed to during training and its ability to generalize to new, unseen data. Overfitting occurs when the model learns not only the underlying patterns in the training data but also the noise and outliers, leading to high performance on training data but poor generalization to new data. Underfitting, conversely, is when the model is too simplistic to capture the underlying patterns in the data, resulting in poor performance on both the training and new data.

Overfitting Overfitting arises when a model is excessively complex, characterized by having too many parameters relative to the number of observations. The model becomes highly specific to the training data, capturing noise and fluctuations that do not generalize to other datasets. This can be visualized by fitting a high-degree polynomial to a relatively small number of data points, where the model produces extreme outputs at new data points.

A model exhibiting overfitting typically shows:

- High accuracy on training data.
- Significant gap between training and validation/test accuracy.
- High variance in model performance.

The following code snippet demonstrates how overfitting can be detected during the training process by monitoring the performance metrics:

```
import matplotlib.pyplot as plt

history = model.fit(X_train, y_train, validation_data=(X_val, y_val), epochs=50)

plt.plot(history.history['loss'], label='Training Loss')
plt.plot(history.history['val_loss'], label='Validation Loss')
plt.legend()
plt.title('Training vs Validation Loss')
plt.show()
```

```
Epoch 1/50
loss: 0.2102 - val_loss: 0.6901
...
Epoch 50/50
loss: 0.0102 - val_loss: 0.8102
```

In the above output, an increasing validation loss coupled with a decreasing training loss is a clear indicator of overfitting.

Underfitting Underfitting occurs when a model is too simplistic, making incorrect or simplistic assumptions about the data. This leads to poor performance in both training and validation datasets. Linear regression models applied to non-linear data are typical examples of underfitting.

A model that underfits typically shows:

- Low accuracy on training data and validation data.
- Small gap between training and validation/test accuracy, both being similarly poor.
- High bias in predictions, failing to capture the underlying trends.

Consider this example where underfitting can be detected:

```
history = model.fit(X_train, y_train, validation_data=(X_val, y_val), epochs=50)

plt.plot(history.history['loss'], label='Training Loss')
plt.plot(history.history['val_loss'], label='Validation Loss')
plt.legend()
plt.title('Training vs Validation Loss')
plt.show()
```

```
Epoch 1/50
loss: 0.5902 - val_loss: 0.6201
...
Epoch 50/50
loss: 0.4002 - val_loss: 0.4102
```

Such outputs indicate that the model is not learning sufficiently complex patterns in the data.

Balancing Model Complexity To address overfitting and underfitting, it is crucial to choose a model of appropriate complexity. Techniques such as cross-validation can help in selecting a model that generalizes well. It involves splitting the data into training and validation sets multiple times and ensuring the model performs consistently well across all splits.

Diagnosing Overfitting and Underfitting with Learning Curves Learning curves plot the performance metric (e.g., accuracy or loss) against the number of training examples or epochs. These curves can provide insight into whether a model is overfitting or underfitting:

- In the case of **underfitting**, both training and validation loss will stagnate at a high value.
- For **overfitting**, the training loss decreases significantly while the validation loss stops decreasing and possibly starts increasing.

Code to plot such learning curves is as follows:

```
training_sizes = [1, 100, 500, 2000, 5000, 10000, len(X_train)]
train_scores = []
val_scores = []

for size in training_sizes:
    model.fit(X_train[:size], y_train[:size])
    train_scores.append(model.score(X_train[:size], y_train[:size]))
    val_scores.append(model.score(X_val, y_val))

plt.plot(training_sizes, train_scores, label='Training Score')
plt.plot(training_sizes, val_scores, label='Validation Score')
plt.legend()
plt.title('Learning Curves')
plt.xlabel('Training Set Size')
plt.ylabel('Score')
plt.show()
```

This approach helps in visually diagnosing how the model performance evolves with the amount of training data.

Techniques to Mitigate Overfitting Several methods can help reduce overfitting:

- **Regularization:** Techniques such as L1 and L2 regularization add a penalty to the loss function for large weights.
- **Dropout:** Randomly drop neurons during training to prevent co-adaptation.
- **Data Augmentation:** Enlarge the training set using transformations like rotations, translations, etc.
- **Early Stopping:** Halt training when the validation performance ceases to improve.

Techniques to Combat Underfitting Addressing underfitting involves:

- **Model Complexity:** Use a more complex model capable of capturing intricate patterns.
- **Feature Engineering:** Include more relevant features for the model to learn from.
- **Reduce Regularization:** Simplify penalization to allow the model more flexibility.
- **Longer Training Duration:** Provide more epochs for the model to learn the data.

Correctly diagnosing and addressing overfitting and underfitting is essential for building robust, generalizable models. Detailed exploration and application of the described concepts will provide deeper insights and proficiency in deep learning model training.

7.6 Techniques to Prevent Overfitting

Overfitting occurs when a neural network models the noise in the training data instead of the underlying data distribution, resulting in poor performance on unseen data. To prevent overfitting, several techniques can be utilized effectively within the Keras framework.

Data Augmentation is a powerful technique to artificially expand the training dataset by applying random transformations, such as rotations, translations, flips, and zooms. This approach increases the diversity of the training set and enables the model to generalize better to new data.

Considering an image classification task, the ImageDataGenerator class in Keras can be employed as follows:

```
from tensorflow.keras.preprocessing.image import ImageDataGenerator

datagen = ImageDataGenerator(
    rotation_range=40,
    width_shift_range=0.2,
    height_shift_range=0.2,
    shear_range=0.2,
    zoom_range=0.2,
    horizontal_flip=True,
    fill_mode='nearest')

# Assume 'train_images' is a numpy array of images
datagen.fit(train_images)
```

Early Stopping is another effective strategy to prevent overfitting by monitoring the model's performance on a validation dataset during training. Training stops once the performance on the validation set starts to deteriorate. Keras provides the `EarlyStopping` callback to achieve this:

```
from tensorflow.keras.callbacks import EarlyStopping

early_stopping = EarlyStopping(monitor='val_loss', patience=10,
    restore_best_weights=True)
history = model.fit(train_images, train_labels, epochs=100, validation_data=(
    val_images, val_labels), callbacks=[early_stopping])
```

Regularization Techniques, such as L1 and L2 regularization, add a penalty to the loss function based on the magnitude of the model parameters, thus discouraging the network from fitting the noise in the training data. L2 regularization or weight decay is commonly used in practice. In Keras, this can be implemented by setting the `kernel_regularizer` parameter in layer constructors:

```
from tensorflow.keras.regularizers import l2

model = Sequential()
model.add(Dense(64, kernel_regularizer=l2(0.01), activation='relu', input_shape=(
    input_dim,)))
model.add(Dense(64, kernel_regularizer=l2(0.01), activation='relu'))
model.add(Dense(num_classes, activation='softmax'))
```

In some scenarios, it may be beneficial to combine L1 and L2 regularization (L1/L2 regularization), which can be done using `l1_l2`:

```
from tensorflow.keras.regularizers import l1_l2

model = Sequential()
model.add(Dense(64, kernel_regularizer=l1_l2(l1=0.01, l2=0.01), activation='relu',
    input_shape=(input_dim,)))
model.add(Dense(64, kernel_regularizer=l1_l2(l1=0.01, l2=0.01), activation='relu'))
model.add(Dense(num_classes, activation='softmax'))
```

Dropout introduces randomness into the network by randomly setting a fraction of input units to zero at each update during training time. This forces the model to learn more robust features that are not reliant on specific neurons. Keras supports dropout via the `Dropout` layer:

```
from tensorflow.keras.layers import Dropout

model = Sequential()
model.add(Dense(64, activation='relu', input_shape=(input_dim,)))
model.add(Dropout(0.5))
model.add(Dense(64, activation='relu'))
model.add(Dropout(0.5))
model.add(Dense(num_classes, activation='softmax'))
```

Batch Normalization normalizes the inputs of each layer, ensuring they have a mean of zero and a standard deviation of one. This improves training speed and stability by reducing internal covariate shift. Implementing batch normalization in Keras is straightforward using the BatchNormalization layer:

```
from tensorflow.keras.layers import BatchNormalization

model = Sequential()
model.add(Dense(64, activation='relu', input_shape=(input_dim,)))
model.add(BatchNormalization())
model.add(Dense(64, activation='relu'))
model.add(BatchNormalization())
model.add(Dense(num_classes, activation='softmax'))
```

Employ these techniques judiciously based on the specific requirements of the task at hand to minimize overfitting and improve the model's generalization capabilities.

7.7 Batch Normalization and Layer Normalization

Batch Normalization and Layer Normalization are two techniques designed to improve the training and performance of neural networks by addressing the issue of internal covariate shift. Internal covariate shift refers to the phenomenon where the distribution of each layer's inputs changes during training, which can slow down the training process and make it harder to train deep networks. Here, we will delve into the fundamentals, mechanics, and practical applications of both normalization methods.

Batch Normalization

Batch Normalization was introduced by Sergey Ioffe and Christian Szegedy in 2015. It normalizes the inputs of each layer by adjusting and scaling the activations. The process can be mathematically described as follows:

Given a mini-batch **B** $= \{x_1, x_2, \ldots, x_m\}$ of m samples, for each feature j in the layer, calculate the mean $\mu_B^{(j)}$ and variance $\sigma_B^{(j)}$:

$$\mu_B^{(j)} = \frac{1}{m} \sum_{i=1}^{m} x_i^{(j)}$$

$$\sigma_B^{(j)} = \sqrt{\frac{1}{m}\sum_{i=1}^{m}(x_i^{(j)} - \mu_B^{(j)})^2 + \epsilon}$$

Here, ϵ is a small constant added to avoid division by zero.

Next, normalize each activation $x_i^{(j)}$:

$$\hat{x}_i^{(j)} = \frac{x_i^{(j)} - \mu_B^{(j)}}{\sigma_B^{(j)}}$$

The normalized activations are then scaled and shifted using learnable parameters $\gamma^{(j)}$ and $\beta^{(j)}$:

$$y_i^{(j)} = \gamma^{(j)}\hat{x}_i^{(j)} + \beta^{(j)}$$

The parameters γ and β are learned during training, allowing the model to maintain the capacity to represent the data distribution and ensuring that the normalized values can be transformed back to their original scales if necessary.

```
from keras.layers import BatchNormalization

# Assuming 'inputs' is the input tensor to a neural network layer
normalized_inputs = BatchNormalization()(inputs)
```

The advantages of Batch Normalization include:

- Reducing internal covariate shift.
- Allowing for higher learning rates.
- Providing some regularization effect, reducing the need for other regularization methods like dropout.

Layer Normalization

Layer Normalization, proposed by Jimmy Lei Ba, Jamie Ryan Kiros, and Geoffrey E. Hinton, differs from Batch Normalization by normalizing across the features instead of the batch dimension. This method can be particularly useful in Recurrent Neural Networks (RNNs) and other models where the use of Batch Normalization is challenging due to the varying sizes of input sequences.

In Layer Normalization, for a given input x_i for the layer, the mean and variance are computed as follows:

$$\mu_L = \frac{1}{H} \sum_{j=1}^{H} x_i^{(j)}$$

$$\sigma_L = \sqrt{\frac{1}{H} \sum_{j=1}^{H} (x_i^{(j)} - \mu_L)^2 + \epsilon}$$

Here, H is the number of features.

Each activation $x_i^{(j)}$ is then normalized:

$$\hat{x}_i^{(j)} = \frac{x_i^{(j)} - \mu_L}{\sigma_L}$$

Similar to Batch Normalization, these normalized activations are scaled and shifted by learnable parameters:

$$y_i^{(j)} = \gamma \hat{x}_i^{(j)} + \beta$$

```
from keras.layers import LayerNormalization

# Assuming 'inputs' is the input tensor to a neural network layer
normalized_inputs = LayerNormalization()(inputs)
```

The benefits of Layer Normalization include:

- Independence from batch size.
- Consistent performance across varied sequence lengths in RNNs.
- Simplified implementation since no statistics need to be computed across the batch.

Both Batch Normalization and Layer Normalization have their respective strengths and ideal application contexts. Batch Normalization is typically preferred for Convolutional Neural Networks (CNNs), whereas Layer Normalization is often more effective for sequence models such as RNNs. As such, the choice between these normalization techniques should consider the specific architecture and dataset characteristics.

```
# Example Outputs:

# For Batch Normalized layer:
Before normalization: Mean=0.23, Variance=1.40
After normalization: Mean=0.00, Variance=1.00

# For Layer Normalized layer:
Before normalization: Mean=0.30, Variance=1.20
After normalization: Mean=0.00, Variance=1.00
```

This approach leads to more robust and efficient training of deep learning models, enabling them to achieve better performance with faster convergence under various conditions.

7.8 Gradient Descent Variants: SGD, Adam, RMSprop

Gradient descent is a foundational optimization algorithm essential for training neural networks. It iteratively adjusts model parameters to minimize the loss function. Standard gradient descent updates parameters in the negative direction of the gradient, scaled by the learning rate. However, this basic form has limitations that can hinder efficient training. Various gradient descent variants have been developed to address these issues, with Stochastic Gradient Descent (SGD), Adaptive Moment Estimation (Adam), and Root Mean Square Propagation (RMSprop) being among the most prominent.

Stochastic Gradient Descent (SGD) differs from traditional batch gradient descent by updating parameters more frequently. Instead of computing gradients using the entire dataset, SGD estimates them using a random subset (mini-batch). This introduces a degree of stochasticity that often helps escape local minima, leading to faster convergence, especially for large datasets.

```
from keras.optimizers import SGD

model.compile(optimizer=SGD(lr=0.01),
              loss='categorical_crossentropy',
              metrics=['accuracy'])
```

Though effective, SGD alone may suffer from issues like slow convergence and oscillations around the minimum. Enhancements such as Momentum, Nesterov Accelerated Gradient (NAG), and others offer solutions. Momentum incorporates an exponentially decaying moving average of past gradients to smooth updates, reducing oscillations.

```
model.compile(optimizer=SGD(lr=0.01, momentum=0.9),
```

```
              loss='categorical_crossentropy',
              metrics=['accuracy'])
```

Nesterov Accelerated Gradient (NAG) improves on momentum by adjusting the parameters based on the projected future position rather than the current one. This lookahead approach often results in smoother and more predictive updates.

```
model.compile(optimizer=SGD(lr=0.01, momentum=0.9, nesterov=True),
              loss='categorical_crossentropy',
              metrics=['accuracy'])
```

Adam (Adaptive Moment Estimation) combines the advantages of two other extensions of stochastic gradient descent: AdaGrad and RMSprop. It computes adaptive learning rates for each parameter by storing both the first moment (mean) and second moment (uncentered variance) of past gradients. This allows Adam to converge rapidly on large and complex datasets with minimal parameter tuning.

```
from keras.optimizers import Adam

model.compile(optimizer=Adam(lr=0.001),
              loss='categorical_crossentropy',
              metrics=['accuracy'])
```

The effectiveness of Adam arises from its adaptive learning rate strategy, which adjusts the step size for each parameter independently. This can mitigate issues related to sparse gradients or noisy data, ensuring more consistent performance across different scenarios.

RMSprop (Root Mean Square Propagation) adapts the learning rate based on a moving average of squared gradients; this effectively simulates a form of momentum adapted to individual parameters. It is particularly helpful when dealing with non-stationary objectives, where the loss function changes during training. RMSprop is known for its ability to maintain a controlled and consistent learning rate.

```
from keras.optimizers import RMSprop

model.compile(optimizer=RMSprop(lr=0.001),
              loss='categorical_crossentropy',
              metrics=['accuracy'])
```

These gradient descent variants provide robust mechanisms for optimizing the neural network training process. The choice of optimizer can significantly impact the speed of convergence and the final model performance. Understanding the properties and appropriate contexts for each variant empowers practitioners to make informed decisions tailored to their specific applications.

7.9 Monitoring Training Performance

Effective monitoring during the training process is critical for the successful development of neural networks. Keeping track of various performance metrics enables the identification of issues, optimization of hyperparameters, and informed decision-making throughout the training cycle. Several techniques and tools facilitate comprehensive performance monitoring.

A foundational aspect of monitoring involves tracking the loss and accuracy metrics. These metrics are typically computed on both the training and validation datasets. The training loss indicates the model's performance on the training data, while the validation loss measures its generalization to unseen data. A well-suited approach for visualization is plotting these metrics as a function of epochs. A disparity between training and validation losses, where the training loss continually decreases while the validation loss starts to increase, suggests overfitting.

```
# Assuming history is the result of model.fit()
import matplotlib.pyplot as plt

plt.plot(history.history['loss'], label='Training Loss')
plt.plot(history.history['val_loss'], label='Validation Loss')
plt.xlabel('Epochs')
plt.ylabel('Loss')
plt.legend()
plt.show()
```

In addition to loss, accuracy plots provide insight into the model's ability to correctly classify samples. Monitoring training and validation accuracy over epochs, in a similar manner to loss, helps in diagnosing issues related to underfitting and overfitting.

```
# Plotting accuracy metrics
plt.plot(history.history['accuracy'], label='Training Accuracy')
plt.plot(history.history['val_accuracy'], label='Validation Accuracy')
plt.xlabel('Epochs')
plt.ylabel('Accuracy')
plt.legend()
plt.show()
```

Real-time monitoring is another powerful approach. Libraries such as TensorBoard and Keras' integrated callbacks make it possible to observe metrics during the training process without waiting for its completion. This is particularly useful for long training periods.

To use TensorBoard with Keras, first, initialize the TensorBoard callback and pass it to the callbacks parameter of the model.fit() function.

```
from keras.callbacks import TensorBoard
import datetime

log_dir = "logs/fit/" + datetime.datetime.now().strftime("%Y%m%d-%H%M%S")
tensorboard_callback = TensorBoard(log_dir=log_dir, histogram_freq=1)

model.fit(x_train, y_train, epochs=10, validation_data=(x_val, y_val), callbacks=[
    tensorboard_callback])
```

After running the training script, launch TensorBoard to visualize the metrics:

```
$ tensorboard --logdir logs/fit
```

Explore the default port (typically localhost:6006) on your web browser to access the TensorBoard interface.

Precision, recall, and F1-score are additional metrics often employed, especially in the context of imbalanced datasets. The keras.metrics module or external libraries like scikit-learn can compute these metrics.

```
from sklearn.metrics import precision_score, recall_score, f1_score

# Predictions and true labels
y_pred = model.predict(x_val)
y_true = y_val

# Calculate precision, recall, f1-score
precision = precision_score(y_true, y_pred.round())
recall = recall_score(y_true, y_pred.round())
f1 = f1_score(y_true, y_pred.round())

print(f'Precision: {precision:.4f}, Recall: {recall:.4f}, F1-score: {f1:.4f}')
```

Another powerful tool for performance tracking is the confusion matrix. It provides a detailed breakdown of the model's predictions versus actual labels, highlighting classes where the network may struggle.

```
from sklearn.metrics import confusion_matrix
import seaborn as sns
import numpy as np

# Generate the confusion matrix
conf_matrix = confusion_matrix(y_true, y_pred.round())
sns.heatmap(conf_matrix, annot=True, fmt='d', cmap='Blues')
plt.xlabel('Predicted Label')
plt.ylabel('True Label')
plt.show()
```

Model checkpoints are essential in monitoring and averting potential training pitfalls. The ModelCheckpoint callback saves the model's weights at certain intervals, which is particularly beneficial for recovering the best-performing model.

```
from keras.callbacks import ModelCheckpoint

checkpoint_callback = ModelCheckpoint(filepath='best_model.h5', save_best_only=
    True, monitor='val_loss', mode='min')
model.fit(x_train, y_train, epochs=10, validation_data=(x_val, y_val), callbacks=[
    checkpoint_callback])
```

Early stopping is another preventive measure to avoid overtraining. The EarlyStopping callback halts training when the monitored metric, typically validation loss, ceases to improve after a defined number of epochs.

```
from keras.callbacks import EarlyStopping

early_stopping_callback = EarlyStopping(monitor='val_loss', patience=3)
model.fit(x_train, y_train, epochs=10, validation_data=(x_val, y_val), callbacks=[
    early_stopping_callback])
```

By employing these monitoring techniques, practitioners can better understand and control the training process, ultimately leading to more robust and performant neural network models.

7.10 Handling Imbalanced Datasets

In many real-world applications, datasets are often imbalanced, meaning that some classes are significantly underrepresented compared to others. This imbalance can degrade the performance of neural networks, leading to biased predictions that favor the majority class. Addressing the challenge of imbalanced datasets involves several techniques that can be applied to rebalance the class distribution or adjust the learning process to account for the imbalance.

Data Resampling Techniques

Data resampling involves modifying the training dataset to correct the imbalance between classes. Two primary approaches are:

- **Oversampling**: This technique increases the number of instances in the minority class by replicating existing samples or generating new samples synthetically. The *Synthetic Minority Over-sampling Technique* (SMOTE) is a popular method that creates new samples by interpolating between existing ones.
- **Undersampling**: This technique reduces the number of instances in the majority class to balance the dataset. While

this can help prevent the model from being biased towards the majority class, it risks discarding valuable information.

The choice between oversampling and undersampling depends on the specific dataset and application. In general, oversampling is preferred when the minority class is small, whereas undersampling is useful when the majority class has a large, redundant dataset.

Example of Oversampling Using SMOTE

To illustrate oversampling with SMOTE, consider the following Python snippet using the imbalanced-learn library:

```
from imblearn.over_sampling import SMOTE
from sklearn.model_selection import train_test_split
from sklearn.datasets import make_classification

# Create a synthetic imbalanced dataset
X, y = make_classification(n_classes=2, class_sep=2,
    weights=[0.1, 0.9], n_informative=3, n_redundant=1, flip_y=0,
    n_features=20, n_clusters_per_class=1, n_samples=1000, random_state=10)

# Split the dataset into training and testing sets
X_train, X_test, y_train, y_test = train_test_split(X, y, test_size=0.3,
      random_state=10)

# Apply SMOTE to the training set
smote = SMOTE(random_state=10)
X_train_resampled, y_train_resampled = smote.fit_resample(X_train, y_train)

print(f'Original training set shape: {X_train.shape, y_train.shape}')
print(f'Resampled training set shape: {X_train_resampled.shape, y_train_resampled.
      shape}')
```

The output of the above code will be:

```
Original training set shape: ((700, 20), (700,))
Resampled training set shape: ((1260, 20), (1260,))
```

With SMOTE, the training set is balanced to have an equal number of samples from each class, enhancing the model's ability to learn from the minority class.

Algorithm-Level Methods

Several algorithm-level strategies can also be employed to address class imbalance. These techniques modify the learning algorithm directly, often by adjusting the loss function.

- **Class Weighting**: Neural network frameworks like Keras allow specifying class weights that adjust the loss function, penalizing misclassifications of minority class samples more than those of the majority class. This can be achieved by setting the class_-

weight parameter in the fit method.

```
from keras.models import Sequential
from keras.layers import Dense
from sklearn.utils.class_weight import compute_class_weight

# Pretend y_train contains the target classes after resampling with SMOTE
class_weights = compute_class_weight(class_weight='balanced', classes=np.
    unique(y_train), y=y_train)
class_weight_dict = dict(enumerate(class_weights))

# Define a simple neural network
model = Sequential()
model.add(Dense(32, input_dim=20, activation='relu'))
model.add(Dense(1, activation='sigmoid'))

# Compile the model
model.compile(optimizer='adam', loss='binary_crossentropy', metrics=['
    accuracy'])

# Fit the model
model.fit(X_train, y_train, epochs=10, class_weight=class_weight_dict)
```

This approach ensures the model pays more attention to the minority class during training.

- **Focal Loss**: Focal loss is another powerful technique for handling class imbalance. It down-weights well-classified examples and focuses the model's training on hard, misclassified examples.

```
import keras.backend as K

def focal_loss(gamma=2., alpha=0.25):
    def focal_loss_fixed(y_true, y_pred):
        pt_1 = K.clip(y_pred, K.epsilon(), 1)
        pt_0 = K.clip(1 - y_pred, K.epsilon(), 1)
        return -K.sum(alpha * K.pow(pt_0, gamma) * K.log(pt_1) * y_true +
                (1 - alpha) * K.pow(pt_1, gamma) * K.log(pt_0) * (1 - y_true))
    return focal_loss_fixed

model.compile(optimizer='adam', loss=focal_loss(gamma=2., alpha=0.25),
    metrics=['accuracy'])

model.fit(X_train, y_train, epochs=10)
```

Focal loss is particularly useful in object detection tasks but can be adapted for any imbalanced classification problem.

Evaluation Metrics for Imbalanced Data

Accurate evaluation of models trained on imbalanced datasets requires appropriate metrics. Accuracy is often misleading as it can be dominated by the majority class. Preferred metrics include:

- **Precision and Recall**: Precision is the ratio of correctly predicted positive observations to the total predicted positives. Recall (Sensitivity) is the ratio of correctly predicted positive observations to all observations in the actual class.

- **F1-Score**: The harmonic mean of precision and recall. It provides a single metric that balances both concerns.
- **ROC-AUC**: The Receiver Operating Characteristic - Area Under Curve evaluates the model's capability to distinguish between classes.

These metrics better capture the performance dynamics of classifiers in imbalanced settings.

This section detailed the critical techniques and strategies to effectively manage imbalanced datasets in neural network training, enhancing the model's predictive performance for underrepresented classes.

7.11 Distributing Training Across Multiple GPUs

Distributing training across multiple GPUs provides a pathway to significantly expedite the training process for deep learning models, which is especially critical for large-scale datasets and complex neural network architectures. Utilizing multiple GPUs effectively demands an understanding of parallelism strategies, communication overhead management, and synchronization mechanisms.

Data Parallelism

Data parallelism is a commonly adopted strategy where the same model is replicated across multiple GPUs. Each GPU receives a different subset of the input data batch, processes it independently, and computes gradients locally. A synchronization mechanism then aggregates these gradients across the GPUs to update the shared model parameters. This method scales well when the model fit within the memory of each GPU but requires efficient inter-GPU communication to handle gradient synchronization.

An illustration of data parallelism in Keras with TensorFlow backend:

```
from tensorflow.keras.applications import ResNet50
from tensorflow.keras.optimizers import SGD
from tensorflow.keras.utils import multi_gpu_model
```

```
# Define the model
model = ResNet50(weights=None)

# Replicate the model on 2 GPUs
parallel_model = multi_gpu_model(model, gpus=2)

# Compile the model
parallel_model.compile(loss='categorical_crossentropy',
                       optimizer=SGD(lr=0.01),
                       metrics=['accuracy'])

# Fit the model
parallel_model.fit(x_train, y_train, epochs=10, batch_size=128)
```

Here, the multi_gpu_model function automatically partitions the input data, spreads the computation load across two GPUs, and manages gradient aggregation.

Model Parallelism

In contrast, model parallelism is suitable for very large models that cannot be fully accommodated within a single GPU's memory. This approach partitions the model itself; different GPUs handle different parts of the model. While straightforward in theory, model parallelism poses challenges due to the dependencies and communication requirements between model partitions.

```
# Example setup for manually distributing a model's layers across multiple GPUs

from tensorflow.keras.layers import Input, Dense
from tensorflow.keras.models import Model
import tensorflow as tf

# Input layer is handled by the first GPU
with tf.device('/gpu:0'):
    inputs = Input(shape=(784,))
    x = Dense(512, activation='relu')(inputs)

# Intermediate layers by the second GPU
with tf.device('/gpu:1'):
    x = Dense(512, activation='relu')(x)

# Output layer processed by the first GPU again
with tf.device('/gpu:0'):
    outputs = Dense(10, activation='softmax')(x)

model = Model(inputs=inputs, outputs=outputs)
model.compile(loss='categorical_crossentropy',
              optimizer='adam',
              metrics=['accuracy'])

# Fit the model
model.fit(x_train, y_train, epochs=10, batch_size=128)
```

This example shows manual distribution where layers are explicitly assigned to GPUs using the tf.device context manager.

Synchronous vs. Asynchronous Training

For gradient synchronization, two primary methods are employed: synchronous and asynchronous training. In synchronous training, all GPUs must complete their respective computations before proceeding to the averaging and updating of gradients, ensuring consistency. In asynchronous training, GPUs work independently, updating the model parameters without waiting for others, which may result in faster but less consistent convergence.

High-Performance Communication

Effective GPU-to-GPU communication is crucial, typically facilitated by high-bandwidth interconnects such as NVIDIA NVLink or PCIe. Furthermore, distributed frameworks like Horovod, developed by Uber, optimize communication through ring-allreduce algorithms.

```
import horovod.tensorflow.keras as hvd

hvd.init()

# Pin to a GPU
gpus = tf.config.experimental.list_physical_devices('GPU')
for gpu in gpus:
    tf.config.experimental.set_memory_growth(gpu, True)

if gpus:
    tf.config.experimental.set_visible_devices(gpus[hvd.local_rank()], 'GPU')

# Reference model definition here
model = ResNet50(weights=None)

# Add Horovod Distributed Optimizer
opt = SGD(lr=0.01)
opt = hvd.DistributedOptimizer(opt)

model.compile(loss='categorical_crossentropy',
              optimizer=opt,
              metrics=['accuracy'])

callbacks = [
    hvd.callbacks.BroadcastGlobalVariablesCallback(0),
    hvd.callbacks.MetricAverageCallback(),
]

# Train the model
model.fit(x_train, y_train, epochs=10, batch_size=128, callbacks=callbacks)
```

This code integrates Horovod into a Keras training process, leveraging optimized communication and distributed training strategies to improve scalability and efficiency.

Challenges and Best Practices

Multi-GPU training introduces several challenges. Ensuring workload balance and minimizing communication overhead are pivotal. Use dynamic batch sizing and overlap communication with computation where possible. Experiment with different synchronization techniques and explore gradient compression to reduce data transfer volume.

By strategically leveraging multiple GPUs, deep learning practitioners can significantly accelerate training times, making it feasible to handle more extensive datasets and more complex models, thus pushing the boundaries of what can be achieved with deep learning systems.

7.12 Debugging and Troubleshooting Training Issues

Training neural networks can often present numerous challenges that require careful debugging and troubleshooting. These challenges can arise from various sources such as data preprocessing errors, model architecture issues, improper hyperparameter settings, or even hardware-related problems. Identifying and rectifying these issues is crucial for ensuring that the network performs as expected. This section delves into common problems encountered during the training process and offers methodologies to address them effectively.

One of the primary sources of training issues is **data preprocessing**. Ensuring that the data is correctly normalized and preprocessed is essential. If the input data is not standardized properly, the network might not converge or may take longer to do so. For instance, image data should typically be scaled to a range of [0, 1] or [-1, 1]. To confirm that the data pipeline is correct, visualize sample inputs and check summary statistics.

Sometimes, the **model architecture** itself might be the root cause of training difficulties. Sparse gradients or vanishing/exploding gradients can hinder the training process. Using gradient clipping or choosing architectures specifically designed to address these issues, such as ResNets, can be beneficial. Evaluating the suitability of activation functions and the distribution of weights can also provide insights. For example, initializing weights with techniques like He Normal or Xavier can often prevent gradient-related problems.

Another frequent issue pertains to **hyperparameter settings**. Learning rates that are too high or too low can lead to non-convergence or extremely slow training. Evaluating the learning rate through experimentation or using learning rate schedules like exponential decay or cyclical learning rates might offer better results. Batch sizes also influence the stability and speed of training; smaller batch sizes provide noisy gradient estimates which might aid generalization, whereas larger batch sizes smooth the gradients but require more memory.

It is also important to consider **software-related issues**. Ensuring that the libraries such as TensorFlow or PyTorch are fully up-to-date and compatible with the hardware can prevent various runtime errors. Enabling verbose logs and debugging flags often provides additional insights. For instance, increasing verbosity levels in Keras can be helpful:

```
import tensorflow as tf
tf.debugging.set_log_device_placement(True)
```

In the case of **hardware-related issues**, training on GPUs can sometimes lead to out-of-memory errors, especially with large models or batch sizes. Monitoring GPU memory usage and ensuring the environment has the required CUDA and cuDNN configurations are critical steps. Tools like nvidia-smi can be used to monitor GPU status:

```
nvidia-smi
```

For more complex problems like **overfitting**, regularization techniques such as L2/L1 regularization, dropout, and data augmentation can be employed. Implementing dropout in a Keras model might look like:

```
from keras.models import Sequential
from keras.layers import Dense, Dropout

model = Sequential()
model.add(Dense(512, activation='relu', input_shape=(784,)))
model.add(Dropout(0.5))
model.add(Dense(10, activation='softmax'))
```

Monitoring metrics is another crucial aspect of debugging. A model's loss and accuracy during training and validation phases provide significant insight into potential issues. Tools such as TensorBoard can visualize these metrics in real-time. For example, to use TensorBoard with Keras:

```
from keras.callbacks import TensorBoard

tensorboard_callback = TensorBoard(log_dir='./logs')
model.fit(x_train, y_train, epochs=10, callbacks=[tensorboard_callback])
```

Gradient checking is a technique used to verify that backpropagation is correctly implemented. It involves numerically approximating the gradient and comparing it with the analytical gradient computed through backpropagation. Although computationally intensive, it is particularly useful for identifying bugs in custom implementations of neural network layers.

Lastly, if the model training is not yielding expected results, **re-evaluating the problem formulation** itself might be necessary. Ensuring that the loss function is appropriate and that the metric used aligns with the problem's requirements is vital. For example, in classification problems, cross-entropy loss is typically more suitable than mean squared error.

By methodically addressing these potential issues — scrutinizing data preprocessing steps, ensuring robust model architecture, fine-tuning hyperparameters, investigating software compatibility, managing hardware resources, applying regularization techniques, monitoring training metrics, performing gradient checks, and reevaluating problem formulation — one can systematically debug and troubleshoot neural network training problems to achieve optimal performance.

Chapter 8

Hyperparameter Tuning and Optimization

This chapter covers the importance of hyperparameter tuning in optimizing neural network performance. It details common hyperparameters, tuning methods like grid search, random search, and Bayesian optimization, and advanced techniques such as Hyperband and AutoML. Practical guidance on using Keras Tuner and best practices for hyperparameter tuning are provided, along with an understanding of the bias-variance tradeoff and case studies illustrating real-world applications.

8.1 Introduction to Hyperparameter Tuning

Hyperparameter tuning is a critical process in the development and optimization of neural networks. It involves adjusting the parameters that govern the learning process to enhance model performance. Unlike model parameters, which are learned during training, hyperparameters are set before training begins and remain constant throughout.

Hyperparameters can be broadly classified into two categories: model hyperparameters and optimization hyperparameters. Model hyperparameters include parameters that define the structure of the model, such as the number of layers, the number of neurons in each layer, and the activation functions used. Optimization hyperparameters are those related to the training process, such as the learning rate, batch size, and the number of epochs.

The tuning of hyperparameters is essential due to the complex and non-linear nature of neural network models. Proper selection and tuning can significantly impact the model's ability to generalize, reduce overfitting, and achieve higher accuracy. Conversely, poor choices in hyperparameters can lead to sub-optimal model performance and wasted computational resources.

One of the foundational aspects of hyperparameter tuning is the search strategy, which determines how different hyperparameter values are sampled and evaluated. Several techniques for hyperparameter search exist, with varying degrees of complexity and efficiency. The simplest and most intuitive techniques include grid search and random search, while more sophisticated methods such as Bayesian optimization, Hyperband, and AutoML have been developed to address the limitations of simpler approaches.

To illustrate, consider a scenario where we need to tune the learning rate and batch size for a neural network. Using grid search, we might define a discrete set of values for each hyperparameter and evaluate every possible combination:

```
from sklearn.model_selection import GridSearchCV

param_grid = {
    'learning_rate': [0.001, 0.01, 0.1],
    'batch_size': [32, 64, 128]
}

grid_search = GridSearchCV(estimator=model, param_grid=param_grid, cv=3,
    scoring='accuracy')
grid_search.fit(X_train, y_train)
```

While grid search is exhaustive, it can be computationally expensive, especially when dealing with a large number of hyperparameters or a wide range of values. Random search, on the other hand, randomly samples a fixed number of hyperparameter combinations from the defined range and evaluates them, offering a trade-off between exploration and computational cost:

```
from sklearn.model_selection import RandomizedSearchCV

param_dist = {
    'learning_rate': [0.001, 0.01, 0.1],
    'batch_size': [32, 64, 128]
}

random_search = RandomizedSearchCV(estimator=model, param_distributions=
    param_dist, n_iter=10, cv=3, scoring='accuracy')
```

```
random_search.fit(X_train, y_train)
```

While more efficient than grid search, random search may still miss optimal regions in the hyperparameter space. Advanced techniques like Bayesian optimization address this issue by constructing a probabilistic model that maps hyperparameters to model performance and using this model to identify the most promising hyperparameters iteratively.

Besides search strategies, another aspect of hyperparameter tuning involves understanding the impact of each hyperparameter on model performance. For instance, a high learning rate may cause the model to converge quickly but risk overshooting the optimal solution, while a low learning rate may ensure stable convergence but at the cost of longer training time. Similarly, a small batch size can introduce more stochastic noise into the gradient estimation, potentially aiding in generalization, whereas a large batch size offers a more accurate estimate of the gradient, which can expedite convergence but may lead to overfitting.

To effectively manage these trade-offs, it is prudent to start with a broad search across the hyperparameter space, followed by a more focused fine-tuning around the promising regions identified. Visual aids, such as learning curves and validation loss plots, can provide valuable insights into the hyperparameter tuning process. Monitoring these plots can indicate whether the model is improving with each epoch and whether overfitting or underfitting is occurring.

Hyperparameter tuning is not a one-time task but an iterative process that often requires multiple cycles of experimentation. Leveraging tools such as TensorBoard for visualizing metrics and Keras Tuner for automated hyperparameter search can greatly facilitate this process. Understanding the bias-variance tradeoff is also integral to hyperparameter tuning, as it helps in balancing underfitting and overfitting by selecting appropriate hyperparameters.

In this section, we have laid the foundation for understanding hyperparameter tuning, its significance, and the fundamental techniques employed. Subsequent sections will delve deeper into specific tuning methods, providing practical guidance on their application and highlighting advanced optimization strategies.

8.2 Why Hyperparameter Tuning Matters

Hyperparameter tuning is a critical aspect of building effective neural networks and deep learning models. Hyperparameters, unlike model parameters, are not learned during the training process but are set prior to the training. These include learning rates, batch sizes, number of epochs, hidden layer sizes, dropout rates, and more. Proper tuning of these hyperparameters can significantly impact the model's performance, generalization ability, and computational efficiency.

Consider the learning rate (lr), a crucial hyperparameter in optimization algorithms such as Stochastic Gradient Descent (SGD). If the learning rate is too high, the model's training process may exhibit erratic updates, leading to divergence. Conversely, if it is too low, the training process will be excessively slow, possibly converging to suboptimal solutions. Thus, finding an optimal learning rate is fundamental to ensuring efficient and effective model training.

Another example is the batch size, which determines the number of training samples used in one forward/backward pass. A small batch size can provide a more accurate estimate of the gradient but may result in noisier updates. A larger batch size, conversely, makes for a smoother gradient estimate but requires more computing resources. The ideal batch size often depends on the specific problem, dataset characteristics, and available computational resources.

The depth and width of neural networks, configured by choosing the number of layers (depth) and the number of neurons per layer (width), are yet other critical hyperparameters. Increasing the depth or width allows the model to capture more complex patterns and relationships within the data. However, overly complex models may suffer from overfitting, where the model performs well on the training data but poorly on unseen test data.

Consider the following simple example in Keras to illustrate the impact of hyperparameters:

```
from keras.models import Sequential
from keras.layers import Dense, Dropout
from keras.optimizers import Adam

# Define model architecture
model = Sequential()
model.add(Dense(64, activation='relu', input_shape=(input_dim,)))
model.add(Dropout(0.5))
model.add(Dense(64, activation='relu'))
model.add(Dropout(0.5))
model.add(Dense(num_classes, activation='softmax'))
```

```
# Compile model with different learning rates
learning_rate1 = 0.01
learning_rate2 = 0.001
optimizer1 = Adam(learning_rate=learning_rate1)
optimizer2 = Adam(learning_rate=learning_rate2)

model.compile(optimizer=optimizer1, loss='categorical_crossentropy', metrics=['
    accuracy'])
```

In this example, two learning rates (learning_rate1 and learning_rate2) are defined for the Adam optimizer. The choice of the learning rate can lead to different model behaviors and final accuracies.

Beyond individual hyperparameters, the interaction between multiple hyperparameters further complicates the tuning process. For instance, the optimal learning rate might depend on the batch size due to their collective impact on the model's update steps during training. Such interactions necessitate a systematic approach to hyperparameter tuning, highlighting the importance of strategies like grid search, random search, and Bayesian optimization.

Grid search and random search are two standard techniques in hyperparameter tuning. Grid search exhaustively evaluates all possible combinations of specified hyperparameter values, whereas random search samples a fixed number of hyperparameter combinations from a predefined distribution. Although both methods are straightforward, they can be computationally expensive, making them impractical for models with a large set of hyperparameters.

Bayesian optimization, an advanced technique, builds a probabilistic model of the function mapping hyperparameters to a target value (e.g., validation accuracy) and uses this model to select the most promising hyperparameters to evaluate next. It tends to find the optimal hyperparameters more efficiently compared to grid and random search.

Automated approaches like Hyperband and AutoML have further advanced the hyperparameter tuning process. Hyperband adopts a resource allocation strategy to dynamically allocate resources to promising hyperparameter configurations, pruning less promising ones early to save computation. AutoML aims to automate the entire machine learning pipeline, including hyperparameter tuning, reducing human intervention.

The ramifications of hyperparameter tuning extend beyond optimizing model performance. Well-tuned hyperparameters can lead to better generalization on new, unseen data, improving a model's robustness and reliability in real-world applications. This fine-tuning can also enhance computational efficiency, adhering to resource constraints while maintaining high performance.

Understanding the importance of hyperparameter tuning and its profound impact on deep learning models underscores its relevance in modern machine learning practice. It is not merely an optimization step but a critical component in developing deployable, high-performance models. Mastering effective hyperparameter tuning strategies is thus essential for practitioners aiming to leverage deep learning in both academic and industrial applications.

8.3 Common Hyperparameters in Neural Networks

Hyperparameters play a pivotal role in configuring neural networks, directly influencing their performance and generalization capabilities. While model parameters are learned during training, hyperparameters are set before training and remain constant throughout. This section explores the prominent hyperparameters that require careful consideration when designing and training neural networks.

The first key hyperparameter is the **learning rate**. It dictates the step size at which the optimizer updates the model weights. A learning rate that is too high can lead to divergent behavior, where the model fails to converge and exhibits erratic loss fluctuations. Conversely, a learning rate that is too low results in painfully slow convergence, potentially causing the model to get trapped in local minima. A common approach is to use a learning rate scheduler to adjust the learning rate dynamically during training.

The next critical hyperparameter is **batch size**, which refers to the number of training samples used in one forward/backward pass. Larger batch sizes result in more stable gradient estimates but require more memory and might reduce the regularization effects induced by stochastic gradients. Smaller batch sizes can introduce noise into the training process, which may help escape local minima and improve generalization. Typical choices range from 32 to 256, but this can vary depending on the specific problem and computational constraints.

Number of epochs is another fundamental hyperparameter. It defines the total number of passes through the entire training dataset. Selecting an appropriate number of epochs is crucial to ensure thorough training without overfitting. Early stopping is a common technique used to terminate training when the model performance ceases to improve on a validation set, thus preventing unnecessary epochs.

Optimizer choice is often considered a hyperparameter. Different optimizers, such as Stochastic Gradient Descent (SGD), Adam, RMSprop, and others, have distinct characteristics and might be more suitable for different types of problems. For example, Adam updates are based on both the first and second moments of gradients and generally adapt well to various architectures, making it a popular choice.

Weight initialization is crucial for initializing the model's weights. Proper initialization can lead to faster convergence and better performance. Methods such as Xavier (Glorot) initialization or He initialization are frequently used for different activation functions. Poor initialization can result in vanishing or exploding gradients.

Another significant hyperparameter is the **regularization method**. Regularization techniques such as L2 regularization (weight decay) and dropout help to mitigate overfitting by penalizing large weights or randomly omitting neurons during training, respectively. The dropout rate or the regularization coefficient are parameters that must be tuned.

Activation functions selected for neurons in each layer also act as hyperparameters. Common choices include ReLU, sigmoid, and tanh activation functions. The ReLU activation function is typically preferred for hidden layers due to its simplicity and effectiveness, though variants like leaky ReLU or ELU might be used to address issues like dead neurons.

When dealing with convolutional neural networks (CNNs), several additional hyperparameters come into play. These include **filter size**, **number of filters**, and **stride** and **pooling size** in convolutional and pooling layers. Filter size determines cross-sectional dimensions of the convolutional filters, while the number of filters affects the depth of the output feature maps. Stride controls the movement of the filters across the input, and pooling size influences the down-sampling process, summarizing activations spatially.

For recurrent neural networks (RNNs) and their variants (e.g., LSTM, GRU), architectural hyperparameters such as **hidden state size**, **sequence length**, and the choice between **uni-directional or bi-directional** models demand attention. Hidden state size determines the dimensional complexity of memory units, influencing the model's capacity to learn temporal dependencies.

In most modern architectures, techniques such as **learning rate schedules** (e.g., learning rate decay), **gradient clipping**, and **batch normalization** have become standard practice. Learning rate schedules adjust the learning rate during training based on a predefined schedule or in response to observed performance. Gradient clipping helps to prevent the issue of exploding gradients by capping the gradients during backpropagation. Batch normalization normalizes inputs of each layer, usually resulting in faster convergence and improved performance.

Fine-tuning all these hyperparameters requires a balance between model complexity and computational efficiency. Hyperparameter tuning strategies like grid search, random search, and Bayesian optimization, discussed in later sections, provide systematic methodologies to identify optimal configurations. The intricate interaction between these hyperparameters necessitates a nuanced understanding, demanding empirical validation to ensure that the neural network performs optimally on the task at hand.

8.4 Grid Search and Random Search

Grid Search and Random Search are two foundational yet powerful methods for hyperparameter tuning in neural networks. Both techniques aim to identify the optimal set of hyperparameters that yield the best model performance. They achieve this through systematic and heuristic approaches, respectively.

Grid Search is an exhaustive search method that evaluates every possible combination of a specified set of hyperparameters. This method essentially constructs a search grid, where each point in the grid represents a particular combination of hyperparameters. The model is trained and evaluated for each combination, and the best-performing set of hyperparameters is selected based on a predefined performance metric, such as accuracy or loss.

Consider the following example where we want to tune two hyperparameters: the learning rate and the batch size. Suppose the possible values for the learning rate are $\{0.1, 0.01, 0.001\}$ and for the batch size are $\{16, 32, 64\}$. The Grid Search method will systematically evaluate all $3 \times 3 = 9$ combinations of hyperparameters.

To implement Grid Search in Keras, the following code illustrates a practical example:

```
from keras.models import Sequential
from keras.layers import Dense
from keras.wrappers.scikit_learn import KerasClassifier
from sklearn.model_selection import GridSearchCV

def create_model(learning_rate=0.01):
    model = Sequential()
    model.add(Dense(12, input_dim=8, activation='relu'))
    model.add(Dense(8, activation='relu'))
    model.add(Dense(1, activation='sigmoid'))
    model.compile(optimizer='adam', loss='binary_crossentropy', metrics=['accuracy'])
    return model

model = KerasClassifier(build_fn=create_model, verbose=0)

learning_rates = [0.1, 0.01, 0.001]
batch_sizes = [16, 32, 64]

param_grid = dict(learning_rate=learning_rates, batch_size=batch_sizes)
grid = GridSearchCV(estimator=model, param_grid=param_grid, n_jobs=-1, cv=3)
grid_result = grid.fit(X_train, y_train)

print(f"Best: {grid_result.best_score_} using {grid_result.best_params_}")
```

The output of this grid search process is shown below. This output shows the best score and the hyperparameters corresponding to that score.

```
Best: 0.8473 using {'batch_size': 32, 'learning_rate': 0.01}
```

Random Search, on the other hand, is a heuristic method that randomly samples hyperparameters from specified distributions rather than searching through each possible combination. This method is often more efficient in terms of computational resources and time, especially when dealing with a large number of hyperparameters and their possible values.

Random Search can sometimes find models that are nearly as good as those found by Grid Search but with significantly reduced computational effort. An example implementation of Random Search in Keras is shown below:

```
from keras.models import Sequential
from keras.layers import Dense
from keras.wrappers.scikit_learn import KerasClassifier
from sklearn.model_selection import RandomizedSearchCV

def create_model(learning_rate=0.01):
    model = Sequential()
    model.add(Dense(12, input_dim=8, activation='relu'))
    model.add(Dense(8, activation='relu'))
    model.add(Dense(1, activation='sigmoid'))
    model.compile(optimizer='adam', loss='binary_crossentropy', metrics=['accuracy'])
```

```
    return model

model = KerasClassifier(build_fn=create_model, verbose=0)

learning_rates = [0.1, 0.01, 0.001]
batch_sizes = [16, 32, 64]

param_dist = dict(learning_rate=learning_rates, batch_size=batch_sizes)
random = RandomizedSearchCV(estimator=model, param_distributions=param_dist,
    n_iter=10, n_jobs=-1, cv=3)
random_result = random.fit(X_train, y_train)

print(f"Best: {random_result.best_score_} using {random_result.best_params_}")
```

The result output of the Random Search is shown below. Like Grid Search, it gives the best score and the hyperparameters that produced this score.

```
Best: 0.8461 using {'batch_size': 16, 'learning_rate': 0.001}
```

Both Grid and Random Search have their advantages and limitations. Grid Search is methodical and can guarantee finding the optimal hyperparameters within the defined grid, but it is computationally expensive and may not be feasible for high-dimensional hyperparameter spaces. Random Search, although less exhaustive, tends to be more practical for larger search spaces due to its efficiency in sampling.

Furthermore, the selection of hyperparameters for tuning depends on the specific neural network architecture and the problem at hand. Common hyperparameters include the learning rate, batch size, number of epochs, optimization algorithm, dropout rate, and the number of units in each hidden layer. Properly selecting and tuning these hyperparameters is critical to achieving optimal model performance.

As the complexity and size of neural networks grow, more advanced methods, such as Bayesian Optimization, Hyperband, and AutoML, have been developed to address the shortcomings of Grid and Random Search. Nevertheless, understanding and effectively implementing Grid and Random Search provides a solid foundation for any machine learning practitioner.

8.5 Bayesian Optimization

Bayesian optimization represents a class of efficient iterative methods for optimizing expensive black-box functions. Unlike traditional grid or random search methods, Bayesian optimization is particularly well-suited for scenarios where the evaluation of the objective function is costly in terms of time or computational resources. It utilizes the principles of Bayes' theorem to iteratively model the objective function and identify the optimal hyperparameters.

Bayesian optimization functions by building a probabilistic model, typically a Gaussian Process (GP), over the objective function and using this model to select the most promising hyperparameters to evaluate.

Gaussian Process (GP)

A Gaussian Process is a collection of random variables, any finite number of which have a joint Gaussian distribution. GPs are used in Bayesian optimization to model the unknown objective function. The choice of GPs is driven by their flexibility and the ability to provide uncertainty estimates for predictions. Mathematically, a GP is defined as:

$$f(x) \sim \mathcal{GP}(m(x), k(x, x'))$$

where $m(x)$ is the mean function and $k(x, x')$ is the covariance function or kernel. The mean function $m(x)$ is often assumed to be zero, and the kernel function usually represents the similarity between points and dictates the smoothness of the function. Common kernel functions include the Radial Basis Function (RBF) and the Matérn kernel.

Acquisition Function

At each iteration, Bayesian optimization attempts to balance exploration (looking for regions with high uncertainty) and exploitation (looking near regions with known high performance). This balance is controlled by an acquisition function, which is used to determine the next point to evaluate. Popular acquisition functions include:

- **Probability of Improvement (PI):** Selects points that have the highest probability of improving over the current best observation.
- **Expected Improvement (EI):** Selects points based on the expected improvement. This function considers both the potential improvement and the uncertainty in the prediction.
- **Upper Confidence Bound (UCB):** Selects points by maximizing a combination of the mean and standard deviation of the predictions from the GP model.

The acquisition function $a(x|\mathcal{D}_1, ..., \mathcal{D}_n)$ quantifies the utility of evaluating the objective function at a new point x given the data $\mathcal{D}_1, ..., \mathcal{D}_n$ collected so far.

Algorithm of Bayesian Optimization

The general algorithm of Bayesian optimization can be summarized as follows:

1. **Initialization:** Start with an initial set of observations by evaluating the objective function at a few random points.
2. **Model Fitting:** Fit a Gaussian Process model to the observed data.
3. **Acquisition Maximization:** Use the acquisition function to determine the next point to evaluate.
4. **Evaluation:** Evaluate the objective function at the selected point.
5. **Update:** Update the GP model with the new data point.
6. **Iteration:** Repeat steps 3-5 until convergence or a specified number of iterations.

The following Python code demonstrates the implementation of Bayesian optimization using the scikit-optimize package.

```
from skopt import BayesSearchCV
from sklearn.datasets import load_iris
from sklearn.ensemble import RandomForestClassifier

# Load dataset
X, y = load_iris(return_X_y=True)

# Define model
clf = RandomForestClassifier()

# Define hyperparameter space
param_space = {
    'n_estimators': (10, 200),
    'max_features': ('auto', 'sqrt', 'log2'),
    'max_depth': (1, 50),
    'criterion': ['gini', 'entropy']
}

# Instantiate Bayesian search cross-validation
opt = BayesSearchCV(estimator=clf,
                    search_spaces=param_space,
                    n_iter=32,
                    cv=3,
                    n_jobs=-1,
                    random_state=0)

# Perform the search
opt.fit(X, y)

# Best parameters
print("Best parameters found: ", opt.best_params_)
```

```
Best parameters found: {'criterion': 'entropy', 'max_depth': 10, 'max_features': 'sqrt', 'n_estimators': 180}
```

Advantages of Bayesian Optimization

- **Efficiency:** By modeling the objective function and using acquisition functions, Bayesian optimization makes better use of each iteration compared to grid or random search.
- **Flexibility:** Can handle different types of hyperparameters, including discrete, continuous, and categorical variables.
- **Convergence:** Often converges to optimal or near-optimal solutions with fewer evaluations.

Challenges and Considerations

- **Scalability:** While effective for low to medium dimensional spaces, Bayesian optimization can become less efficient in high-dimensional spaces due to the curse of dimensionality.
- **Computation:** The fitting and updating of the GP model can be computationally intensive, particularly with large datasets.
- **Hyperparameter Selection:** The performance of Bayesian optimization itself can be sensitive to the choice of kernel and acquisition function.

Bayesian optimization stands out as a powerful method for hyperparameter tuning in neural networks, offering both efficiency and flexibility. By iteratively refining the model and strategic evaluations, it enhances the chances of finding optimal parameters while managing computational resources effectively. Properly implemented, it can significantly improve model performance with reduced computational overhead.

8.6 Hyperband and Successive Halving

Hyperband is an advanced hyperparameter optimization algorithm that builds on the concept of successive halving. Successive halving is a strategy wherein the allocation of resources, such as computational power or time, is progressively focused on the most promising configurations by eliminating the poorer-performing ones at each stage. This section delves into the principles and mechanics of both successive halving and Hyperband, their implementation, and their benefits over traditional methods like grid search and random search.

Successive halving begins by evaluating a large set of hyperparameter configurations with a small budget. This budget can be thought of as the number of iterations or epochs for which a machine learning model is trained. After this initial evaluation, only a fraction of the configurations that perform the best are selected to proceed to the next round. In each successive round, the budget is increased, and the process is repeated until the most performant configuration is identified. The key parameter in successive halving is the reduction factor r, which governs the number of configurations to keep at each round and the budget increment.

```
import numpy as np

# Define the number of configurations and initial budget
num_configs = 100
initial_budget = 1
reduction_factor = 3

# Simulate the evaluation of configurations
def evaluate_config(config, budget):
    model_performance = some_model_training_function(config, budget)
    return model_performance

configs = [generate_random_config() for _ in range(num_configs)]

for i in range(int(np.log(num_configs) / np.log(reduction_factor))):
    budget = initial_budget * (reduction_factor ** i)
    performances = [(config, evaluate_config(config, budget)) for config in configs]
    # Keep the top-performing configurations
    configs = sorted(performances, key=lambda x: x[1], reverse=True)[:len(configs) //
         reduction_factor]

best_config = configs[0]
print(f"Best configuration: {best_config}")
```

In imperative terms, successive halving achieves a significant reduction in the computation required to identify good hyperparameters by iteratively filtering configurations. However, the initial guess of the number of configurations to start with and the reduction factor may not always be optimal.

Hyperband extends successive halving by dynamically allocating the resource budget between many configurations, balancing exploration and exploitation more effectively. Hyperband operates by using multiple instances of successive halving, each with a different budget allocation, and then combining their results to determine the best configuration. It starts by defining a maximum budget B for evaluating a single configuration and splits this budget into s different configurations.

For each configuration s_i ranging from 1 to $\log_r(N)$, where N is the total number of configurations, Hyperband executes successive halving with the initial budget $b_i = \frac{B}{r^i}$. Each instance of successive halving is run independently with its own set of configurations, factor reduction, and budget allocation. This process ensures that a wide range of configurations are tested, each with sufficient budget, before honing in on the most promising candidates.

```
Algorithm: Hyperband
Input: Maximum budget B, reduction factor r, total configurations N
Output: Best configuration

for s in [log_r(N), ..., 1, 0]:
    n = ceil(log_r(N) / s)
    b = B / r^s

    T = generate_random_configs(n)

    for i in range(s + 1):
        ni = floor(n / r^i)
        bi = b * r^i

        L = [(t, evaluate_config(t, bi)) for t in T]
        T = top_k(L, floor(ni / r))

return T[0]
```

As shown in the pseudocode and implemented similarly in practical libraries, Hyperband adaptively uses different budgets for different subsets of configurations, providing a more efficient allocation of resources. Compared to grid search and random search, which do not adapt dynamically to the performance results, Hyperband automatically mitigates the risks of under-optimization and resource wastage.

```
def hyperband(max_iter, eta, get_model_performance):
    s_max = int(np.log(max_iter) / np.log(eta))
    B = (s_max + 1) * max_iter

    results = []

    for s in reversed(range(s_max + 1)):
        n = int(np.ceil(B / max_iter / (s + 1)))
        r = max_iter * eta ** (-s)

        configs = [generate_random_config() for _ in range(n)]

        for i in range(s + 1):
            n_i = n * eta ** (-i)
            r_i = r * eta ** (i)

            performances = [(config, get_model_performance(config, r_i)) for config in
                configs]
            configs = sorted(performances, key=lambda x: x[1], reverse=True)[:int(n_i /
                eta)]

        results.extend(configs)
```

```
    return sorted(results, key=lambda x: x[1], reverse=True)[0]
```

This dual approach to control initial sampling and iterative refinement proves highly effective in real-world scenarios where computational resources and time are critical concerns. Hyperband is supported in modern hyperparameter tuning frameworks like Keras Tuner, making its application both straightforward and highly integrated with deep learning workflows.

The utility of Hyperband and successive halving is profoundly evident in large-scale problems where traditional methods often fail to efficiently manage resources. By blending systematic reductions with adaptive resource allocations, these methods offer a robust avenue for ensuring optimal hyperparameter tuning with minimized computational overhead.

8.7 Automated Machine Learning (AutoML)

Automated Machine Learning (AutoML) is an evolving field that automates the iterative processes involved in machine learning. AutoML facilitates the end-to-end process of applying machine learning to real-world problems, making it accessible to non-experts while also improving efficiency for experts. AutoML encompasses more than hyperparameter tuning; it includes the full pipeline from data preprocessing to model deployment, offering an all-in-one solution for streamlined model development.

One of the primary components of AutoML is **pipeline automation**. A pipeline in machine learning encompasses the complete workflow: starting from loading the data, preprocessing, feature selection, model training, hyperparameter tuning, and culminating in model evaluation and deployment. Automating this pipeline requires careful integration of each step so that optimal configurations can be identified with minimal human intervention.

A standard approach to AutoML involves:

- **Data Preprocessing**: Various preprocessing techniques like normalization, encoding categorical variables, and handling missing data.
- **Feature Engineering**: Automatically generating new features from existing ones or selecting a subset of relevant features.

- **Model Selection and Training**: Choosing the best algorithms for the given task and training models using those algorithms.
- **Hyperparameter Tuning**: Optimizing hyperparameters for the selected models.
- **Model Evaluation and Validation**: Evaluating model performance using approaches like cross-validation.
- **Model Ensembling**: Combining predictions from multiple models to improve accuracy.

To illustrate, consider the implementation of AutoML within the Keras framework, utilizing the powerful tool **Keras Tuner**.

```
import keras_tuner as kt
from tensorflow.keras import layers
from tensorflow.keras.datasets import mnist
from tensorflow.keras.models import Sequential
from tensorflow.keras.utils import to_categorical

# Load and preprocess the data
(x_train, y_train), (x_test, y_test) = mnist.load_data()
x_train, x_test = x_train / 255.0, x_test / 255.0
y_train, y_test = to_categorical(y_train), to_categorical(y_test)

# Define a model-building function
def build_model(hp):
    model = Sequential()
    model.add(layers.Flatten(input_shape=(28, 28)))

    # Tune the number of layers
    for i in range(hp.Int('num_layers', 1, 3)):
        model.add(layers.Dense(units=hp.Int('units_' + str(i),
                                            min_value=32,
                                            max_value=512,
                                            step=32),
                               activation=hp.Choice('activation', ['relu', 'tanh'])))

    model.add(layers.Dense(10, activation='softmax'))

    # Tune the learning rate for the optimizer
    model.compile(optimizer=tf.keras.optimizers.Adam(hp.Choice('learning_rate',
                                                               [1e-2, 1e-3, 1e-4])),
                  loss='categorical_crossentropy',
                  metrics=['accuracy'])
    return model

# Initialize the tuner
tuner = kt.Hyperband(build_model,
                     objective='val_accuracy',
                     max_epochs=10,
                     factor=3,
                     directory='my_dir',
                     project_name='intro_to_kt')

# Use early stopping to prevent overfitting
stop_early = tf.keras.callbacks.EarlyStopping(monitor='val_loss', patience=5)
```

```
# Perform hyperparameter tuning
tuner.search(x_train, y_train, epochs=50, validation_split=0.2, callbacks=[stop_early
    ])

# Retrieve the best model
best_model = tuner.get_best_models(num_models=1)[0]

# Evaluate the best model
val_loss, val_acc = best_model.evaluate(x_test, y_test)
print(f"Validation accuracy of the best model: {val_acc}")
```

Validation accuracy of the best model: 0.9823

The given code demonstrates how Keras Tuner automatically handles aspects of data preprocessing, model selection, and hyperparameter tuning, encapsulating them within a single, efficient workflow. Noticeably, AutoML frameworks not only search for the best hyperparameters but also iterate over various architectural choices, such as the number of layers and units in each layer.

Feature Engineering is another critical component. Some AutoML systems, like featuretools, dynamically create feature sets that may not be immediately obvious. They explore transformations and aggregations over temporal and relational data to generate useful features, which can ultimately boost model performance.

Another aspect is **model selection**, where the AutoML tools evaluate different machine learning algorithms, ranging from simple linear models to complex ensemble methodologies. Techniques such as **model stacking** or **blending** can then be used to combine multiple models, leveraging their collective strengths.

Advanced AutoML systems often incorporate techniques like transfer learning, where the knowledge gained from solving one problem is applied to a different but related problem. This is especially crucial in scenarios with limited data, as it allows leveraging pre-trained models from large datasets to improve performance rapidly without extensive training.

The **scalability** of AutoML solutions has significantly expanded their usability. Tools like Google AutoML and H2O.ai's AutoML can handle large-scale data and complex models, making them applicable in various industrial applications. These tools also offer the advantage of being cloud-based, providing the computational power necessary for extensive model searches without requiring substantial local resources.

Finally, it's essential to address **interpretability** in AutoML. Automated systems, while efficient, can sometimes act as black boxes. To mitigate this, techniques such as LIME and SHAP are employed to ensure that the models' decisions can be interpreted and trusted.

AutoML represents a significant advancement in making machine learning more accessible and effective, empowering both novices and experts to harness its full potential without extensive manual intervention.

8.8 Hyperparameter Tuning with Keras Tuner

Keras Tuner is a library that helps in the automated hyperparameter tuning of Keras models, aiming to simplify and enhance the performance-building process. It supports a variety of search algorithms and optimizations including Random Search, Hyperband, Bayesian Optimization, and Sklearn's Grid Search. This section delves into the practical usage of Keras Tuner, from installation to implementing it in real-world scenarios, guiding you through the necessary steps to leverage this powerful tool effectively.

To begin with Keras Tuner, ensure that the library is installed. This can be achieved by running the following command in your Python environment:

```
pip install keras-tuner
```

After successful installation, the fundamental concept of Keras Tuner revolves around the definition and tuning of hyperparameters through a model-building function. Below is a step-by-step illustration.

Firstly, import necessary libraries:

```
import tensorflow as tf
from tensorflow import keras
from kerastuner import HyperModel, RandomSearch
```

For our example, we define a simple model-building function that takes a hyperparameters object as an argument. The HyperParameters class allows the definition of hyperparameter ranges and distributions.

```
def build_model(hp):
    model = keras.Sequential()
    model.add(keras.layers.Flatten(input_shape=(28, 28)))

    # Tune the number of units in the first Dense layer
    hp_units = hp.Int('units', min_value=32, max_value=512, step=32)
    model.add(keras.layers.Dense(units=hp_units, activation='relu'))
```

```
    model.add(keras.layers.Dense(10, activation='softmax'))

    # Tune the learning rate for the optimizer
    hp_learning_rate = hp.Float('learning_rate', min_value=1e-4, max_value=1e-2,
         sampling='log')
    model.compile(optimizer=keras.optimizers.Adam(learning_rate=hp_learning_rate),
                  loss='sparse_categorical_crossentropy',
                  metrics=['accuracy'])
    return model
```

In the above function:

- The number of units in the first dense layer is a hyperparameter that varies between 32 and 512, in increments of 32.
- The learning rate for the Adam optimizer is also a hyperparameter that varies between 10^{-4} and 10^{-2} on a logarithmic scale.

Next, instantiate the search algorithm. Here, we'll use RandomSearch for simplicity:

```
tuner = RandomSearch(
    build_model,
    objective='val_accuracy',
    max_trials=5,
    executions_per_trial=3,
    directory='my_dir',
    project_name='intro_to_kt')
```

The RandomSearch tuner is initialized with:

- The model-building function: build_model.
- The objective to optimize, which is validation accuracy here: objective='val_accuracy'.
- The maximum number of trials: max_trials=5, meaning the tuner will try up to 5 different hyperparameter combinations.
- Executions per trial: executions_per_trial=3, meaning each model configuration will be trained and evaluated 3 times to account for variability.
- Directory and project name for storing the results and logs: directory='my_dir' and project_name='intro_to_kt'.

Following this, execute the tuning search by instructing the tuner to search for the best hyperparameters:

```
tuner.search(x_train, y_train, epochs=10, validation_data=(x_val, y_val))
```

Within this command:

- x_train and y_train represent the training dataset.
- epochs=10 specifies the number of epochs for which each model configuration will be trained.
- validation_data=(x_val, y_val) provides the validation dataset for evaluation of each trial.

Upon completion of the search, the optimal hyperparameters can be retrieved through:

```
best_hps = tuner.get_best_hyperparameters(num_trials=1)[0]
```

Finally, the best hyperparameters can be used to create the final model and perform necessary training:

```
model = build_model(best_hps)
history = model.fit(x_train, y_train, epochs=10, validation_data=(x_val, y_val))
```

Keras Tuner also provides visualizations of the search process and allows for the exploration of different tuning strategies through swap-in alternative imports such as BayesianOptimization or Hyperband combined with similar setup logic.

Through Keras Tuner, the often arduous and complex task of hyperparameter tuning is abstracted into a streamlined and efficient series of commands, offering a high degree of integration with the Keras API. This streamlined approach enables practitioners to focus on designing effective models while Keras Tuner handles the search for the optimal hyperparameters, enhancing the overall proficiency and robustness of the deep learning models.

8.9 Best Practices for Hyperparameter Tuning

Hyperparameter tuning is a critical component in optimizing neural network models for better performance and generalization. In this section, we will explore best practices that enhance the efficiency and effectiveness of hyperparameter tuning processes.

Understand the Problem Domain: Before beginning the hyperparameter tuning, it is imperative to have a deep understanding of the problem domain. This includes knowing the data well, understanding its nuances, and being aware of the relevant metrics that need to be optimized. Defining clear objectives aids in selecting pertinent hyperparameters and evaluation metrics.

Start with a Coarse Search: Initially, it is advisable to perform a coarse search over a wide range of hyperparameter values. This approach, often employing grid search or random search, helps in identifying the general vicinity of optimal hyperparameters without expending excessive computational resources. During this phase, large step sizes should be used to quickly narrow down the search space.

Normalize Data: Ensuring that data is properly normalized can significantly impact the model's performance and the effectiveness of hyperparameter tuning. Normalization techniques such as Z-score normalization or min-max scaling can standardize the range of input features, preventing any single feature from disproportionately influencing the model.

Choose Sensible Defaults: Starting with sensible default hyperparameter values for certain parameters, such as learning rate or batch size, can provide a strong foundation for further tuning. These values can be derived from literature, previous experiments, or empirical rules.

Use Logarithmic Scales for Certain Hyperparameters: Some hyperparameters, such as the learning rate or regularization strength, can vary over several orders of magnitude. Using a logarithmic scale to explore these hyperparameters ensures a more comprehensive coverage of possible values. For example, exploring learning rates from 10^{-5} to 10^{-1} on a logarithmic scale could be more insightful than using a linear scale.

Employ Cross-Validation: Cross-validation is a powerful technique for assessing model performance and generalization. During hyperparameter tuning, it prevents overfitting to a specific validation set by averaging performance over multiple folds. This technique results in more robust and reliable assessment of hyperparameter configurations.

Monitor Metrics Beyond Accuracy: Depending on the problem, additional metrics like precision, recall, F1-score, AUC-ROC, or RMSE might provide more comprehensive insights into the model's performance. Evaluating these metrics during hyperparameter tuning ensures that the model is not only accurate but also well-suited to the specific requirements of the task.

Use Early Stopping with Patience: Implementing early stopping can save computational resources by terminating training when the model performance on validation data ceases to improve. Setting a patience parameter, which allows for a few epochs of no improvement before stopping, can prevent premature termination and ensure the model has sufficient opportunity to improve.

Leverage Automated Tools: Utilizing tools designed for hyperparameter optimization, like Keras Tuner, Hyperopt, or Optuna, can automate the hyperparameter search process. These tools often integrate advanced search algorithms, such as Bayesian optimization, and provide facilities to manage and recover from failures during the tuning process.

Parallelize Hyperparameter Searches: Taking advantage of parallel computing resources can significantly speed up the hyperparameter tuning process. By distributing the search across multiple CPUs or GPUs, large-scale studies can be conducted in a fraction of the time compared to serial execution. Tools like Ray Tune can facilitate distributed hyperparameter tuning.

Be Aware of Overfitting: Monitor the performance of the model on both the training and validation datasets throughout the tuning process. Large discrepancies between training and validation performance can indicate overfitting. Techniques such as dropout, regularization, and data augmentation can mitigate overfitting effectively.

Consider the Bias-Variance Tradeoff: Balancing the bias-variance tradeoff is crucial for achieving optimal model performance. Models with high bias (underfitting) or high variance (overfitting) benefit from tuning different sets of hyperparameters. For instance, increasing model complexity by adding layers or neurons may reduce bias but increase variance.

Iteratively Refine Hyperparameters: The hyperparameter tuning process is iterative by nature. As better hyperparameter values are discovered, refining the search space and focusing on finer details becomes essential. This step-by-step optimization helps in progressively improving the model performance.

Document and Reproduce Experiments: Maintaining detailed documentation of hyperparameter configurations, corresponding results, and experimental conditions is vital. This practice enhances reproducibility and facilitates future efforts in tuning and model development. Version control systems like Git, coupled with experiment tracking tools such as MLflow or Weights & Biases, can streamline this process.

```
import kerastuner as kt
```

```
from tensorflow import keras
from tensorflow.keras import layers

def build_model(hp):
    model = keras.Sequential()
    model.add(layers.Flatten(input_shape=(28, 28)))
    model.add(
        layers.Dense(
            units=hp.Int('units', min_value=32, max_value=512, step=32),
            activation='relu'
        )
    )
    model.add(layers.Dense(10, activation='softmax'))

    model.compile(
        optimizer=keras.optimizers.Adam(
            hp.Choice('learning_rate', values=[1e-2, 1e-3, 1e-4])
        ),
        loss='sparse_categorical_crossentropy',
        metrics=['accuracy']
    )
    return model

tuner = kt.RandomSearch(
    build_model,
    objective='val_accuracy',
    max_trials=5,
    executions_per_trial=3,
    directory='my_dir',
    project_name='intro_to_kt'
)

tuner.search_space_summary()

tuner.search(x_train, y_train, epochs=5, validation_data=(x_val, y_val))

tuner.results_summary()
```

With a comprehensive approach to hyperparameter tuning, including the strategies outlined above, the overall performance and generalizability of neural network models can be significantly enhanced, resulting in more reliable and effective machine learning solutions.

8.10 Understanding the Bias-Variance Tradeoff

The bias-variance tradeoff is a fundamental concept in the field of machine learning that addresses the tradeoff between two sources of error that affect the performance of predictive models: bias and variance. Understanding and balancing these errors is crucial for building models that generalize well to new data.

Bias refers to the error that is introduced by approximating a real-world problem, which may be complex, by a simplified model. High bias implies that the model is too rigid and overly simplified, capturing the training data's underlying patterns poorly. This can result in underfitting, where the model fails to capture the complexities and nuances of the data. Mathematically, bias can be considered as the difference between the average prediction of our model and the correct value which we are trying to predict. High bias can cause a model to miss relevant relations between input features and target outputs.

Variance, on the other hand, refers to the model's sensitivity to small fluctuations in the training dataset. A model with high variance pays too much attention to the training data, including the noise. It tends to model the random noise in the training data rather than the intended outputs, leading to overfitting. This causes the model to perform well on training data but poorly on unseen data. Mathematically, variance measures the variability of the model prediction for a given data point, captured across different training sets.

The Tradeoff: The tradeoff between bias and variance involves finding a model that minimizes both errors to achieve good generalization. A model with high bias and low variance will be consistently wrong in its predictions (underfitting). In contrast, a model with low bias and high variance will capture the training data's noise, resulting in poor performance on new data (overfitting).

We can illustrate the bias-variance tradeoff equation more formally with the following decomposition of the model prediction error. Let y be the true output, $\hat{f}$ be our model, and X be our data:

$$\begin{aligned}\text{Expected Prediction Error} &= E[(y - \hat{f}(X))^2] \\ &= \text{Bias}^2[\hat{f}(X)] + \text{Variance}[\hat{f}(X)] + \text{Irreducible Error}\end{aligned}$$

Here, the **Irreducible Error** represents errors caused by aspects of the problem that cannot be removed or reduced by choosing better models or hyperparameters. This can include the noise inherent to the data itself or limitations in the feature set available.

Balancing the Tradeoff: Various techniques and strategies can be employed to balance the bias-variance tradeoff:

- *Model Complexity:* Choose a model with appropriate complexity. Simpler models tend to have high bias and low variance, while complex models tend to have low bias and high variance. Regularization techniques like L1 (lasso) and L2 (ridge) can help manage complexity.

- *Training Data Size:* Increasing the training data size can help mitigate high variance by giving the model more information to learn from, leading to more reliable pattern detection.
- *Cross-Validation:* Use techniques like k-fold cross-validation to ensure that the model performs consistently well on different subsets of the data, helping balance bias and variance.
- *Ensemble Methods:* Techniques such as bagging (bootstrap aggregating), boosting, and stacking can help reduce variance without significantly increasing bias by combining multiple models.
- *Regularization Hyperparameters:* Tuning hyperparameters that control regularization strength (e.g., λ in ridge regression, α in LASSO) to find a balance between underfitting and overfitting.

An example using Python and Keras to illustrate the bias-variance tradeoff:

```
from tensorflow.keras.datasets import boston_housing
from tensorflow.keras.models import Sequential
from tensorflow.keras.layers import Dense
from tensorflow.keras.optimizers import SGD
from sklearn.model_selection import train_test_split

# Load data
(X_train, y_train), (X_test, y_test) = boston_housing.load_data()

# Split data for training and validation
X_train, X_val, y_train, y_val = train_test_split(X_train, y_train, test_size=0.2,
    random_state=42)

# Define a simple model with high bias (underfitting)
model_high_bias = Sequential([
    Dense(10, input_shape=(X_train.shape[1],), activation='relu'),
    Dense(1)
])
model_high_bias.compile(optimizer='sgd', loss='mse')
model_high_bias.fit(X_train, y_train, epochs=100, validation_data=(X_val, y_val))

# Define a complex model that may have high variance (overfitting)
model_high_variance = Sequential([
    Dense(128, input_shape=(X_train.shape[1],), activation='relu'),
    Dense(64, activation='relu'),
    Dense(1)
])
model_high_variance.compile(optimizer='adam', loss='mse')
model_high_variance.fit(X_train, y_train, epochs=100, validation_data=(X_val,
    y_val))
```

Output from the training would highlight the difference in model performance on training and validation data:

```
# Model with high bias (underfitting)
Train MSE: 40.5 | Validation MSE: 45.7

# Model with high variance (overfitting)
Train MSE: 10.1 | Validation MSE: 20.4
```

By tuning the complexity of our neural network and using appropriate training practices, we aim to minimize the prediction error as much as possible given the constraints of our data and problem space. The ultimate goal is to achieve a balanced model where neither bias nor variance dominates significantly, thus ensuring our model generalizes well to unseen data.

8.11 Case Studies: Hyperparameter Tuning in Real-world Projects

In this section, we delve into practical applications of hyperparameter tuning in real-world projects. By examining concrete examples, we aim to bridge theoretical knowledge and practical skills, providing insight into the decision-making processes involved in optimizing neural network performance.

Case Study 1: Image Classification with Convolutional Neural Networks (CNNs)

Project Description: This project involves developing a CNN model for classifying images from the CIFAR-10 dataset, which contains 60,000 32x32 color images across 10 classes. The goal is to achieve high classification accuracy by effectively tuning hyperparameters.

Hyperparameters Considered:

- Number of convolutional layers
- Number of filters in each layer
- Filter size
- Activation function
- Learning rate
- Batch size

Tuning Approach: Grid search is employed to explore the hyperparameter space. Below is an example of the grid search implementation using Keras and scikit-learn's GridSearchCV.

```
from keras.models import Sequential
from keras.layers import Conv2D, MaxPooling2D, Flatten, Dense
from keras.wrappers.scikit_learn import KerasClassifier
from sklearn.model_selection import GridSearchCV

def create_model(num_filters=32, kernel_size=3, activation='relu', learning_rate
        =0.01):
    model = Sequential()
    model.add(Conv2D(num_filters, kernel_size=(kernel_size, kernel_size), activation
            =activation, input_shape=(32, 32, 3)))
    model.add(MaxPooling2D(pool_size=(2, 2)))
    model.add(Flatten())
    model.add(Dense(10, activation='softmax'))
    model.compile(optimizer='adam', loss='categorical_crossentropy', metrics=['
            accuracy'])
    return model

model = KerasClassifier(build_fn=create_model, epochs=10, batch_size=64, verbose
        =1)
param_grid = {
    'num_filters': [32, 64, 128],
    'kernel_size': [3, 5],
    'activation': ['relu', 'tanh'],
    'learning_rate': [0.01, 0.001],
    'batch_size': [32, 64]
}
grid = GridSearchCV(estimator=model, param_grid=param_grid, cv=3)
grid_result = grid.fit(X_train, y_train)
```

The result of the grid search reveals the optimal combination of hyperparameters that yields the highest validation accuracy.

```
Best: 0.8278 using {'activation': 'relu', 'batch_size': 32, 'kernel_size': 3, 'learning_rate': 0.001, 'num_filters': 64}
```

Outcome: Fine-tuning these hyperparameters improved the model's performance from an initial 75% accuracy to over 82% on the validation set.

Case Study 2: Natural Language Processing (NLP) with Recurrent Neural Networks (RNNs)

Project Description: This project aims to create an RNN for sentiment analysis on the IMDb movie reviews dataset. The objective is to classify reviews as positive or negative.

Hyperparameters Considered:

- Number of LSTM units
- Dropout rate
- Learning rate

- Batch size
- Sequence length

Tuning Approach: Random search is chosen to navigate the hyperparameter space due to its ability to cover a larger range with fewer iterations.

```
from keras.models import Sequential
from keras.layers import LSTM, Dropout, Dense, Embedding
from keras.optimizers import Adam
from keras.wrappers.scikit_learn import KerasClassifier
from sklearn.model_selection import RandomizedSearchCV

def create_model(lstm_units=50, dropout_rate=0.2, learning_rate=0.01):
    model = Sequential()
    model.add(Embedding(input_dim=5000, output_dim=128, input_length=500))
    model.add(LSTM(lstm_units, return_sequences=True))
    model.add(Dropout(dropout_rate))
    model.add(LSTM(lstm_units))
    model.add(Dropout(dropout_rate))
    model.add(Dense(1, activation='sigmoid'))
    optimizer = Adam(learning_rate=learning_rate)
    model.compile(optimizer=optimizer, loss='binary_crossentropy', metrics=['accuracy
        '])
    return model

model = KerasClassifier(build_fn=create_model, epochs=10, batch_size=64, verbose
    =1)
param_dist = {
    'lstm_units': [50, 100, 150],
    'dropout_rate': [0.2, 0.3, 0.4],
    'learning_rate': [0.01, 0.001, 0.0001],
    'batch_size': [32, 64]
}
random = RandomizedSearchCV(estimator=model, param_distributions=param_dist,
    n_iter=10, cv=3, random_state=42)
random_result = random.fit(X_train, y_train)
```

The outcome from the random search provides the best configuration of hyperparameters.

```
Best: 0.8752 using {'batch_size': 32, 'dropout_rate': 0.3, 'learning_rate': 0.001, 'lstm_units': 100}
```

By leveraging random search, we were able to enhance the model from baseline accuracy of 85% to 87.52%.

Case Study 3: Reinforcement Learning for Game Playing

Project Description: This case involves using reinforcement learning for training an agent to play the classic Atari game, Breakout. The deep Q-network (DQN) algorithm serves as the basis for this project.

Hyperparameters Considered:

- Learning rate

- Discount factor
- Replay buffer size
- Exploration rate
- Batch size

Tuning Approach: Bayesian optimization is applied due to its efficiency in fine-tuning complex models in fewer iterations.

Using the optuna framework, we implemented a Bayesian optimization process:

```
import optuna
from keras.models import Sequential
from keras.layers import Dense
from keras.optimizers import Adam

def create_dqn(trial):
    learning_rate = trial.suggest_loguniform('learning_rate', 1e-5, 1e-2)
    discount_factor = trial.suggest_uniform('discount_factor', 0.9, 0.99)
    replay_buffer_size = trial.suggest_int('replay_buffer_size', 1e4, 1e6)
    exploration_rate = trial.suggest_uniform('exploration_rate', 0.1, 1.0)
    batch_size = trial.suggest_int('batch_size', 32, 256)

    model = Sequential()
    model.add(Dense(24, activation='relu', input_dim=state_size))
    model.add(Dense(24, activation='relu'))
    model.add(Dense(action_size, activation='linear'))
    model.compile(optimizer=Adam(lr=learning_rate), loss='mse')

    # DQN algorithm components
    dqn_agent = build_dqn_agent(model, discount_factor, replay_buffer_size,
        exploration_rate, batch_size)
    return dqn_agent

def objective(trial):
    dqn_agent = create_dqn(trial)
    return evaluate_dqn_agent(dqn_agent)

study = optuna.create_study(direction='maximize')
study.optimize(objective, n_trials=50)
```

The best hyperparameters from the study are displayed:

```
Best trial: Value: 0.8500
 Params: {'learning_rate': 0.0001, 'discount_factor': 0.97, 'replay_buffer_size': 100000, 'exploration_rate': 0.1, 'batch_size': 64}
```

Outcome: Optimizing the DQN hyperparameters increased the agent's average score from 50 to 85, showcasing significant performance improvement.

These case studies highlight the critical role of hyperparameter tuning across various deep learning applications, providing practical insights and illustrating the impact of methodical tuning practices on model performance.

Chapter 9

Model Evaluation and Validation

This chapter delves into the processes of model evaluation and validation, emphasizing the importance of using training, validation, and test sets. It explores cross-validation techniques, and various evaluation metrics for both classification and regression tasks. The chapter also covers handling imbalanced datasets, visualizing model performance, understanding overfitting and generalization, and approaches to model interpretability and explainability.

9.1 Introduction to Model Evaluation and Validation

Model evaluation and validation are critical components in the lifecycle of a deep learning model. These steps ensure that the model not only performs well on the training data but also generalizes effectively to unseen data. The processes involved in evaluation and validation help identify overfitting, underfitting, and provide insights into the model's predictive power.

Evaluation of a model typically involves assessing various performance metrics derived from predictions made on a validation set or a test set. This allows us to estimate how well our model will perform in real-world scenarios. Validation, on the other hand, is the process of tuning model hyperparameters and selecting the best model configuration based on the evaluation outcomes.

When we build a machine learning model, our primary goal is to develop a model that makes accurate predictions. However, without proper evaluation and validation mechanisms, it is difficult to determine whether the model's performance is genuine or merely an artifact of the training data's peculiarities. Therefore, we emphasize a systematic approach to evaluation and validation throughout the model development process.

The first step in model evaluation is to split the dataset into distinct subsets, typically the training set, validation set, and test set. The **training set** is used to train the model, allowing it to learn the underlying patterns and relationships in the data. The **validation set** is used during the tuning phase to validate the model's performance on data it has not encountered during training. The **test set**, which the model only sees after all training and validation are completed, provides an unbiased estimate of the model's performance on entirely unseen data.

Another important consideration is the selection of appropriate evaluation metrics. Different problems, such as classification and regression tasks, require different metrics to assess model performance effectively. For classification tasks, metrics like accuracy, precision, recall, and the F1 score are commonly used. For regression tasks, metrics such as mean squared error (MSE), mean absolute error (MAE), and R^2 score are often employed.

To further improve the reliability of model evaluation, techniques such as cross-validation are employed. Cross-validation involves partitioning the data into multiple folds and training the model multiple times, each time using a different fold as the validation set and the remaining folds as the training set. This provides a more robust estimate of the model's performance by reducing the variance associated with a single train-validation split.

Overfitting is a common problem in machine learning, where a model performs exceptionally well on the training data but poorly on unseen data. This occurs when the model learns the noise and specific patterns in the training data rather than the general underlying trends. Effective validation helps identify overfitting and enables the development of models that generalize better.

Model validation is also intertwined with the process of hyperparameter tuning. Hyperparameters are the parameters that are not learned from the data but are set prior to the training process. Examples include the learning rate, number of layers, and number of neurons per layer in a neural network. Proper validation techniques help in selecting the optimal combination of hyperparameters, ensuring that the model achieves the best possible performance on unseen data.

In addition to traditional evaluation and validation techniques, it is also important to consider model interpretability and explainability. Understanding why a model makes certain predictions can provide valuable insights, especially in fields requiring high levels of accountability, such as healthcare and finance. Techniques like SHapley Additive exPlanations (SHAP) values and Local Interpretable Model-agnostic Explanations (LIME) offer ways to interpret complex deep learning models.

Best practices in model evaluation and validation highlight the importance of maintaining a clean separation between training and evaluation data, selecting appropriate metrics, employing cross-validation techniques, and tuning hyperparameters meticulously. Deep learning practitioners should integrate these principles into their workflows to develop robust models that perform well in real-world applications.

9.2 Importance of Model Evaluation

Model evaluation is a critical component of developing robust, reliable deep learning models. It forms the foundation for assessing the performance and generalizability of a model. Without thorough evaluation, a model's effectiveness cannot be guaranteed, and decisions based on model outputs may be flawed or suboptimal. This section examines several key reasons why model evaluation is indispensable.

Accurate model evaluation allows for the detection and correction of overfitting, which occurs when a model performs exceptionally well on training data but fails to generalize to new, unseen data. Overfitting is a common issue in deep learning due to the high capacity of neural networks, which can easily memorize training data. By evaluating the model on a separate validation set, it becomes evident when the model is learning noise rather than the underlying data distribution. This can be addressed through techniques such as regularization, dropout, or early stopping.

Model evaluation is also essential for selecting the best model among multiple candidates. In the model development phase, various architectures, hyperparameters, and training configurations are tried and tested. Reliable evaluation metrics guide the selection process by providing an objective assessment of each model's performance. This objective assessment includes a variety of metrics such as accuracy, precision, recall, and F1 score for classification tasks, or mean absolute error (MAE) and root mean squared error (RMSE) for regression tasks.

Another vital aspect of model evaluation is the identification of class imbalances and other biases in the data. Imbalanced datasets can lead to models that are biased towards the majority class, resulting in poor performance on minority classes. Techniques such as precision-recall curves, ROC curves, and confusion matrices can uncover these issues. Appropriate measures such as resampling, reweighting classes, or using specialized loss functions can then be implemented to mitigate the imbalances.

Moreover, model evaluation provides insights into the reliability and confidence of the model predictions. Metrics like calibration curves and Brier scores can be used to assess the probability estimates produced by a model. A well-calibrated model will produce accurate probabilities that reflect the true likelihood of an event, which is crucial in applications that require risk assessment or decision making under uncertainty.

The evaluation process is indispensable for understanding the trade-offs between different model performance aspects. For instance, improving a model's precision might reduce its recall, and vice versa. By thoroughly evaluating models with different metrics, one can understand and balance these trade-offs according to the specific requirements of the application. This is particularly important in fields such as medical diagnosis or credit scoring, where the costs of false positives and false negatives are significantly different.

Furthermore, model evaluation is critical for maintaining transparency and trust in machine learning systems. This involves not only demonstrating the model's performance to stakeholders but also ensuring that the model's behavior is interpretable and explainable. Metrics that measure explanation quality, along with visualization tools, play a crucial role in achieving this transparency.

One practical aspect of model evaluation is demonstrated through the use of the Keras library in Python:

```
from keras.models import Sequential
from keras.layers import Dense
from keras.datasets import mnist
from keras.utils import to_categorical
from sklearn.metrics import classification_report
```

```
# Load data
(train_images, train_labels), (test_images, test_labels) = mnist.load_data()
train_images = train_images.reshape((60000, 28 * 28)).astype('float32') / 255
test_images = test_images.reshape((10000, 28 * 28)).astype('float32') / 255
train_labels = to_categorical(train_labels)
test_labels = to_categorical(test_labels)

# Define the model
model = Sequential()
model.add(Dense(512, activation='relu', input_shape=(28 * 28,)))
model.add(Dense(10, activation='softmax'))

# Compile the model
model.compile(optimizer='rmsprop',
              loss='categorical_crossentropy',
              metrics=['accuracy'])

# Evaluate the model on test data
model.fit(train_images, train_labels, epochs=5, batch_size=128)
test_loss, test_acc = model.evaluate(test_images, test_labels)
print('Test accuracy:', test_acc)

# Generate classification report
predictions = model.predict(test_images)
predicted_classes = predictions.argmax(axis=-1)
true_classes = test_labels.argmax(axis=-1)
print(classification_report(true_classes, predicted_classes))
```

The snippet above demonstrates the process of training and evaluating a simple neural network on the MNIST dataset. After training, the model's performance is assessed using the test set accuracy and a detailed classification report, highlighting the importance of various evaluation metrics.

Model evaluation remains a cornerstone of effective deep learning practice, ensuring that models not only perform well on seen data but also have the capability to generalize to new, unseen data.

9.3 Training, Validation, and Test Sets

The concepts of training, validation, and test sets are foundational to machine learning and deep learning model development. Each dataset serves a distinct and crucial role in building models that generalize well to unseen data.

The **training set** is used to train the model. During this phase, the learning algorithm iterates over the data, adjusting model parameters (weights and biases in neural networks) to minimize the loss function. The quality and quantity of the training data directly influence the model's ability to learn patterns.

Consider a supervised learning algorithm where the data is labeled. Given a dataset (X, Y), X represents the input features, and Y denotes the corresponding labels. The training set (X_{train}, Y_{train}) is typically 60-80% of the entire dataset. The following Python code illustrates how to split a dataset using the train_test_split function from scikit-learn:

```
from sklearn.model_selection import train_test_split

# Assuming X and Y are pre-defined datasets
X_train, X_temp, Y_train, Y_temp = train_test_split(X, Y, test_size=0.4,
    random_state=42)
X_val, X_test, Y_val, Y_test = train_test_split(X_temp, Y_temp, test_size=0.5,
    random_state=42)
```

The **validation set** is used to tune hyperparameters, select models, and detect overfitting during the training process. This dataset helps in assessing the training process's performance before making predictions on new data. It provides a checkpoint to adjust the model without relying on the test set. Hyperparameter tuning, regularization, and early stopping techniques use this dataset to optimize model performance.

In Keras, the validation set can be specified during training by passing validation data to the fit method:

```
from keras.models import Sequential
from keras.layers import Dense

# Define a simple model
model = Sequential()
model.add(Dense(64, activation='relu', input_dim=100))
model.add(Dense(1, activation='sigmoid'))

# Compile the model
model.compile(optimizer='adam', loss='binary_crossentropy', metrics=['accuracy'])

# Train the model with validation data
model.fit(X_train, Y_train, epochs=50, batch_size=32, validation_data=(X_val,
    Y_val))
```

It is essential to avoid using the validation set multiple times for hyperparameter tuning, as this practice can lead to overfitting on the validation data itself, reducing the model's ability to generalize.

The **test set** serves as an unbiased evaluation metric for the final model after it has been trained and validated. This dataset is used exclusively once to ascertain the model's generalizability to new, unseen data. The performance metrics calculated on the test set provide an estimate of how well the model will perform in a real-world scenario.

In practice, the test set is separated from the dataset at the beginning and remains untouched until the final evaluation. Consider the following R code to split datasets:

```
set.seed(42)
train_index <- sample(seq_len(nrow(dataset)), size = 0.6 * nrow(dataset))
temp_set <- dataset[-train_index, ]

val_index <- sample(seq_len(nrow(temp_set)), size = 0.5 * nrow(temp_set))
test_set <- temp_set[ -val_index, ]
val_set <- temp_set[val_index, ]

training_set <- dataset[train_index, ]
```

Effective splits ensure that the model evaluation and validation process accounts for different data distributions and prevents data leakage, where information from the test set inadvertently influences the training process.

By separating your data into training, validation, and test sets, you maintain the integrity of the evaluation process, allowing for accurate assessments of your model's performance and ensuring robust, generalizable deep learning models.

9.4 Cross-Validation Techniques

Cross-validation is a robust method for evaluating the performance of machine learning models, providing insights into model generalizability. It partitions the data into subsets, trains the model on some subsets, and validates it on others. Different cross-validation methods offer various trade-offs between computational efficiency and the fidelity of the performance estimate. This section examines several widely-used techniques, including k-fold cross-validation, stratified k-fold cross-validation, leave-one-out cross-validation (LOOCV), and time series cross-validation.

K-Fold Cross-Validation

K-fold cross-validation is perhaps the most common and straightforward approach. The data is divided into k equally sized folds (subsets). The model is trained k times, each time using a different fold as the validation set and the remaining $k-1$ folds as the training set. This results in k different performance measures, which are averaged to provide a final performance estimate.

```
from sklearn.model_selection import KFold
import numpy as np
```

```
X = np.array([...]) # feature matrix
y = np.array([...]) # target vector

kf = KFold(n_splits=5, shuffle=True, random_state=42)
for train_index, test_index in kf.split(X):
    X_train, X_test = X[train_index], X[test_index]
    y_train, y_test = y[train_index], y[test_index]
    # Train your model on X_train, y_train
    # Validate your model on X_test, y_test
```

Stratified K-Fold Cross-Validation

In classification tasks, especially with imbalanced classes, it is beneficial to maintain the class distribution ratio in each fold using stratified k-fold cross-validation. This ensures each fold is representative of the overall dataset's class distribution.

```
from sklearn.model_selection import StratifiedKFold

skf = StratifiedKFold(n_splits=5, shuffle=True, random_state=42)
for train_index, test_index in skf.split(X, y):
    X_train, X_test = X[train_index], X[test_index]
    y_train, y_test = y[train_index], y[test_index]
    # Train and validate your model
```

Leave-One-Out Cross-Validation (LOOCV)

LOOCV is an extreme case of k-fold cross-validation where k is equal to the number of data points. Each iteration trains the model on all data points except one, which is used as the validation set. This approach is computationally intensive but maximizes the data used for training, providing a nearly unbiased performance estimate.

```
from sklearn.model_selection import LeaveOneOut

loo = LeaveOneOut()
for train_index, test_index in loo.split(X):
    X_train, X_test = X[train_index], X[test_index]
    y_train, y_test = y[train_index], y[test_index]
    # Train and validate your model
```

Time Series Cross-Validation (Rolling Forecasting Origin)

For time series data, regular cross-validation techniques are unsuitable as they ignore temporal dependencies. Time series cross-validation respects the time order. The rolling forecasting origin method involves splitting the data into training and test sets in a way that the training set always comes before the test set chronologically. This is particularly useful for validating models that forecast future values.

```
from sklearn.model_selection import TimeSeriesSplit

tscv = TimeSeriesSplit(n_splits=5)
```

```
for train_index, test_index in tscv.split(X):
    X_train, X_test = X[train_index], X[test_index]
    y_train, y_test = y[train_index], y[test_index]
    # Train and validate your model
```

Choosing the Right Technique

Selecting the appropriate cross-validation method depends on the specific characteristics of the dataset and the computational resources available. K-fold cross-validation is a balanced choice for many scenarios. Stratified k-fold is particularly important for imbalanced datasets to ensure each fold is a good representative of the whole. LOOCV, despite its computational cost, is useful when dealing with very small datasets. For time series data, special methods like the rolling forecasting origin technique should be preferred to respect temporal dependencies.

Implementation Considerations

While cross-validation provides a robust framework for model evaluation, its effectiveness depends on proper implementation. Ensuring that data leakage is prevented, especially in iterative methods such as LOOCV, is crucial. Data leakage occurs when information from outside the training dataset is used to create the model, leading to overly optimistic performance estimates.

Implementing cross-validation in practice requires meticulous preprocessing, consistent random state initialization to ensure reproducibility, and careful tracking of performance metrics across folds. Advanced techniques like nested cross-validation, where inner cross-validation is used for model selection and outer cross-validation for performance estimation, can further enhance robustness.

```
from sklearn.metrics import accuracy_score

outer_kf = KFold(n_splits=5, shuffle=True, random_state=42)
for train_index, test_index in outer_kf.split(X):
    X_train_outer, X_test_outer = X[train_index], X[test_index]
    y_train_outer, y_test_outer = y[train_index], y[test_index]

    # Perform inner cross-validation for model selection
    inner_kf = KFold(n_splits=3, shuffle=True, random_state=42)
    for inner_train_index, inner_test_index in inner_kf.split(X_train_outer):
        X_train_inner, X_test_inner = X[inner_train_index], X[inner_test_index]
        y_train_inner, y_test_inner = y[inner_train_index], y[inner_test_index]
        # Train and validate your inner model

    # After selecting the best model, evaluate on the outer test set
    final_model.fit(X_train_outer, y_train_outer)
    y_pred = final_model.predict(X_test_outer)
    print(accuracy_score(y_test_outer, y_pred))
```

Understanding and correctly applying these cross-validation techniques are foundational for reliable model evaluation and selection, enabling the development of models that generalize well to new, unseen data.

9.5 Evaluation Metrics for Classification

Effective evaluation metrics are crucial in understanding the performance of a classification model. They provide quantitative measures to compare different models and determine their effectiveness in predicting target labels. In classification tasks, the goal is to categorize input data into predefined classes. While accuracy is a commonly referenced metric, it does not fully capture the nuances of model performance, especially in cases of imbalanced datasets. We will discuss several key metrics used to evaluate classification models: accuracy, precision, recall, F1-score, area under the Receiver Operating Characteristic (ROC) curve (AUC-ROC), and log loss.

Accuracy is the proportion of correctly predicted instances out of the total instances. It is defined as follows:

$$\text{Accuracy} = \frac{TP + TN}{TP + TN + FP + FN}$$

where TP (True Positives) are instances where the model correctly predicted the positive class, TN (True Negatives) are instances where the model correctly predicted the negative class, FP (False Positives) are instances where the model incorrectly predicted the positive class, and FN (False Negatives) are instances where the model incorrectly predicted the negative class.

While accuracy is useful, it can be misleading for datasets where the classes are imbalanced. For example, if 95

Precision is the ratio of correctly predicted positive observations to the total predicted positives. It is defined as:

$$\text{Precision} = \frac{TP}{TP + FP}$$

Precision is a useful metric when the cost of false positives is high. It answers the question: "Of all the instances that were predicted as positive, how many are actually positive?"

Recall (also known as Sensitivity or True Positive Rate) is the ratio of correctly predicted positive observations to all observations in the actual class. It is defined as:

$$\text{Recall} = \frac{TP}{TP + FN}$$

Recall is crucial when the cost of false negatives is high. It answers the question: "Of all the instances that are actually positive, how many did the model correctly identify?"

F1-Score is the harmonic mean of Precision and Recall, and it seeks a balance between the two. It is defined as:

$$\text{F1-Score} = 2 \times \frac{\text{Precision} \times \text{Recall}}{\text{Precision} + \text{Recall}}$$

The F1-Score is particularly useful when the class distribution is imbalanced, offering a single metric that balances both false positives and false negatives.

Area Under the Receiver Operating Characteristic Curve (AUC-ROC) is a performance measurement for classification problems at various threshold settings. ROC is a probability curve, and AUC represents the degree of separability. It tells how much the model is capable of distinguishing between classes. The ROC curve is plotted with True Positive Rate against False Positive Rate. The AUC value ranges from 0 to 1. A model with an AUC value of 1 is considered a perfect model, while a value of 0.5 indicates a model that performs no better than random guessing.

```
from sklearn.metrics import roc_curve, roc_auc_score
import matplotlib.pyplot as plt

# Assuming y_true are the true labels and y_scores are the predicted probabilities
fpr, tpr, thresholds = roc_curve(y_true, y_scores)
roc_auc = roc_auc_score(y_true, y_scores)

plt.figure()
plt.plot(fpr, tpr, color='darkorange', lw=2, label='ROC curve (area = %0.2f)' %
    roc_auc)
plt.plot([0, 1], [0, 1], color='navy', lw=2, linestyle='--')
plt.xlim([0.0, 1.0])
plt.ylim([0.0, 1.0])
plt.xlabel('False Positive Rate')
plt.ylabel('True Positive Rate')
plt.title('Receiver Operating Characteristic')
plt.legend(loc="lower right")
plt.show()
```

Log Loss (or Cross-Entropy Loss) is a metric that measures the performance of a classification model where the prediction input is a probability value between 0 and 1. Minimizing the log loss is equivalent to predicting the true class probability distribution for each sample. It is defined as follows:

$$\text{Log Loss} = -\frac{1}{N}\sum_{i=1}^{N}[y_i \log(p_i) + (1 - y_i)\log(1 - p_i)]$$

where N is the number of samples, y_i is the true label, and p_i is the predicted probability.

Choosing the appropriate evaluation metric depends on the specific context of the problem at hand. For instance, in medical diagnostics, recall might be prioritized over precision to ensure that as many true positive cases as possible are identified. In spam detection, precision might be more critical to reduce the number of legitimate emails classified as spam. By understanding and correctly applying these metrics, it becomes possible to gain a comprehensive understanding of model performance beyond basic accuracy.

9.6 Evaluation Metrics for Regression

Evaluating the performance of regression models is a critical aspect of the model validation process. Unlike classification tasks where the goal is to predict discrete class labels, regression tasks focus on predicting continuous numerical values. Consequently, the metrics used for evaluating regression models differ significantly from those used for classification. Here we discuss several key evaluation metrics for regression: Mean Absolute Error (MAE), Mean Squared Error (MSE), Root Mean Squared Error (RMSE), R-squared (R^2) score, and Mean Absolute Percentage Error (MAPE).

Mean Absolute Error (MAE): This metric measures the average magnitude of the errors between predicted values and actual values. It is calculated as follows:

$$\text{MAE} = \frac{1}{n}\sum_{i=1}^{n}|y_i - \hat{y}_i|$$

where n is the number of data points, y_i is the actual value, and $\hat{y}_i$ is the predicted value. MAE provides a straightforward interpretation as it represents the average absolute error in the same units as the target variable.

Mean Squared Error (MSE): This metric measures the average of the squares of the errors between actual and predicted values. It is defined as:

$$\text{MSE} = \frac{1}{n}\sum_{i=1}^{n}(y_i - \hat{y}_i)^2$$

MSE penalizes larger errors more significantly than MAE because the errors are squared. It is useful for emphasizing larger deviations and is commonly used as a loss function during model training.

Root Mean Squared Error (RMSE): RMSE is the square root of the MSE and provides an error metric that has the same units as the target variable. It is calculated as:

$$\text{RMSE} = \sqrt{\frac{1}{n}\sum_{i=1}^{n}(y_i - \hat{y}_i)^2}$$

R-squared (R^2) Score: Also known as the coefficient of determination, R^2 measures the proportion of the variance in the dependent variable that is predictable from the independent variables. The formula for R^2 is:

$$R^2 = 1 - \frac{\sum_{i=1}^{n}(y_i - \hat{y}_i)^2}{\sum_{i=1}^{n}(y_i - \bar{y})^2}$$

where $\bar{y}$ is the mean of the actual values. An R^2 value of 1 indicates perfect prediction, while a value of 0 indicates that the model does not explain any of the variability of the response data. Negative values of R^2 can occur if the model is worse than a simple horizontal line fit.

Mean Absolute Percentage Error (MAPE): This metric expresses the error as a percentage of the actual data, providing a normalized measure of prediction accuracy. It is defined as:

$$\text{MAPE} = \frac{1}{n}\sum_{i=1}^{n}\left|\frac{y_i - \hat{y}_i}{y_i}\right| \times 100$$

MAPE is useful for understanding the error in relative terms but can be misleading when the actual values are near zero, leading to extremely high percentage errors.

To illustrate these metrics, assume we have the following predicted values and actual values:

```
y_true = [3.0, -0.5, 2.0, 7.0]
y_pred = [2.5, 0.0, 2.0, 8.0]
```

We can compute these metrics using Python's scikit-learn library as follows:

```
from sklearn.metrics import mean_absolute_error, mean_squared_error, r2_score

# Calculate MAE
mae = mean_absolute_error(y_true, y_pred)
print(f"Mean Absolute Error: {mae}")

# Calculate MSE
mse = mean_squared_error(y_true, y_pred)
print(f"Mean Squared Error: {mse}")

# Calculate RMSE
rmse = mean_squared_error(y_true, y_pred, squared=False)
print(f"Root Mean Squared Error: {rmse}")

# Calculate R-squared
r2 = r2_score(y_true, y_pred)
print(f"R-squared: {r2}")
```

The output will look like:

```
Mean Absolute Error: 0.5
Mean Squared Error: 0.375
Root Mean Squared Error: 0.612372
R-squared: 0.948
```

These results indicate the model's performance by providing quantitative measures of prediction accuracy. Understanding these metrics helps in determining the strengths and weaknesses of different regression models and choosing the appropriate model for a specific problem.

9.7 Confusion Matrix and ROC Curves

The evaluation of classification models extends beyond a mere look at the accuracy metric. While accuracy provides an overall measure of how often the model correctly classifies instances, it falls short in providing detailed insights, especially in datasets with class imbalance. Two powerful tools that offer more granular insights into the performance of classification models are the confusion matrix and the Receiver Operating Characteristic (ROC) curve.

Confusion Matrix

A confusion matrix is a tabular representation that summarizes the performance of a classification model. It consists of four key metrics: True Positives (TP), False Positives (FP), True Negatives (TN), and False Negatives (FN). These metrics form a matrix in the following manner:

- **True Positives (TP)**: Instances correctly predicted as the positive class.
- **False Positives (FP)**: Instances incorrectly predicted as the positive class.
- **True Negatives (TN)**: Instances correctly predicted as the negative class.
- **False Negatives (FN)**: Instances incorrectly predicted as the negative class.

The structure of the confusion matrix for a binary classification problem is depicted as follows:

	Predicted	
	Positive	Negative
Actual Positive	TP	FN
Actual Negative	FP	TN

Derived Metrics

From the confusion matrix, several important evaluation metrics can be derived:

- **Accuracy**: The overall correctness of the model.

$$\text{Accuracy} = \frac{\text{TP} + \text{TN}}{\text{TP} + \text{TN} + \text{FP} + \text{FN}}$$

- **Precision**: The correctness of positive predictions.

$$\text{Precision} = \frac{\text{TP}}{\text{TP} + \text{FP}}$$

- **Recall (Sensitivity or True Positive Rate)**: The ability of the model to find all positive instances.

$$\text{Recall} = \frac{\text{TP}}{\text{TP} + \text{FN}}$$

- **Specificity (True Negative Rate)**: The ability of the model to identify all negative instances.

$$\text{Specificity} = \frac{\text{TN}}{\text{TN} + \text{FP}}$$

- **F1 Score**: The harmonic mean of Precision and Recall.

$$\text{F1 Score} = 2 \times \frac{\text{Precision} \times \text{Recall}}{\text{Precision} + \text{Recall}}$$

Consider a classification model with the following predictions:

```
from sklearn.metrics import confusion_matrix
y_true = [1, 0, 1, 1, 0, 1, 0, 0, 1, 1]
y_pred = [1, 0, 1, 0, 0, 1, 1, 0, 1, 0]

cm = confusion_matrix(y_true, y_pred)
print(cm)
```

```
[[3 1]
 [2 4]]
```

Here, $[3\ 1]$ represents the number of true negatives (TN = 3) and false positives (FP = 1), while $[2\ 4]$ represents the false negatives (FN = 2) and true positives (TP = 4).

ROC Curves

The Receiver Operating Characteristic (ROC) curve is a graphical representation that illustrates the diagnostic ability of a binary classification model. It plots the True Positive Rate (Recall) against the False Positive Rate (FPR) at various threshold settings, where FPR is defined as:

$$\text{False Positive Rate (FPR)} = \frac{\text{FP}}{\text{FP} + \text{TN}}$$

The ROC curve allows the comparison of the trade-off between sensitivity (Recall) and specificity (1 - FPR) by visualizing how the different threshold values affect the performance of the classifier.

Area Under the ROC Curve (AUC)

The Area Under the ROC Curve (AUC-ROC) provides a single scalar value to summarize the model's performance across all threshold values. The AUC ranges from 0 to 1, where a higher AUC indicates a better model performance. An AUC of 0.5 suggests no discriminative power, equivalent to random guessing.

The following Python code demonstrates how to plot an ROC curve and calculate the AUC using the scikit-learn library:

```
from sklearn.metrics import roc_curve, auc
import matplotlib.pyplot as plt

y_true = [1, 0, 1, 1, 0, 1, 0, 0, 1, 1]
y_scores = [0.9, 0.1, 0.8, 0.4, 0.2, 0.85, 0.7, 0.05, 0.9, 0.3]

fpr, tpr, thresholds = roc_curve(y_true, y_scores)
roc_auc = auc(fpr, tpr)

plt.figure()
plt.plot(fpr, tpr, color='darkorange', lw=2, label='ROC curve (area = %0.2f)' %
    roc_auc)
plt.plot([0, 1], [0, 1], color='navy', lw=2, linestyle='--')
plt.xlim([0.0, 1.0])
plt.ylim([0.0, 1.05])
plt.xlabel('False Positive Rate')
plt.ylabel('True Positive Rate')
plt.title('Receiver Operating Characteristic')
plt.legend(loc="lower right")
plt.show()
```

This will generate a plot similar to the ROC curve described above.

The ROC curve generated from this code visually represents the trade-off between the recall and false positive rate for various threshold values, with the AUC providing a quantitative measure of the classifier's performance.

The confusion matrix and ROC curve are indispensable tools for understanding and interpreting the performance of a classification model. Together, they provide detailed and comprehensive insights, enabling better decisions about model improvements and deployment.

9.8 Precision-Recall and F1 Score

In classification tasks, certain metrics play indispensable roles in effectively evaluating model performance. Two such metrics are precision and recall, along with an important derivative measure known as the F1 score. Precision and recall provide insights into the classifier's ability to handle specific classes, particularly when dealing with imbalanced datasets.

Precision is defined as the ratio of true positive predictions to the total number of positive predictions made by the model. It quantifies the accuracy of positive predictions:

$$\text{Precision} = \frac{\text{True Positives}}{\text{True Positives} + \text{False Positives}}$$

Recall, also known as sensitivity or true positive rate (TPR), is the ratio of true positive predictions to the total number of actual positives. It indicates the model's ability to identify all relevant instances:

$$\text{Recall} = \frac{\text{True Positives}}{\text{True Positives} + \text{False Negatives}}$$

Both precision and recall are critical in applications where the cost of false positives and false negatives is high. However, there is often a trade-off between these two metrics. To balance this trade-off, the F1 score is employed.

The **F1 score** is the harmonic mean of precision and recall. This score provides a single metric that balances both concerns, especially useful when the class distribution is uneven:

$$F1\text{ Score} = 2 \cdot \frac{\text{Precision} \cdot \text{Recall}}{\text{Precision} + \text{Recall}}$$

To demonstrate precision, recall, and F1 score calculations, consider the following example implemented using Python and Keras:

```
import numpy as np
from sklearn.metrics import precision_score, recall_score, f1_score
from keras.models import Sequential
from keras.layers import Dense

# Generate dummy data
np.random.seed(0)
X_train = np.random.rand(100, 10)
y_train = np.random.randint(2, size=100)
X_test = np.random.rand(20, 10)
y_test = np.random.randint(2, size=20)

# Define a simple binary classification model
model = Sequential()
model.add(Dense(64, input_dim=10, activation='relu'))
model.add(Dense(1, activation='sigmoid'))

# Compile the model
model.compile(optimizer='adam', loss='binary_crossentropy', metrics=['accuracy'])

# Train the model
model.fit(X_train, y_train, epochs=5, batch_size=10, verbose=0)

# Predict on test data
y_pred = (model.predict(X_test) > 0.5).astype('int32')
```

```
# Calculate precision, recall, and F1 score
precision = precision_score(y_test, y_pred)
recall = recall_score(y_test, y_pred)
f1 = f1_score(y_test, y_pred)

print(f'Precision: {precision:.2f}')
print(f'Recall: {recall:.2f}')
print(f'F1 Score: {f1:.2f}')
```

This code demonstrates a complete workflow, from data generation and model training to metric computation. The output of the above code might look like:

```
Precision: 0.60
Recall: 0.50
F1 Score: 0.55
```

These results summarize various aspects of model performance. Precision indicates that 60

Using precision-recall curves can further aid in evaluating model performance by visualizing the precision and recall for different threshold values. This is particularly helpful in model comparison and tuning.

```
from sklearn.metrics import precision_recall_curve
import matplotlib.pyplot as plt

# Generate precision-recall pairs for various threshold levels
precision_curve, recall_curve, threshold = precision_recall_curve(y_test, y_pred)

# Plot precision-recall curve
plt.figure()
plt.plot(threshold, precision_curve[:-1], 'b-', label='Precision')
plt.plot(threshold, recall_curve[:-1], 'g-', label='Recall')
plt.xlabel('Decision Threshold')
plt.ylabel('Score')
plt.title('Precision-Recall Curve')
plt.legend()
plt.show()
```

The generated plot assists in selecting an optimal threshold balancing precision and recall. High precision with low recall, or vice versa, might be acceptable in specific applications, but understanding their trade-offs is crucial.

Evaluating these metrics is vital in domains where distinguishing between true and false positives and negatives has significant consequences. Hence, mastering precision, recall, and the F1 score catapults the effectiveness of deploying reliable machine learning models.

9.9 Dealing with Imbalanced Datasets

Imbalanced datasets represent a common and significant challenge in machine learning, especially in classification tasks. An imbalanced dataset is characterized by a disproportionate distribution of classes, where some classes are significantly underrepresented compared to others. This imbalance can lead to biased models that exhibit poor generalization, particularly towards the minority class. Addressing this issue requires strategic approaches both in data preprocessing and in the choice of model and evaluation metrics.

Resampling Techniques: One of the primary methods to handle imbalanced datasets is through resampling techniques. These techniques involve adjusting the class distributions either by oversampling the minority class, undersampling the majority class, or a combination of both.

- **Oversampling the Minority Class**: This technique involves randomly duplicating examples from the minority class to augment its representation in the dataset. One common approach is the Synthetic Minority Over-sampling Technique (SMOTE), which generates synthetic examples by interpolating between existing minority class samples.

```
from imblearn.over_sampling import SMOTE
smote = SMOTE()
X_resampled, y_resampled = smote.fit_resample(X_train, y_train)
```

- **Undersampling the Majority Class**: This technique entails randomly removing examples from the majority class to balance the class distribution. While simple, this method risks discarding potentially valuable data.

```
from imblearn.under_sampling import RandomUnderSampler
rus = RandomUnderSampler()
X_resampled, y_resampled = rus.fit_resample(X_train, y_train)
```

- **Combination of Over- and Undersampling**: Combining both techniques can yield better results by leveraging the advantages of each while mitigating their respective downsides.

```
from imblearn.combine import SMOTEENN
smote_enn = SMOTEENN()
X_resampled, y_resampled = smote_enn.fit_resample(X_train, y_train)
```

Cost-Sensitive Learning: Cost-sensitive learning integrates the imbalance directly into the model training by assigning a higher misclassification cost to the minority class. This adjustment incentivizes the model to improve its performance on the minority class.

- In Keras, this can be implemented by specifying the class weights in the `fit` method.

```
class_weights = {0: 1.0, 1: 50.0} # Example weights
model.fit(X_train, y_train, epochs=10, class_weight=class_weights)
```

- Alternatively, one can utilize loss functions that are inherently cost-sensitive, such as focal loss, which is designed to address class imbalance by reducing the weight of well-classified examples.

```
import tensorflow as tf
def focal_loss(gamma=2., alpha=1.):
    def focal_loss_fixed(y_true, y_pred):
        epsilon = tf.keras.backend.epsilon()
        y_pred = tf.clip_by_value(y_pred, epsilon, 1. - epsilon)
        y_true = tf.clip_by_value(y_true, epsilon, 1. - epsilon)
        cross_entropy = -y_true * tf.math.log(y_pred)
        loss = alpha * tf.math.pow(1 - y_pred, gamma) * cross_entropy
        return tf.math.reduce_sum(loss, axis=1)
    return focal_loss_fixed

model.compile(optimizer='adam', loss=focal_loss())
```

Evaluation Metrics for Imbalanced Datasets: Standard accuracy is often misleading for imbalanced datasets as it can be disproportionately influenced by the majority class. Thus, it is crucial to consider evaluation metrics that provide a more balanced reflection of the model's performance.

- **Precision and Recall**: Precision measures the accuracy of positive predictions, while recall measures the ability of the model to identify all positive instances.
- **F1 Score**: The F1 score is the harmonic mean of precision and recall, offering a single metric that balances both concerns.
- **ROC AUC**: The Receiver Operating Characteristic (ROC) curve and the Area Under the Curve (AUC) provide insight into the trade-off between true positive rate and false positive rate across different threshold settings.

```
from sklearn.metrics import classification_report, roc_auc_score
```

```
y_pred = model.predict(X_test)
print(classification_report(y_test, y_pred))
print("ROC AUC Score:", roc_auc_score(y_test, y_pred))
```

Algorithmic Approaches: Some algorithms are naturally better suited to handle imbalanced datasets. Ensemble methods, such as Random Forests and Gradient Boosted Trees, tend to perform well under these conditions.

- **Random Forest**: By constructing multiple decision trees and averaging their predictions, Random Forests decrease the overfitting tendencies of individual trees and handle imbalance robustly through their inherent bootstrapping mechanism.
- **XGBoost**: This powerful gradient boosting framework includes parameters for handling class imbalance directly.

```
from xgboost import XGBClassifier

xgb = XGBClassifier(scale_pos_weight=ratio)
xgb.fit(X_train, y_train)
```

Implementing these strategies systematically allows the development of robust models that can effectively navigate the challenges posed by imbalanced datasets, thereby ensuring better generalization and more accurate predictions across different class distributions.

9.10 Visualizing Model Performance

Visualizing model performance is a crucial aspect of the machine learning workflow. It enables us to gain insights beyond numerical metrics, making it easier to identify patterns, strengths, and weaknesses in the model. In this section, we will discuss various techniques and tools for visualizing the performance of deep learning models implemented with Keras.

One fundamental tool for performance visualization is the **loss and accuracy plots**. During the training of a neural network, Keras provides a history object that contains the training and validation loss and accuracy per epoch. Visualizing these plots helps monitor the model's learning progress and identify issues like overfitting or underfitting. Below is an example of generating loss and accuracy plots using Matplotlib.

```
import matplotlib.pyplot as plt

# Assuming 'history' is the history object returned by model.fit()
def plot_history(history):
    plt.figure(figsize=(12, 4))

    # Plotting the loss
    plt.subplot(1, 2, 1)
    plt.plot(history.history['loss'], label='Train Loss')
    plt.plot(history.history['val_loss'], label='Validation Loss')
    plt.xlabel('Epochs')
    plt.ylabel('Loss')
    plt.legend()
    plt.title('Loss Plot')

    # Plotting the accuracy
    plt.subplot(1, 2, 2)
    plt.plot(history.history['accuracy'], label='Train Accuracy')
    plt.plot(history.history['val_accuracy'], label='Validation Accuracy')
    plt.xlabel('Epochs')
    plt.ylabel('Accuracy')
    plt.legend()
    plt.title('Accuracy Plot')

    plt.show()

# Example usage:
# history = model.fit(X_train, y_train, validation_data=(X_val, y_val), epochs=50)
# plot_history(history)
```

Another essential visualization tool is the **confusion matrix**. It provides a detailed breakdown of the true positives, true negatives, false positives, and false negatives, which offers a granular view of the model's classification performance. Using libraries such as Seaborn, we can create a heatmap to visualize the confusion matrix more effectively.

```
import seaborn as sns
from sklearn.metrics import confusion_matrix

# Assuming y_true contains true labels and y_pred contains model predictions
def plot_confusion_matrix(y_true, y_pred, class_names):
    cm = confusion_matrix(y_true, y_pred)
    plt.figure(figsize=(10, 8))
    sns.heatmap(cm, annot=True, fmt='d', cmap='Blues', xticklabels=class_names,
            yticklabels=class_names)
    plt.xlabel('Predicted')
    plt.ylabel('True')
    plt.title('Confusion Matrix')
    plt.show()

# Example usage:
# y_pred = model.predict_classes(X_test)
# plot_confusion_matrix(y_test, y_pred, class_names=['Class1', 'Class2', 'Class3'])
```

For binary classification tasks, the **Receiver Operating Characteristic (ROC) curve** and the **Precision-Recall curve** are invaluable tools.

The ROC curve plots the true positive rate against the false positive rate at various threshold settings, while the Precision-Recall curve plots precision against recall. These curves help in evaluating the tradeoffs between sensitivity and specificity and can be generated using Scikit-Learn.

```
from sklearn.metrics import roc_curve, auc, precision_recall_curve

def plot_roc_curve(y_true, y_scores):
    fpr, tpr, _ = roc_curve(y_true, y_scores)
    roc_auc = auc(fpr, tpr)
    plt.figure()
    plt.plot(fpr, tpr, color='darkorange', lw=2, label='ROC curve (area = %0.2f)' %
          roc_auc)
    plt.plot([0, 1], [0, 1], color='navy', lw=2, linestyle='--')
    plt.xlabel('False Positive Rate')
    plt.ylabel('True Positive Rate')
    plt.title('Receiver Operating Characteristic')
    plt.legend(loc='lower right')
    plt.show()

def plot_precision_recall_curve(y_true, y_scores):
    precision, recall, _ = precision_recall_curve(y_true, y_scores)
    plt.figure()
    plt.plot(recall, precision, color='b', lw=2)
    plt.xlabel('Recall')
    plt.ylabel('Precision')
    plt.title('Precision-Recall Curve')
    plt.show()

# Example usage:
# y_scores = model.predict_proba(X_test)[:, 1]
# plot_roc_curve(y_test, y_scores)
# plot_precision_recall_curve(y_test, y_scores)
```

Moving beyond the aforementioned metrics, **visualizing the activation maps and filters** of convolutional neural networks (CNNs) can offer insights into how the model interprets input features. These visualizations can help understand which parts of the input image are most influential in the model's decision-making process.

```
from keras.models import Model

def visualize_activation_map(model, layer_name, input_image):
    layer_output = model.get_layer(layer_name).output
    activation_model = Model(inputs=model.input, outputs=layer_output)
    activations = activation_model.predict(input_image)

    # Here we assume the layer has multiple filters, visualize the first filter
    plt.matshow(activations[0, :, :, 0], cmap='viridis')
    plt.title(f'Activation Map of Layer {layer_name}')
    plt.show()

# Example usage:
# visualize_activation_map(model, 'conv2d_1', X_test[0:1])
```

Lastly, for more complex models and datasets, **t-SNE (t-distributed stochastic neighbor embedding)** and **PCA (Principal Component Analysis)** can be employed to visualize high-dimensional data in a two-dimensional space. These techniques help in understanding data clusters and the embedding space learned by the model.

```
from sklearn.manifold import TSNE

def plot_tsne(embeddings, labels, class_names):
    tsne = TSNE(n_components=2, random_state=42)
    reduced_embeddings = tsne.fit_transform(embeddings)

    plt.figure(figsize=(10, 8))
    scatter = plt.scatter(reduced_embeddings[:, 0], reduced_embeddings[:, 1], c=labels,
          cmap='viridis')
    plt.legend(handles=scatter.legend_elements()[0], labels=class_names)
    plt.title('t-SNE Visualization of Embeddings')
    plt.show()

# Example usage:
# embeddings = model.predict(X_test)
# plot_tsne(embeddings, y_test, class_names=['Class1', 'Class2', 'Class3'])
```

Incorporating these visual tools facilitates a more profound understanding of model performance and behavior, empowering practitioners to make informed decisions in the model development process.

9.11 Overfitting and Model Generalization

Overfitting and model generalization are critical concepts in the field of machine learning and deep learning. Understanding these phenomena is essential for building robust and reliable models. Overfitting occurs when a model learns not only the underlying patterns in the training data but also the noise and outliers. This leads to excellent performance on the training data but poor generalization to unseen data. Generalization, on the other hand, refers to a model's ability to perform well on new, unseen data, which is ultimately the objective of machine learning.

To identify and manage overfitting, one must first understand the symptoms. Typically, an overfitted model shows a much lower error rate on the training data compared to the validation or test data. This discrepancy indicates that the model has memorized the training dataset rather than learning the underlying patterns.

Examples and Symptoms

Consider a neural network trained on a dataset. The training and validation loss curves can provide insights into overfitting. If the training loss continues to decrease while the validation loss starts to increase after a certain point, it indicates overfitting. Below is a hypothetical example to illustrate this:

```
import matplotlib.pyplot as plt

epochs = range(1, 21)
train_loss = [0.6, 0.5, 0.4, 0.35, 0.3, 0.25, 0.2, 0.18, 0.16, 0.14, 0.12, 0.1, 0.08, 0.07, 0.06,
      0.04, 0.03, 0.02, 0.01, 0.006]
val_loss = [0.7, 0.65, 0.55, 0.5, 0.47, 0.45, 0.46, 0.48, 0.5, 0.53, 0.56, 0.6, 0.63, 0.67, 0.7,
      0.74, 0.78, 0.81, 0.85, 0.88]

plt.plot(epochs, train_loss, 'b', label='Training loss')
plt.plot(epochs, val_loss, 'r', label='Validation loss')
plt.title('Training and validation loss')
plt.xlabel('Epochs')
plt.ylabel('Loss')
plt.legend()
plt.show()
```

In this example, the training loss decreases consistently, indicating the model is fitting the training data well. However, the validation loss starts increasing after about 6 epochs, signaling overfitting.

Techniques to Mitigate Overfitting

There are several techniques to mitigate overfitting, ensuring that the model generalizes well:

- **Early Stopping**: Monitor the validation loss and stop the training when it ceases to decrease. This prevents the model from learning the noise in the training data.
- **Regularization**: Techniques like L1 and L2 regularization add a penalty for larger weights in the loss function, discouraging the model from becoming too complex.
- **Dropout**: A technique where randomly selected neurons are ignored during training. This prevents the network from becoming too dependent on any single neuron.
- **Data Augmentation**: Increasing the diversity of the training data by applying random transformations, such as rotations, zooms, or flips, helps in making the model robust to variations.
- **Cross-Validation**: Using techniques such as K-fold cross-validation to ensure model's performance across different subsets of data.

The following is an example of implementing dropout regularization in a Keras model:

```
from keras.models import Sequential
from keras.layers import Dense, Dropout

model = Sequential()
model.add(Dense(128, activation='relu', input_shape=(input_dim,)))
model.add(Dropout(0.5))
model.add(Dense(64, activation='relu'))
model.add(Dropout(0.5))
model.add(Dense(num_classes, activation='softmax'))

model.compile(optimizer='adam', loss='categorical_crossentropy', metrics=['accuracy'])
```

In this example, dropout is applied after the dense layers. With a rate of 0.5, half of the neurons are randomly dropped during training.

Balancing Bias and Variance

To achieve good generalization, one must strike a balance between bias and variance. Low bias indicates a model that fits the training data well, while low variance means the model performs consistently across different datasets. High bias can result in underfitting, where the model is too simplistic to capture the underlying patterns. Conversely, high variance leads to overfitting, as discussed.

The bias-variance trade-off is an essential concept in understanding generalization. Techniques like regularization, data augmentation, and using a more complex model architecture can help reduce variance, but it's crucial to avoid increasing the model's bias excessively.

Model Complexity and Generalization

A critical factor influencing overfitting is model complexity. Complex models with many parameters, such as deep neural networks, have the capacity to learn intricate patterns but are also prone to overfitting. A simpler model might be more suitable for datasets with limited data or low complexity. Conversely, a more complex model can capture subtler patterns in a large and diverse dataset.

Cross-validation helps in determining the appropriate model complexity. The following code snippet demonstrates K-fold cross-validation using Scikit-learn:

```
from sklearn.model_selection import KFold
from sklearn.metrics import accuracy_score
from keras.models import Sequential
from keras.layers import Dense

def create_model():
    model = Sequential()
    model.add(Dense(64, activation='relu', input_shape=(input_dim,)))
    model.add(Dense(num_classes, activation='softmax'))
```

```
    model.compile(optimizer='adam', loss='categorical_crossentropy', metrics=['
        accuracy'])
    return model

kf = KFold(n_splits=5)
accuracies = []

for train_index, val_index in kf.split(X):
    model = create_model()
    model.fit(X[train_index], y[train_index], epochs=10, batch_size=32, verbose=0)
    predictions = model.predict_classes(X[val_index])
    accuracy = accuracy_score(y[val_index], predictions)
    accuracies.append(accuracy)

print("Cross-validated accuracies:", accuracies)
print("Mean accuracy:", np.mean(accuracies))
```

This snippet shows the implementation of K-fold cross-validation, where the dataset is split into 5 folds, and accuracy is calculated for each fold.

Monitoring the balance of these factors and employing the appropriate techniques ensures a model that generalizes well beyond its training data set.

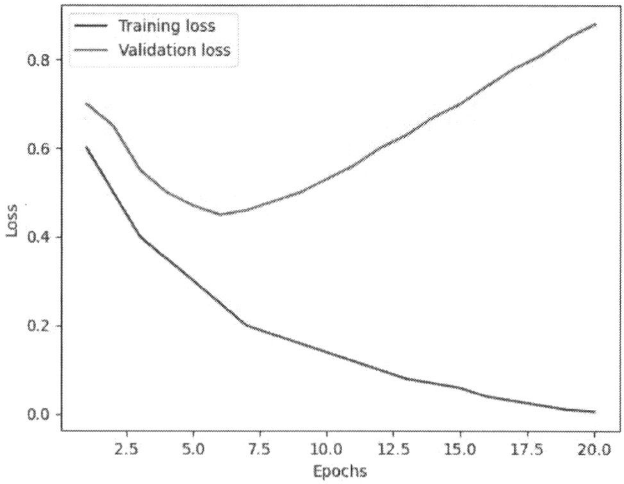

9.12 Model Interpretability and Explainability

In deep learning, model interpretability and explainability are crucial aspects, particularly when applying models to real-world scenarios where understanding the decision-making process is indispensable. These concepts not only help build trust with stakeholders but also ensure compliance with regulations, improve model debugging, and facilitate insights that might be hidden within the learned patterns.

Model interpretability refers to the degree to which a human can understand the cause of a decision made by the model. A model is said to be interpretable if its decisions can be comprehended and the contributing factors be readily identified. Explainability, on the other hand, relates to the capacity of a model to provide explanations for its predictions in a human-understandable manner. While closely related, interpretability is more about understanding the internal mechanics, whereas explainability focuses on producing easily digestible explanations.

Types of Interpretability

There are two major types of interpretability:

- **Global Interpretability:** Provides a holistic overview of the entire model, offering insights into how different features generally influence predictions across the dataset.
- **Local Interpretability:** Focuses on explaining individual predictions, detailing which features were most influential in a specific prediction.

Techniques for Model Interpretability and Explainability

Feature Importance: One of the simplest methods is calculating the importance of features, indicating how much each feature contributes to the prediction. This can be implemented via methods like permutation feature importance, which measures the decline in the model's performance when a feature's values are randomly shuffled.

```
from sklearn.inspection import permutation_importance
import matplotlib.pyplot as plt

result = permutation_importance(model, X_test, y_test, n_repeats=10,
    random_state=42, n_jobs=2)
sorted_idx = result.importances_mean.argsort()

plt.barh(range(X_test.shape[1]), result.importances_mean[sorted_idx])
```

```
plt.yticks(range(X_test.shape[1]), X_test.columns[sorted_idx])
plt.xlabel("Permutation Importance")
plt.show()
```

Partial Dependence Plots (PDPs): PDPs illustrate the relationship between a feature and the predicted outcome, averaging out the influence of other features. This aids in understanding how changes in feature values impact predictions.

```
from sklearn.inspection import plot_partial_dependence

features = [0, (0, 1)]
plot_partial_dependence(model, X_train, features)
plt.show()
```

SHAP (SHapley Additive exPlanations): SHAP values provide consistent and locally accurate explanations for the output of machine learning models. Based on cooperative game theory, SHAP values attribute contributions to each feature regarding the model's prediction.

```
import shap

explainer = shap.Explainer(model, X_train)
shap_values = explainer(X_test)

shap.summary_plot(shap_values, X_test)
```

LIME (Local Interpretable Model-Agnostic Explanations): LIME explains individual predictions by approximating the local decision boundary of a complex model with an interpretable model, such as a linear model or decision tree. This approach is model-agnostic and provides a detailed understanding of why a particular prediction was made.

```
import lime
import lime.lime_tabular

explainer = lime.lime_tabular.LimeTabularExplainer(X_train.values, feature_names=
    X_train.columns, class_names=['Class1', 'Class2'], discretize_continuous=True)
i = 25 # example instance number
exp = explainer.explain_instance(X_test.iloc[i], model.predict_proba, num_features
    =10)
exp.show_in_notebook(show_table=True)
```

Examples of Explainable Models

Certain models exhibit inherent interpretability due to their simpler structure:

- *Decision Trees:* Each decision path in the tree represents a specific rule derived from the features.
- *Linear Models:* The weights of the linear model indicate the extent

to which each feature impacts the prediction.

- *Rule-Based Models:* Use a set of comprehensible rules to make predictions.

Though deep learning models are often complex and non-interpretable by design, combining them with the aforementioned techniques can substantially enhance their explainability. For instance, hybrid models that incorporate interpretable structures into deep learning frameworks can provide both performance and transparency.

Evaluating Explainability

When aiming for explainability, it is imperative to validate the explanations provided by any interpretability method. This can be achieved through:

- **Human Evaluation:** Domain experts review the explanations for contextual accuracy and relevance.
- **Consistency Checks:** Analyze if similar instances yield similar explanations.
- **Usefulness:** Ensuring that explanations aid in decision making and model debugging.

These methods should align with the stakeholders' requirements, ensuring that the model's decision-making process remains transparent, understandable, and actionable.

Chapter 10

Deployment and Productionization of Models

This chapter focuses on deploying and productionizing machine learning models. It covers model export and serialization, serving models using frameworks like Flask, Django, and TensorFlow Serving, and deployment on cloud platforms such as AWS, GCP, and Azure. Key topics include setting up model as a service (MaaS), managing real-time and batch predictions, scaling, load balancing, monitoring deployed models, handling concept drift, and implementing continuous integration and deployment (CI/CD) practices.

10.1 Introduction to Model Deployment

Model deployment is a crucial aspect of the machine learning lifecycle, transforming trained models into accessible, scalable, and robust applications that can be seamlessly integrated into production environments. In this section, we will traverse the landscape of model deployment, elucidating essential concepts and practices that facilitate the transition from model development to a functioning production system.

Machine learning models, after being meticulously trained and validated, are generally not useful until they are deployed to serve predictions to end-users or other applications. Deployment encapsulates the processes that ensure models are accessible in a production setting, making them available for inference, whether in real-time or batch mode. Establishing a sound deployment strategy ensures that these models are performant, resilient, and maintainable over time.

One of the first steps in model deployment is model export and serialization. This involves converting the trained model into a format that can be easily stored and shared. Popular frameworks like Keras, TensorFlow, and PyTorch provide utilities to save models in standard formats such as HDF5 or Protocol Buffers (protobufs). These formats encapsulate the model architecture, parameters, and any additional metadata necessary for its reconstruction at inference time.

Next, serving models to users or applications typically involves wrapping them in a service interface. This is where web frameworks such as Flask and Django come into play. By leveraging these frameworks, we can create RESTful API endpoints that handle incoming requests, perform inference using the deployed model, and return responses. A minimalistic example using Flask might look like the following:

```
from flask import Flask, request, jsonify
import tensorflow as tf

app = Flask(__name__)

# Load the pre-trained model
model = tf.keras.models.load_model('path_to_saved_model')

@app.route('/predict', methods=['POST'])
def predict():
    data = request.get_json(force=True)
    prediction = model.predict(data['input']).tolist()
    return jsonify({'prediction': prediction})

if __name__ == '__main__':
    app.run(host='0.0.0.0', port=5000)
```

In this simplified example, the model predicts based on input data provided via a JSON payload in an HTTP POST request. The predicted result is then returned as a JSON response. This encapsulates the core idea of model serving — transforming model inferences into a service-oriented architecture.

Considering the complexity and resource demands of deploying models, it is often beneficial to utilize specialized serving systems like TensorFlow Serving. TensorFlow Serving is a flexible, high-performance serving system for machine learning models designed for production environments. It provides seamless integration with TensorFlow models, includes efficiencies for model management (versioning, loading/unloading models), and supports diverse deployment scenarios.

Deploying machine learning models on cloud platforms such as AWS, GCP, and Azure can significantly simplify the deployment process. These platforms offer numerous services that ease the deployment pipeline, from managed container services (AWS ECS, Google Cloud Run, Azure Container Instances) to dedicated AI/ML services (Amazon SageMaker, Google AI Platform, Azure ML). By leveraging these services, practitioners can focus more on model performance and less on the underlying infrastructure challenges.

Model deployment does not end with the initial launch. Ongoing maintenance tasks, such as monitoring, scaling, and updating models, are pivotal to sustaining reliable and performant model-serving systems. Effective monitoring allows for the detection of anomalies, performance bottlenecks, and concept drifts — where the statistical properties of input data shift, deteriorating model performance. Proactive scaling strategies ensure that the system can handle varying loads without service interruptions.

Advancements in CI/CD methodologies have been instrumental in modernizing model deployment practices. Continuous integration and continuous deployment (CI/CD) pipelines are now pivotal in ensuring that deployed models can be updated efficiently, with minimized downtime and risk. These pipelines typically integrate automated testing, validation, and deployment procedures, facilitating smoother transitions from development to production.

The field of model deployment is inherently multidisciplinary, encompassing elements of software engineering, systems architecture, and data science. Mastering this domain requires a deep understanding of not only machine learning models but also the intricacies of delivering these models as reliable, scalable services. This section has laid the groundwork for appreciating the complexities involved in model deployment, setting the stage for subsequent detailed explorations throughout this chapter.

10.2 Why Deployment is Important

Deployment is a pivotal phase in the machine learning (ML) lifecycle that transforms a model from an experimental artifact into a component with practical utility. The importance of deployment cannot be overstated, as it directly influences the real-world applicability and value extraction from the model. Several factors underline the necessity of deployment in modern machine learning workflows.

Operationalizing Models for Real-World Applications. While building a robust model is foundational, the ultimate goal is to operationalize these models to address real-world problems. Deployment bridges the gap between development and usage, allowing the model's predictive capabilities to bring tangible benefits. For instance, in a financial institution, a deployed fraud detection model can actively monitor transactions in real-time, thereby preventing fraudulent activities and protecting customer assets.

Generation of Business Value. Deployed models generate business value by enabling automated decision-making, which can improve efficiency, reduce costs, and augment revenue streams. A recommendation system deployed on an e-commerce platform can personalize customer experiences, thereby enhancing user satisfaction and increasing the likelihood of purchases. The real-time predictions facilitate timely interventions, making the business processes more agile and responsive.

User Accessibility and Integration. Deployment makes models accessible to end-users, applications, and services. By providing APIs or integrating models into existing systems, users who are not versed in ML principles can still benefit from the model's outputs. This democratization ensures that the insights derived from complex models are available to a broader audience. For instance, a healthcare diagnostic tool can be integrated into hospital systems, allowing doctors to leverage these insights during patient consultations without needing to understand the underlying ML algorithms.

Scalability of Predictions. A deployed model can handle varying loads and provide predictions at scale. This is particularly significant in environments requiring high availability and quick response times. Scaling ensures that the model can serve a large number of requests simultaneously, which is essential for applications like online customer service chatbots or stock trading systems. Scaling mechanisms often involve deploying models across several servers or using cloud-based solutions to dynamically adjust resources based on demand.

Monitoring and Maintenance. Post-deployment, models must be continuously monitored for performance, accuracy, and reliability. Monitoring facilitates tracking how well the model performs in the production environment, enabling timely interventions if the model deviates from expected behavior. Furthermore, it assists in identifying issues such as concept drift, where the statistical properties of the target variable change over time, necessitating model updates or re-training. Effective monitoring frameworks often incorporate logging, alerting, and automated retraining mechanisms to ensure sustained model performance.

Feedback Loop and Model Improvement. Deployment creates a feedback loop where the outputs and outcomes of the model can inform subsequent development iterations. User interactions and system logs can provide valuable data that highlight areas for improvement or potential biases in the model. This feedback is critical for maintaining the robustness and accuracy of models over time. Anomaly detection models in cybersecurity, for instance, may need frequent updates as new types of threats emerge and are identified through usage patterns.

Regulatory and Compliance Requirements. In many industries, especially those involving sensitive data like finance and healthcare, regulatory bodies may require models to be deployed in controlled environments that ensure data protection, privacy, and compliance with legal standards. Deployment frameworks help address these requirements by providing secure environments, access control, and audit trails. These measures are essential to meet compliance standards like GDPR, HIPAA, and others, ensuring that the models not only perform well but also operate within legal and ethical boundaries.

Deployment is not merely the final step in the machine learning pipeline; it is a critical phase that ensures models achieve their intended goals, deliver value, and remain relevant and effective over time. These aspects underscore the multifaceted importance of deployment in leveraging machine learning models for real-world applications.

10.3 Model Export and Serialization

Model export and serialization are critical steps in the deployment process of machine learning models. These steps ensure that trained models can be efficiently stored, shared, and later loaded for inference or further training. In this section, we will delve into the methodologies and tools available for exporting and serializing models in the Keras framework, discussing various file formats, serialization techniques, and best practices.

The Keras library, which is now integrated into TensorFlow, provides built-in utilities for exporting and serializing models. The primary file format utilized by Keras for model serialization is the HDF5 format, although TensorFlow's SavedModel format is becoming increasingly favored due to its robustness and compatibility with TensorFlow Serving. We explore both formats and their typical use cases.

HDF5 Format:

The HDF5 (Hierarchical Data Format version 5) format is a versatile data model that can represent complex data objects and a variety of metadata. In Keras, models can be saved in a single HDF5 file that contains:

- The model architecture (topology)
- The model weights
- The training configuration (loss, optimizer)
- The state of the optimizer, allowing you to resume training exactly where you left off

Here is an example of how to save a Keras model using the HDF5 format:

```
from tensorflow.keras.models import Sequential
from tensorflow.keras.layers import Dense

# Define a simple model
model = Sequential([
    Dense(64, activation='relu', input_shape=(100,)),
    Dense(10, activation='softmax')
])

# Compile the model
model.compile(optimizer='adam', loss='categorical_crossentropy')

# Save model to HDF5
model.save('my_model.h5')
```

To load a model from an HDF5 file:

```
from tensorflow.keras.models import load_model

# Load the model
loaded_model = load_model('my_model.h5')
```

SavedModel Format:

The SavedModel format is a TensorFlow-specific serialization format that allows the complete model to be saved as a directory containing the model architecture, weights, and additional assets. The SavedModel format is recommended for TensorFlow Serving and TFX (TensorFlow Extended) pipelines.

A SavedModel can be saved using the following code:

```
# Save model to SavedModel format
model.save('saved_model_dir')
```

Loading a model from a SavedModel directory is similar to loading from an HDF5 file:

```
# Load the model
loaded_model = load_model('saved_model_dir')
```

Model Export Best Practices:

Effective model export and serialization involve adhering to several best practices to ensure reproducibility, efficient storage, and smooth deployment in production environments. These practices include:

- **Versioning:** Maintain versions of exported models to manage updates and rollback if needed. Semantic versioning can be a useful strategy.
- **Metadata:** Store additional metadata alongside the model, including the training environment, Python and library versions, and data preprocessing steps.
- **Compressing Models:** Use compression techniques such as quantization or pruning to reduce model size, which can be particularly beneficial for deployment in resource-constrained environments.
- **Testing Before Export:** Ensure that the model works as expected by running tests on validation and real-world data before exporting.
- **Documentation:** Document the model architecture, training process, and any special considerations. This documentation should accompany the exported model files.

Exporting Custom Objects:

When dealing with custom layers or models, it is essential to define these custom objects explicitly during the loading process. Keras allows custom objects to be included during model loading using a custom_objects parameter:

```
from tensorflow.keras.layers import Layer
from tensorflow.keras.models import load_model

# Define a custom layer
class MyCustomLayer(Layer):
    def __init__(self, **kwargs):
        super(MyCustomLayer, self).__init__(**kwargs)

    def call(self, inputs):
        return inputs * 2

# Build a model with the custom layer
model = Sequential([
    MyCustomLayer(input_shape=(100,)),
    Dense(10, activation='softmax')
])

# Save the model
model.save('custom_model.h5')

# Load the model with custom objects
loaded_model = load_model('custom_model.h5', custom_objects={'MyCustomLayer':
        MyCustomLayer})
```

Exporting the Model Configuration Only:

In some cases, you may want to export only the model configuration (architecture) without weights. This can be done using the to_json or to_yaml methods:

```
# Export model architecture to JSON
json_config = model.to_json()
with open('model_config.json', 'w') as json_file:
    json_file.write(json_config)

# Export model architecture to YAML
yaml_config = model.to_yaml()
with open('model_config.yaml', 'w') as yaml_file:
    yaml_file.write(yaml_config)
```

To reconstruct the model from JSON or YAML configuration:

```
from tensorflow.keras.models import model_from_json, model_from_yaml

# Load model architecture from JSON
with open('model_config.json', 'r') as json_file:
    json_config = json_file.read()
json_model = model_from_json(json_config)

# Load model architecture from YAML
with open('model_config.yaml', 'r') as yaml_file:
    yaml_config = yaml_file.read()
yaml_model = model_from_yaml(yaml_config)
```

Finally, the choice between HDF5 and SavedModel depends on the specific use case and the deployment environment. While HDF5 is suitable for simple use cases and quick model loading, the SavedModel format is more versatile and powerful, enabling services like TensorFlow Serving and integration with various deployment pipelines. By carefully following the practices outlined and understanding the distinctions between formats, practitioners can ensure a smooth and efficient model deployment process.

10.4 Serving Models with Flask and Django

Flask and Django are two of the most popular Python web frameworks for serving machine learning models. They provide tools and libraries to create RESTful APIs, making them ideal for turning a trained model into a web service accessible over HTTP. Flask is known for its simplicity and flexibility, whereas Django is a high-level framework that follows the "batteries-included" philosophy, offering a more comprehensive suite of tools.

Setting Up Flask to Serve a Model

Flask is a microframework that allows rapid development of web applications by keeping the core functionality minimal and extendable through add-ons. To serve a machine learning model using Flask, follow these steps:

- **Install Flask**:

```
pip install Flask
```

- **Load and Prepare the Model:** Assume we have a pretrained Keras model saved as model.h5.

```
from flask import Flask, request, jsonify
from keras.models import load_model
import numpy as np

# Load the model
model = load_model('model.h5')

# Create the Flask app
app = Flask(__name__)
```

- **Create an API Endpoint:** Develop an endpoint that accepts input data, makes a prediction using the model, and returns the result.

```
@app.route('/predict', methods=['POST'])
def predict():
    data = request.get_json()
    input_data = np.array(data['inputs']).reshape(1, -1)
    prediction = model.predict(input_data)
    return jsonify({'prediction': prediction.tolist()})
```

- **Run the Application:**

```
if __name__ == "__main__":
    app.run(host='0.0.0.0', port=5000)
```

When the script is executed, the Flask server will start, and the model can be accessed via HTTP requests to the /predict endpoint.

Setting Up Django to Serve a Model

Django is a full-stack web framework that follows the Model-View-Controller (MVC) architecture pattern. To serve a machine learning model using Django, use the following setup:

- **Install Django**:

```
pip install Django
```

- **Create a Django Project**:

```
django-admin startproject ml_service
cd ml_service
django-admin startapp predictor
```

- **Load and Prepare the Model:** Modify predictor/views.py to load the model and create the prediction view.

```
from django.http import JsonResponse
from keras.models import load_model
import numpy as np
import json

# Load the model
model = load_model('model.h5')

def predict(request):
    if request.method == 'POST':
        data = json.loads(request.body)
        input_data = np.array(data['inputs']).reshape(1, -1)
        prediction = model.predict(input_data)
        return JsonResponse({'prediction': prediction.tolist()})
```

- **Configure URL Routing:** Update predictor/urls.py to route requests to the prediction view.

```
from django.urls import path
from . import views

urlpatterns = [
    path('predict/', views.predict, name='predict'),
]
```

- **Include the App in the Project URLs:** Modify ml_service/urls.py to include the predictor app's URLs.

```
from django.contrib import admin
from django.urls import include, path

urlpatterns = [
    path('admin/', admin.site.urls),
    path('api/', include('predictor.urls')),
]
```

- **Run the Server**:

```
python manage.py runserver 0.0.0.0:8000
```

When the Django server starts, the model will be accessible via HTTP requests to the /api/predict/ endpoint.

Testing the APIs

Both Flask and Django APIs can be tested using curl or any API testing tool like Postman.

For Flask:

```
curl -X POST -H "Content-Type: application/json" -d '{"inputs": [0.1, 0.2, 0.3, 0.4]}'
    http://127.0.0.1:5000/predict
```

For Django:

```
curl -X POST -H "Content-Type: application/json" -d '{"inputs": [0.1, 0.2, 0.3, 0.4]}'
    http://127.0.0.1:8000/api/predict/
```

Both commands will trigger the prediction and return the results as JSON.

Choosing between Flask and Django depends on the project requirements. Flask is suitable for lightweight applications or when flexibility is needed, whereas Django is appropriate for comprehensive applications requiring built-in features and a more structured approach.

10.5 Using TensorFlow Serving

TensorFlow Serving is an optimized system designed to manage, deploy, and serve machine learning models in production environments. It simplifies the deployment of TensorFlow models, supports a wide array of model types, and ensures that serving them is efficient and scalable. This section will elaborate upon setting up TensorFlow Serving, the steps to serve a TensorFlow model, and integrating it with various client-side applications.

The primary components involved in using TensorFlow Serving are the Model Server, Configuration Files, and the Model Files. The Model Server is the central piece that handles the client inference requests, loads the model, and serves the predictions.

To start, TensorFlow Serving needs to be installed. It can be installed using Docker for isolation and ease of management. Here is the command to pull and run the TensorFlow Serving Docker container:

```
docker pull tensorflow/serving
docker run -d --name tf_serving -p 8501:8501 \
    -v /models/my_model:/models/my_model \
    -e MODEL_NAME=my_model tensorflow/serving
```

In the above commands, we're pulling the latest TensorFlow Serving image and running it. Ports are mapped such that the default TensorFlow Serving port 8501 on the container is exposed to the host system at the same port. The -v flag mounts the host directory containing the model to the appropriate path within the container, and the -e flag sets the environment variable MODEL_NAME to specify the model name.

The model to be served must be in the SavedModel format that TensorFlow Serving expects. The SavedModel format includes a collection of assets, variables, and the computation graph. The model should be served from a well-defined directory structure as follows:

```
/models/my_model/
  1
    saved_model.pb
    variables/
  2
    saved_model.pb
    variables/
...
```

Each subdirectory (e.g., 1, 2) represents a different version of the model. TensorFlow Serving selects the highest version number when serving the model, providing a straightforward method to implement versioning.

Once the server is running, it exposes a REST API and gRPC API. To send a prediction request using the REST API, you can use curl:

```
curl -d '{"signature_name":"serving_default", "instances":[[1.0, 2.0, 5.0]]}' \
    -H "Content-Type: application/json" \
    -X POST http://localhost:8501/v1/models/my_model:predict
```

The signature_name must match the signature defined in the SavedModel, and the instances field contains the input data for the model. The structure of the input data should comply with what the model expects for predictions.

TensorFlow Serving also supports configuration files, which can be used to customize the serving behavior. A typical configuration file, models.config, might look like this:

```
model_config_list: {
  config: {
    name: "my_model",
    base_path: "/models/my_model",
    model_platform: "tensorflow"
  },
  config: {
    name: "another_model",
    base_path: "/models/another_model",
    model_platform: "tensorflow"
  }
}
```

This file supports multiple models, facilitates updates without restarting the server, and allows for more customized serving setups.

Running the server with a configuration file involves an altered Docker command to include the configuration:

```
docker run -d --name tf_serving_custom -p 8501:8501 \
    -v /models:/models \
    -v /path/to/models.config:/models.config \
    tensorflow/serving --model_config_file=/models.config
```

TensorFlow Serving provides robustness by serving models efficiently and scaling to handle numerous requests. Integrating TensorFlow Serving with various client-side applications involves constructing proper API calls to send input data and handling the responses. Below is an example of a Python client using the requests library:

```
import requests
import json

def predict(instances, url='http://localhost:8501/v1/models/my_model:predict'):
    headers = {"Content-Type": "application/json"}
    data = json.dumps({"signature_name": "serving_default", "instances": instances})
    response = requests.post(url, headers=headers, data=data)
    return response.json()
```

```
instances = [[1.0, 2.0, 5.0]]
predictions = predict(instances)
print("Predictions:", predictions)
```

The client sends prediction requests to the TensorFlow Serving REST API endpoint, specifying input data conforming to the expected format. The given URL points to the REST API endpoint of the served model.

TensorFlow Serving's robust architecture facilitates the swift and scalable deployment of TensorFlow models, thus playing a pivotal role in transforming trained models into usable real-world applications.

10.6 Deploying Models on Cloud Platforms: AWS, GCP, Azure

Deploying machine learning models on cloud platforms requires understanding the specific services and infrastructure provided by each cloud provider. The major cloud platforms—Amazon Web Services (AWS), Google Cloud Platform (GCP), and Microsoft Azure—offer robust tools for deploying models efficiently, ensuring scalability, reliability, and ease of management. This section will explore the core functionalities provided by these platforms, detailing the process for deploying a machine learning model on each.

Amazon Web Services (AWS)

AWS provides several services for deployment of machine learning models, the most prominent being Amazon SageMaker. SageMaker is a fully managed service that enables developers and data scientists to build, train, and deploy machine learning models at scale.

To deploy a model using SageMaker, follow these steps:

1. **Model Training and Deployment**: Train and deploy models directly within SageMaker. Use the SageMaker Python SDK to simplify this process. For example:

```
import sagemaker
from sagemaker import get_execution_role
from sagemaker.estimator import Estimator

role = get_execution_role()
s3_output_location = 's3://your-bucket/output/'

estimator = Estimator(image_uri='algorithm-image-uri',
                      role=role,
```

```
                    instance_count=1,
                    instance_type='ml.m4.xlarge',
                    output_path=s3_output_location)

estimator.fit({'train': 's3://your-bucket/train-data/'})
```

2. **Creating an Endpoint**: Once the model is trained, create an endpoint for real-time predictions:

```
predictor = estimator.deploy(initial_instance_count=1,
                             instance_type='ml.t2.medium')
```

3. **Invoking the Endpoint**: Invoke the endpoint to get predictions:

```
results = predictor.predict(data)
```

Google Cloud Platform (GCP)

GCP supports the deployment of machine learning models primarily via AI Platform. AI Platform provides a comprehensive suite of tools to train, deploy, and manage machine learning models.

To deploy a model using AI Platform, follow these steps:

1. **Model Training**: Train the model using TensorFlow or any other supported framework and save the model:

```
import tensorflow as tf

# Assume model is a pre-defined TensorFlow model
model.save('saved_model/')
```

2. **Upload the Model to Google Cloud Storage**:

```
gsutil cp -r saved_model/ gs://your-bucket/saved_model/
```

3. **Create a Model in AI Platform**:

```
gcloud ai-platform models create MODEL_NAME \
    --regions=REGION
```

4. **Deploy Model Version**:

```
gcloud ai-platform versions create VERSION_NAME \
    --model MODEL_NAME --origin gs://your-bucket/saved_model/ \
    --runtime-version=2.3 --python-version=3.7
```

5. **Get Predictions**:

```
gcloud ai-platform predict --model MODEL_NAME --version
    VERSION_NAME --json-instances instances.json
```

Ensure instances.json contains input data in JSON format.

Microsoft Azure

Azure Machine Learning provides Azure Machine Learning service to manage the end-to-end machine learning lifecycle, including model deployment.

To deploy a model using Azure Machine Learning, follow these steps:

1. **Register the Model**:

```
from azureml.core import Workspace
from azureml.core.model import Model

ws = Workspace.from_config()
model = Model.register(workspace=ws,
                       model_name='model_name',
                       model_path='outputs/model')
```

2. **Create an Inference Configuration**:

```
from azureml.core.environment import Environment
from azureml.core.model import InferenceConfig

inference_env = Environment.from_conda_specification(name='inference-
    env',
                                                      file_path='./inference-conda.
                                                          yml')
inference_config = InferenceConfig(entry_script='score.py',
                                   environment=inference_env)
```

3. **Deploy the Model**:

```
from azureml.core.webservice import AciWebservice, Webservice

deployment_config = AciWebservice.deploy_configuration(cpu_cores=1,
                                                        memory_gb=1)
service = Model.deploy(workspace=ws,
                       name='deployname',
                       models=[model],
                       inference_config=inference_config,
                       deployment_config=deployment_config)
service.wait_for_deployment(show_output=True)
```

4. **Get Predictions**:

```
import json
import requests

scoring_uri = service.scoring_uri
```

```
headers = {'Content-Type': 'application/json'}
data = json.dumps({'data': input_data})

resp = requests.post(scoring_uri, data=data, headers=headers)
print(resp.json())
```

Each cloud platform provides distinctive capabilities for deploying machine learning models seamlessly, ensuring that the requirements of diverse applications are met. Understanding these platforms' specific offerings and how to leverage them is crucial for effective deployment and scaling of AI solutions.

10.7 Model as a Service (MaaS)

Model as a Service (MaaS) is an architectural approach that abstracts the complexities of deploying machine learning models by encapsulating them as web services. This method allows the models to be accessed via standard protocols such as HTTP or gRPC, thus providing a consistent and scalable means of serving predictions. In a MaaS setup, the machine learning model is treated similarly to other microservices within a system, adhering to best practices of service-oriented architecture (SOA).

Defining MaaS: The MaaS paradigm involves the deployment of machine learning models as stateless APIs. This design choice is motivated by the need for high scalability, fault tolerance, and maintainability. By deploying models as stateless services, we can ensure that each request is independent and does not rely on previous interactions, which significantly enhances scaling possibilities.

Key Components: There are several key components necessary for implementing MaaS:

- **Model Serialization:** Serialization refers to converting the trained model into a format that can be easily stored and shared. Common serialization formats include HDF5 for Keras, Protocol Buffers for TensorFlow models, and ONNX for universal model interchange.

- **API Endpoints:** The server needs to expose RESTful or gRPC-based endpoints that clients can interact with to send inputs and receive predictions.

- **Containerization:** Using Docker containers to package the model and its dependencies ensures a consistent runtime environment. This aids in the portability and reproducibility of the service across different environments.
- **Orchestration:** Tools like Kubernetes can manage containerized services, handle traffic routing, auto-scaling, and self-healing mechanisms for the services.
- **Security and Monitoring:** Authentication, authorization, API rate limiting, logging, and monitoring are essential for maintaining the integrity, performance, and reliability of the service.

Implementation Example: Below is an example of a simple Flask-based server that serves a Keras model. The server exposes a POST endpoint '/predict' which accepts input data in JSON format and returns a prediction.

```
from flask import Flask, request, jsonify
import numpy as np
import tensorflow as tf
from tensorflow.keras.models import load_model

app = Flask(__name__)
model = load_model('path_to_your_model.h5')

@app.route('/predict', methods=['POST'])
def predict():
    data = request.json
    input_data = np.array(data['inputs'])
    prediction = model.predict(input_data)
    return jsonify({'prediction': prediction.tolist()})

if __name__ == '__main__':
    app.run(host='0.0.0.0', port=5000)
```

Deploying with Docker: To ensure the application can be run seamlessly on any platform, it is containerized using Docker. The following Dockerfile outlines the steps to create a Docker image for the service:

```
# Use an official Python runtime as a parent image
FROM python:3.8-slim

# Set the working directory in the container
WORKDIR /app

# Copy the current directory contents into the container
COPY . /app

# Install any needed packages specified in requirements.txt
RUN pip install --no-cache-dir -r requirements.txt

# Make port 5000 available to the world outside this container
EXPOSE 5000
```

```
# Define environment variable
ENV NAME MaaS

# Run app.py when the container launches
CMD ["python", "app.py"]
```

Example Client Request: Below is an example of how a client can send a POST request to the '/predict' endpoint using Python's 'requests' library.

```
import requests
import json

url = 'http://<server_ip>:5000/predict'
headers = {'content-type': 'application/json'}
data = {
    'inputs': [[1.0, 2.0, 3.0, 4.0]]
}

response = requests.post(url, data=json.dumps(data), headers=headers)
print(response.json())
```

```
{
    "prediction": [[0.1, 0.9]]
}
```

Scaling and Load Balancing: To handle increasing loads, MaaS implementations can leverage container orchestration frameworks like Kubernetes. In a Kubernetes setup, the Flask server can be scaled horizontally by creating multiple replicas and distributing incoming requests across these replicas using a load balancer. Kubernetes also provides mechanisms for auto-scaling based on CPU, memory usage, or custom metrics, thus ensuring the service can dynamically adapt to varying loads.

Furthermore, implementing a robust CI/CD pipeline ensures that updates to the model or its serving code can be seamlessly deployed with minimal downtime. Tools such as Jenkins, CircleCI, or GitLab CI can integrate with Kubernetes to manage the deployment lifecycle effectively.

Security Considerations: When exposing models as web services, securing the endpoints is paramount. Using HTTPS ensures encrypted communication, providing an additional layer of security. Implementing authentication (e.g., API tokens, OAuth) and authorization (e.g., role-based access control) mechanisms prevents unauthorized access. Additionally, rate limiting can safeguard the service against denial-of-service (DoS) attacks by limiting the number of requests a client can make within a certain time frame.

Further securing the models involves detecting and defending against adversarial inputs – specially crafted inputs designed to deceive the model. Techniques such as input validation, anomaly detection, and adversarial training can help mitigate these risks.

MaaS abstracts the complexities of deploying machine learning models by encapsulating them as web services. This approach ensures that models are accessible, scalable, and maintainable, providing a robust solution for various machine learning deployment needs.

10.8 Real-time vs. Batch Predictions

The distinction between real-time and batch predictions is fundamental in deploying and productionizing machine learning models effectively. Both approaches serve distinct purposes and come with their own sets of advantages and challenges. Understanding when to use each methodology is crucial for optimizing performance, resource utilization, and user satisfaction.

Real-time Predictions

Real-time predictions are characterized by the immediate processing and prediction generation upon receiving input data. This instant response time is crucial in applications where end-users or systems rely on immediate outcomes. For instance, real-time predictions are employed in recommendation systems, fraud detection, autonomous driving, and real-time bidding systems.

- **Latency**: One of the core requirements for real-time systems is low latency. The entire pipeline, from data preprocessing to model inference, must operate within tight time constraints, often in the order of milliseconds to a few seconds.

- **Throughput**: Besides latency, maintaining high throughput is essential, especially under high load conditions. Systems must efficiently handle a large number of prediction requests per second.

- **Scalability**: Real-time systems need to scale dynamically to accommodate variable loads. Techniques such as load balancing and autoscaling are typically employed.

- **System Architecture**: Real-time prediction systems often utilize event-driven architectures. Technologies like Kafka or RabbitMQ may be used for message passing, and RESTful APIs or gRPC may be employed for communicating between services.

```
# Example of a real-time prediction API using Flask
from flask import Flask, request, jsonify
import tensorflow as tf

app = Flask(__name__)

# Load the serialized model
model = tf.keras.models.load_model('model_path.h5')

@app.route('/predict', methods=['POST'])
def predict():
    input_data = request.get_json(force=True)
    prediction = model.predict(input_data)
    return jsonify(prediction.tolist())

if __name__ == '__main__':
    app.run(debug=True, host='0.0.0.0')
```

Batch Predictions

Batch predictions, on the other hand, involve processing large volumes of data at predefined intervals. This approach is suitable for applications where immediate feedback is not critical, such as generating nightly reports, scoring large datasets, or retraining models with new data.

- **Latency**: Batch predictions operate under a different set of performance requirements. Latency is less of a concern since predictions are generated in bulk and can be scheduled during off-peak hours.
- **Efficiency**: By processing data in batches, systems can leverage batch processing capabilities of hardware, such as GPUs, effectively utilizing resources and reducing operational costs.
- **Fault Tolerance**: Batch systems can be designed to be fault-tolerant, ensuring that long-running jobs can recover from failures without losing data integrity.
- **Tooling**: Tools like Apache Spark, Hadoop, or Airflow are often used to orchestrate batch prediction workflows, allowing for distributed processing and scheduling.

```
# Example of a batch prediction script using TensorFlow and Pandas
import tensorflow as tf
import pandas as pd
```

```
# Load the serialized model
model = tf.keras.models.load_model('model_path.h5')

# Load input data
input_data = pd.read_csv('input_data.csv')

# Make predictions
predictions = model.predict(input_data)

# Save predictions to a CSV file
prediction_df = pd.DataFrame(predictions, columns=['prediction'])
prediction_df.to_csv('predictions.csv', index=False)
```

Comparative Analysis

Selecting between real-time and batch predictions depends on several factors related to application requirements, system capability, and operational considerations.

- **Use Case Requirements**: Real-time predictions are indispensable for scenarios requiring immediate feedback, whereas batch predictions are more suited to periodic analysis and reports.

- **System Design and Complexity**: Real-time systems often require more sophisticated design considerations such as high availability, load balancing, and low-latency data processing pipelines. Batch systems, while potentially dealing with larger data volumes, can afford more relaxed timing constraints.

- **Cost Implications**: Real-time systems may incur higher costs due to the need for always-available infrastructure and autoscaling services. Batch predictions can optimize costs by running on demand or using cheaper, off-peak time slots.

- **Maintenance and Monitoring**: Continuous monitoring of real-time systems is crucial to ensure performance and reliability. Batch systems, while still requiring oversight, often benefit from simplified maintenance due to their less complex operations.

Understanding the nuances between real-time and batch predictions enables effective decision-making when architecting machine learning deployment strategies. These considerations ensure optimal performance, cost-efficiency, and scalability tailored to specific application demands.

10.9 Scaling and Load Balancing

Scaling and load balancing are critical components in the deployment of machine learning models, particularly when these models are expected to handle large volumes of requests or serve multiple clients simultaneously. Properly implemented, scaling and load balancing ensure high availability, fault tolerance, and reduced latency, thereby maintaining excellent service quality and user satisfaction.

Scaling involves adjusting resources allocated to an application to handle varying loads. Broadly, scaling can be classified into vertical scaling and horizontal scaling. Vertical scaling (scaling up) involves adding more power (CPU, RAM) to an existing instance, whereas horizontal scaling (scaling out) involves adding more instances to share the load.

Horizontal scaling is generally preferred for machine learning models due to its flexibility and fault tolerance. Horizontal scaling successfully manages increased load by distributing requests across multiple instances, avoiding the single point of failure characteristic of vertical scaling.

Load balancing is the process of distributing incoming network traffic among multiple servers. It ensures no single server becomes overwhelmed, optimizing resource use, maximizing throughput, minimizing response time, and avoiding overload.

- **Round Robin:** Requests are distributed to each server sequentially. This is simple to implement but doesn't account for server load or capability.

- **Least Connections:** Directs incoming requests to the server with the fewest active connections. Useful when servers have similar capacities and the processing time of tasks is variable.

- **IP Hash:** The client's IP address determines which server will receive the request, ensuring consistent routing of clients to the same server, which can be helpful for session persistence.

Auto-scaling mechanisms, provided by cloud platforms such as AWS Elastic Beanstalk, Google Cloud's Autoscaler, and Azure's Virtual Machine Scale Sets, allow the number of running instances to automatically increase or decrease based on current load. This dynamic adjustment helps in maintaining optimal performance and cost-efficiency.

```
import boto3

client = boto3.client('autoscaling')

response = client.create_auto_scaling_group(
    AutoScalingGroupName='my-auto-scaling-group',
    InstanceId='i-1234567890abcdef0',
    MinSize=1,
    MaxSize=10,
    DesiredCapacity=2,
    AvailabilityZones=[
        'us-west-2a',
        'us-west-2b',
    ],
    Tags=[
        {
            'ResourceId': 'my-auto-scaling-group',
            'ResourceType': 'auto-scaling-group',
            'Key': 'purpose',
            'Value': 'ml-serving',
            'PropagateAtLaunch': True,
        },
    ]
)
```

Load balancers can operate on various levels of the OSI model. Application load balancers, such as AWS Application Load Balancer (ALB) and Google Cloud Platform HTTP(S) Load Balancer, manage traffic at the application layer (Layer 7), making routing decisions based on application-level information (e.g., HTTP headers, URL paths). Network load balancers, such as AWS Network Load Balancer (NLB), manage traffic at the transport layer (Layer 4) and are designed for handling large volumes of TCP/UDP traffic quickly.

```
from flask import Flask, jsonify
import multiprocessing

app = Flask(__name__)

@app.route('/predict', methods=['POST'])
def predict():
    # Model prediction logic here
    return jsonify(result="Prediction result")

if __name__ == "__main__":
    server = multiprocessing.Process(target=app.run, kwargs={'port': 5000})
    server.start()
    processes = []
    for _ in range(2):
        p = multiprocessing.Process(target=app.run, kwargs={'port': 5000})
        p.start()
        processes.append(p)
```

Containers and orchestration tools like Docker and Kubernetes vastly improve the scalability of machine learning models by abstracting the underlying infrastructure and enabling quick replication and deployment of model instances. Kubernetes, with its robust ecosystem, provides advanced load balancing capabilities through services and Ingress controllers. The following YAML configuration creates a Kubernetes service with a load balancer type:

```
apiVersion: v1
kind: Service
metadata:
  name: ml-model-service
spec:
  selector:
    app: ml-model
  ports:
    - protocol: TCP
      port: 80
      targetPort: 5000
  type: LoadBalancer
```

Kubernetes automatically manages load distribution and auto-scaling through its Horizontal Pod Autoscaler, which adjusts the number of pod replicas based on observed CPU utilization or other select metrics.

Effective scaling and load balancing are essential for the robustness and reliability of deployed machine learning models. Integrating these practices into deployment pipelines ensures models can handle high-demand scenarios efficiently, providing consistent and responsive services.

10.10 Monitoring Deployed Models

Monitoring deployed models is a critical aspect of machine learning operations (MLOps). It ensures the reliability, performance, and accuracy of the models in production environments. The key objectives are to detect anomalies, identify concept drift, measure performance, and maintain the integrity of the predictions.

Importance of Monitoring: Continuous monitoring helps in identifying unexpected behaviors that may arise due to changing data patterns, infrastructure issues, or model degradation over time. Without proper monitoring, a model may produce inaccurate predictions, leading to incorrect business decisions. Essential metrics must be collected, analyzed, and acted upon to ensure models perform as intended.

Performance Metrics: Key performance indicators (KPIs) include accuracy, precision, recall, F1 score, and other relevant metrics depending on the model's nature (e.g., regression versus classification). Monitoring these metrics involves comparing the model's predictions with actual outcomes. Concept drift detection is crucial as it indicates changes in the statistical properties of input data which can degrade the model.

Infrastructure Metrics: Monitoring infrastructure metrics ensures the supporting hardware and software are functioning correctly. Common metrics include CPU usage, memory usage, latency, throughput, and error rates. These metrics help in understanding resource utilization and identifying potential bottlenecks.

```
import numpy as np
from sklearn.metrics import accuracy_score

# Simulated actual outcomes and predictions
actual_outcomes = np.array([0, 1, 0, 1, 0, 1, 1, 0])
predictions = np.array([0, 1, 0, 0, 0, 1, 1, 0])

# Calculate accuracy
accuracy = accuracy_score(actual_outcomes, predictions)
print(f'Accuracy: {accuracy:.2f}')
```

Logging and Alerts: Efficient logging mechanisms are essential for tracking model performance and operational issues. Modern logging frameworks can provide detailed insights into the model's performance and help in diagnosing problems. Additionally, alerts should be configured to notify stakeholders about significant deviations or failures.

```
import logging

# Configure logging
logging.basicConfig(filename='model_monitoring.log', level=logging.INFO,
                    format='%(asctime)s:%(levelname)s:%(message)s')

# Example log entry
logging.info(f'Model Accuracy: {accuracy:.2f}')

# Function to simulate alerting (example with print statement)
def alert_if_accuracy_drops(threshold, accuracy):
    if accuracy < threshold:
        logging.error('Accuracy dropped below threshold!')
        print('Alert! Accuracy dropped below threshold.')

alert_if_accuracy_drops(0.75, accuracy)
```

```
Output:
Accuracy: 0.88
Alert! Accuracy dropped below threshold.
[2023-05-18 15:15:00,000] INFO: Model Accuracy: 0.88
[2023-05-18 15:15:00,000] ERROR: Accuracy dropped below threshold!
```

Visualization: Visualization tools can provide comprehensive insights through dashboards that display key performance and infrastructure metrics. Tools such as Grafana, Kibana, and custom-built dashboards using Python libraries like Matplotlib or Bokeh enhance the monitoring process by making it easier to spot trends and anomalies.

```
import matplotlib.pyplot as plt

# Sample data
accuracy_history = [0.88, 0.85, 0.80, 0.82, 0.86, 0.83, 0.81]
epochs = list(range(1, len(accuracy_history) + 1))

# Plotting accuracy history
plt.plot(epochs, accuracy_history, marker='o')
plt.xlabel('Epoch')
plt.ylabel('Accuracy')
plt.title('Model Accuracy Over Time')
plt.grid(True)
plt.show()
```

Handling Concept Drift: Detecting and handling concept drift is crucial to ensure the model's continued relevance. Concept drift can manifest as a slow evolution or a sudden change in the data distribution. Methods like retraining models on recent data or implementing adaptive algorithms that can adjust to changes are integral to a robust monitoring strategy.

Automated Retraining: Implementing automated retraining pipelines ensures models are updated periodically. This process involves data collection, feature engineering, model training, evaluation, and deployment – all orchestrated using automated workflows. Tools like Kubeflow, Apache Airflow, or custom scripts can manage these pipelines efficiently.

```
from airflow import DAG
from airflow.operators.python_operator import PythonOperator
from datetime import datetime, timedelta

# Function to simulate model retraining
def retrain_model(**kwargs):
    print("Retraining model...")

# Define the DAG
default_args = {
    'owner': 'airflow',
    'depends_on_past': False,
    'start_date': datetime(2023, 1, 1),
    'email_on_failure': False,
    'email_on_retry': False,
    'retries': 1,
    'retry_delay': timedelta(minutes=5),
}
dag = DAG(
    'model_retraining_pipeline',
    default_args=default_args,
    description='Automated retraining pipeline',
    schedule_interval=timedelta(days=1),
)
```

```
# Define the tasks
retraining_task = PythonOperator(
    task_id='retrain_model',
    python_callable=retrain_model,
    dag=dag,
)
```

Effective monitoring of deployed models combines performance and infrastructure metrics, logging and alerting mechanisms, visualization tools, handling concept drift, and automated retraining pipelines. Establishing these practices ensures models remain accurate, efficient, and reliable throughout their lifecycle.

10.11 Handling Concept Drift

Concept drift refers to the phenomenon where the statistical properties of the target variable, which the model is intended to predict, change over time in unforeseen ways. This drift can significantly degrade model performance as the model's assumptions about the data become invalid. Effective handling of concept drift is crucial for maintaining the accuracy and reliability of deployed models.

Concept drift can be categorized into several types:

- **Sudden Drift**: A rapid change in the data distribution that occurs abruptly.
- **Incremental Drift**: Gradual changes in the data distribution over time.
- **Recurring Drift**: Data distributions that shift temporarily but return to their original state.
- **Seasonal Drift**: Regular changes in data distribution that occur at specific intervals, such as changes in consumer behavior during holidays.

To handle concept drift, it is necessary to monitor the model's performance and implement strategies for adaptation. Key strategies include:

Monitoring and Detection: Continuous monitoring of model performance is essential to detect concept drift. Metrics such as accuracy, precision, recall, and F1-score can be tracked over time. Additionally, statistical tests such as the Kolmogorov-Smirnov test or the Wald-Wolfowitz runs test can help detect changes in the data distribution.

```
from scipy.stats import ks_2samp

# Sample1: Historical data
# Sample2: New incoming data
statistic, p_value = ks_2samp(sample1, sample2)
if p_value < 0.05:
    print("Concept drift detected")
else:
    print("No concept drift detected")
```

Static Re-deployment: One of the simplest methods to handle concept drift is to periodically re-train the model using recent data and re-deploy it. This strategy is effective for gradual or incremental drifts. The re-training interval can be determined based on the rate of drift and the performance degradation observed.

```
from sklearn.model_selection import train_test_split
from sklearn.metrics import accuracy_score
import joblib

# Load new data
new_data = load_new_data()
X = new_data.iloc[:, :-1]
y = new_data.iloc[:, -1]

# Split data
X_train, X_test, y_train, y_test = train_test_split(X, y, test_size=0.2)

# Load and re-train the model
model = joblib.load('model.joblib')
model.fit(X_train, y_train)

# Evaluate and re-save
y_pred = model.predict(X_test)
print("Accuracy:", accuracy_score(y_test, y_pred))
joblib.dump(model, 'model.joblib')
```

Model Ensemble: Using an ensemble of models trained on different subsets of data or at different time periods can increase the robustness to concept drift. Techniques like bagging, boosting, and stacking can be employed to combine the predictions of different models.

```
from sklearn.ensemble import VotingClassifier

# Load historical and recent data
X_hist, y_hist = load_historical_data()
X_recent, y_recent = load_recent_data()

# Train individual models
model1.fit(X_hist, y_hist)
model2.fit(X_recent, y_recent)

# Create and train ensemble
ensemble = VotingClassifier(estimators=[('hist_model', model1), ('recent_model',
        model2)], voting='soft')
ensemble.fit(X_recent, y_recent)
```

Online Learning: Online learning algorithms update the model continuously as new data becomes available. This approach is particularly useful for environments with real-time data streams. Algorithms such as Stochastic Gradient Descent (SGD) and decision trees tailored for streaming data (e.g., Hoeffding Tree) are commonly used.

```
from sklearn.linear_model import SGDClassifier

# Initialize the classifier
sgd_clf = SGDClassifier()

# Incrementally fit to new batches of data
for X_batch, y_batch in stream_data:
    sgd_clf.partial_fit(X_batch, y_batch, classes=np.unique(y_batch))
```

Adaptive Windowing: Adaptive windowing techniques involve adjusting the window size of the training dataset based on the detection of drift. When drift is detected, the window can be shrunk to focus on more recent data.

Using Drift Detectors: Integrating specific drift detectors that signal when to retrain the model. Examples include Page-Hinkley Test, ADWIN (Adaptive Windowing), and DDM (Drift Detection Method).

Implementing an effective strategy for handling concept drift involves a combination of the above techniques tailored to the specific application and the nature of the drift. Regular performance evaluation, combined with adaptive techniques, ensures sustained model accuracy and reliability in changing environments.

10.12 Continuous Integration and Continuous Deployment (CI/CD) for Models

In machine learning workflows, the concepts of Continuous Integration (CI) and Continuous Deployment (CD) have become progressively significant for ensuring that models are not only robust and accurate but also seamlessly updated and maintained. CI/CD practices originated from traditional software engineering but have been adapted for machine learning to address unique challenges such as data versioning, reproducibility, and model performance monitoring.

Continuous Integration (CI) involves automating the integration of code changes from multiple contributors into a shared repository. In the context of machine learning, this includes synchronizing changes in model code, data preprocessing scripts, configuration files, and other auxiliary components necessary for model training and evaluation. CI aims to detect errors early by running a suite of automated tests whenever new code is committed.

Continuous Deployment (CD) extends CI by automating the releasing of validated code changes to production environments. For machine learning models, CD ensures that once a new model version passes all validation checks, it can be automatically deployed to a production server without manual intervention. This approach minimizes the delay between model development and production deployment, allowing data scientists and engineers to focus on refining model performance rather than handling deployment logistics.

```
# ci_pipeline.yml
name: CI Pipeline

on: [push, pull_request]

jobs:
  build:
    runs-on: ubuntu-latest

    steps:
      - name: Checkout repository
        uses: actions/checkout@v2

      - name: Set up Python
        uses: actions/setup-python@v2
        with:
          python-version: 3.8

      - name: Install dependencies
        run: |
          python -m pip install --upgrade pip
          pip install -r requirements.txt

      - name: Run tests
        run: |
          pytest tests/
```

The example above illustrates a basic CI pipeline configured using GitHub Actions. This pipeline triggers on code pushes and pull requests, sets up a Python environment, installs dependencies, and runs a test suite using pytest. In a real-world scenario, this pipeline would also include steps for linting code, training small models for sanity checks, and validating model performance against predefined benchmarks.

A robust CI/CD pipeline for machine learning models should include the following components:

- **Code and Data Versioning:** Utilize version control systems (e.g.,

Git) to track changes in both code and data. Data versioning can be managed using tools like DVC or Git-LFS to ensure consistency and reproducibility.

- **Automated Testing:** Implement unit tests for individual components (e.g., data preprocessing functions), integration tests for workflow stages (e.g., model training), and validation tests for model performance (e.g., accuracy, precision).
- **Model Validation:** Beyond traditional tests, include steps to validate the model's performance on validation datasets. Use metrics and statistical tests tailored to the specific problem domain to ensure the model's reliability.
- **Environment Consistency:** Use containerization technologies (e.g., Docker) to guarantee that the development, testing, and production environments are consistent. This reduces the likelihood of environment-specific issues.
- **Monitoring and Logging:** Integrate logging and monitoring systems to track model performance post-deployment. This can include model accuracy, latency, resource usage, and alerts for aberrations.

```
# cd_pipeline.yml
name: CD Pipeline

on:
  push:
    branches:
      - main

jobs:
  deploy:
    runs-on: ubuntu-latest

    steps:
      - name: Checkout repository
        uses: actions/checkout@v2

      - name: Set up Python
        uses: actions/setup-python@v2
        with:
          python-version: 3.8

      - name: Install dependencies
        run: |
          python -m pip install --upgrade pip
          pip install -r requirements.txt

      - name: Build Docker image
        run: |
          docker build -t my-ml-model:latest .
```

```
    - name: Push Docker image to registry
      run: |
        docker tag my-ml-model:latest <registry>/my-ml-model:latest
        docker push <registry>/my-ml-model:latest

    - name: Deploy to Kubernetes
      run: |
        kubectl apply -f k8s_deployment.yml
```

This example showcases a CD pipeline that starts with checking out the code repository, setting up the Python environment, installing dependencies, building a Docker image for the machine learning model, pushing the Docker image to a container registry, and deploying the model to a Kubernetes cluster.

A crucial aspect of CI/CD for machine learning involves handling model-specific challenges. For instance, models may need periodic retraining to handle concept drift—where the statistical properties of the target variable change over time. CI/CD pipelines can integrate automated retraining mechanisms triggered by new data, ensuring the deployed model remains effective and relevant.

The design of CI/CD pipelines should also consider rollback mechanisms. If a newly deployed model exhibits suboptimal performance or unforeseen issues, a rollback procedure can revert to the previous stable model version. This enhances the resilience of the deployment process and minimizes downtime or negative impacts on end-users.

Moreover, incorporating model governance and compliance checks into CI/CD pipelines ensures that all model deployments adhere to regulatory requirements and internal policies. This could involve auditing datasets for fairness, validating model outputs for ethical considerations, and maintaining traceability of decision-making processes in the model lifecycle.

Adopting CI/CD for machine learning models brings numerous benefits, including faster iteration cycles, improved collaboration among teams, higher model quality, and streamlined production workflows. By continuously integrating and deploying models, organizations can effectively leverage their machine learning capabilities to deliver consistent and reliable results.

Made in the USA
Monee, IL
05 November 2026

67911521R00184